DOES FINANCIAL
DEREGULATION WORK?

NEW DIRECTIONS IN MODERN ECONOMICS
General Editor: Malcolm C. Sawyer,
Professor of Economics, University of Leeds

New Directions in Modern Economics presents a challenge to orthodox economic thinking. It focuses on new ideas emanating from radical traditions including post-Keynesian, Kaleckian, neo-Ricardian and Marxian. The books in the series do not adhere rigidly to any single school of thought but attempt to present a positive alternative to the conventional wisdom.

A list of published titles in this series is printed at the end of this volume.

Does Financial Deregulation Work?

A Critique of Free Market Approaches

Bruce Coggins

Graduate, University of California, Riverside

NEW DIRECTIONS IN MODERN ECONOMICS

Edward Elgar
Cheltenham, UK • Northampton, MA, USA

Published by
Edward Elgar Publishing Limited
8 Lansdown Place
Cheltenham
Glos GL50 2HU
UK

Edward Elgar Publishing, Inc.
6 Market Street
Northampton
Massachusetts 01060
USA

A catalogue record for this book
is available from the British Library

Library of Congress Cataloguing in Publication Data

Coggins, Bruce, 1958–
    Does financial deregulation work?: a critique of free market approaches / Bruce Coggins.
    (New directions in modern economics series)
    Includes bibliographical references and index.
    1. Financial services industry—Deregulation—United States.
I. Title. II. Series.
HG185.U6C64 1998
332.1—dc21
                                          97–30627
                                                CIP

ISBN 1 85898 638 9

Printed and bound in Great Britain by
Biddles Ltd, Guildford and King's Lynn

To

Janet and Elizabeth

Contents

Acknowledgements

I must thank the people at the University of California, Riverside who made this book possible. Some worked with me for many years and others jumped in to help without knowing me very well. These people include James S. Earley, Robert Pollin, Gary Dymski, Jonathan Langford and Patty Sorrels.

I must also thank those in the medical community that have made life itself possible. I thank all the members of the lung transplant team at the University of California, San Diego Medical Center. However, I especially want to thank Dr. Stuart Jamieson, Dr. Jolene Kriett, Ann Hayden and Becky Robert. I should also thank those I have known for many years at the Kaiser Medical Facility in Fontana, California. They are Dr. Crawford Judge, Dr. Craig Arakaki and Kathy Snow.

Lastly, I must thank my family. My wife and daughter I thank for their extraordinary patience. My parents and brothers I thank for their unwavering support.

1. An Introduction to the Deregulation Controversy

THE SAVINGS AND LOAN DEBACLE

The United States' Savings and Loan (S&L) crisis of the 1980s, and the legislative response to it, ignited a debate over the causes of, and possible solutions to, instability in the industry. The difficulties in the S&L industry also sparked debates over the same issues in other depository financial sectors suffering similar but lesser difficulties. The legislative response to the mounting difficulties came in the form of the Depository Institutions and Deregulation and Monetary Control Act of 1980 and the Garn–St. Germain Act of 1982. The intent of the two acts was to aid ailing S&Ls by phasing out interest-rate ceilings on deposits, by lifting restrictions on their activities and investments, and by making it easier to merge, including mergers across state lines. It was reasoned that this would relieve troubled S&Ls by enabling them to compete on an equal footing with other institutions for funds, by allowing them to enter more profitable, but previously prohibited, fields of business, and by allowing healthy depository institutions (both S&Ls and banks) to merge with troubled S&Ls. The problems were not alleviated by the legislation. They grew larger, and ended in the collapse and bailout of the Federal Savings and Loan Insurance Corporation (FSLIC), the insurer of S&L deposits, at tremendous taxpayer expense.

THE TWO SIDES OF THE DEBATE

Those Favoring a New Approach to Regulation

On one side of the debate, it is thought that the distress in the S&L industry grew larger through the 1980s because of the piecemeal deregulation which took effect at the beginning of the decade. Their position is that the lifting of some regulatory restrictions increased instability in the industry. This happened because S&Ls were allowed to enter risky fields of business in which they did not have experience. Most S&Ls were already contending for growth to overcome earnings that had soured with the rise in interest rates. Earnings had evaporated because S&Ls were caught carrying portfolios heavily laden with lower-interest, long-term mortgage loans as the costs of the short-term deposits which financed those loans rose. In this solvency-threatening atmosphere, previously prohibited outlets for growth were fiercely pursued by desperate S&Ls. This aggressive striving for growth, with the passage of time, made competition increasingly more intense. This, in turn, made it even more necessary for S&Ls to succeed in not only their new, but also their old, ventures.

In essence, what happened is that what I call 'competitive risk', basically the likelihood that a firm's competitive capabilities and market share will be eroded by the growth and innovations of others,[1] rose substantially. This resulted in many S&Ls recklessly pursuing growth, at the expense of greater portfolio risk, in order to remain competitive and survive. It ended with the failure of many S&Ls and the collapse of the industry. With this outlook, the solution which will bring about greater stability is the establishment of a new regulatory structure which, to some extent, limits competition and restricts S&L behavior.

Those Favoring Deregulation

The other side of the debate, and the assumptions which underlie it, will be the initial focus of the thesis. This side contends that instability was fostered by insufficient deregulation. In fact, they claim that the troubles in the S&L industry were the result of restrictive regulations which prevented the use of diversification designed to avoid potential mismatches between borrowing and lending rates. The limited deregulation allowed S&Ls to expose themselves to greater portfolio risks, but still left intact a regulatory structure which insulated the firm from the potential costs of its risk-taking while allowing it full enjoyment of any potential gains. This created a moral hazard problem.

When such a moral hazard exists, each S&L has an incentive to expose itself to risks it would not expose itself to if subjected more fully to the risks and rigors, or discipline, of the market. This moral hazard problem, or incentive incompatibility between regulator and regulated, prompted naturally self-interested S&Ls to acquire excessive, and destabilizing, portfolio risk. Over time, portfolio risk rose and many S&Ls failed, taking down the industry. With this outlook, destabilizing risk is brought into check through extensive deregulation which strips away protective regulatory barriers, strengthening market discipline.

THE TOPIC TO BE STUDIED

The S&L industry is only a part of a much broader issue of how to regulate financial intermediaries. Other financial sectors, especially the commercial banking industry, have developed problems similar to those just depicted in the S&L industry. Given these widespread, or universal, difficulties, the controversy and debate over deregulation extends to all financial intermediaries operating in the United States.[2] The purpose of this book is to demonstrate that this controversy over deregulation is rooted in differing assumptions regarding both depository financial firms (DFFs) and the financial markets in which they operate. The initial focus will be the deregulatory proposals made by a cohesive and influential group of economists. I refer to this group of economists as Deregulationists. All of them have either been, or currently are, members of the Shadow Financial Regulatory Committee (SFRC), or are closely affiliated, in their reasoning, with members of the committee. The contention will be that the argumentation supporting the Deregulationists' proposals is built on a foundation of assumptions. Most of these assumptions are implicit, within their reasoning, and are rarely explicitly stated. Nonetheless, the assumptions the Deregulationists employ are discernible.

At one level, the Deregulationists' arguments that the market discipline generated by deregulation will promote financial system soundness and stability are very powerful and convincing. This persuasive power, however, only remains intact as long as the foundational assumptions remain unquestioned. When the assumptions are made explicit, the Deregulationists' proposals lose credibility. Credibility is lost because the assumptions fall short of being sufficiently realistic generalizations about the current and historically observed behaviors of both DFFs and financial markets.

When an alternative approach is adopted employing assumptions which more fully mirror the real-world behaviors of both DFFs and financial markets, the Deregulationists' proposals are found to be destabilizing, not stabilizing. Under the alternative assumptions, stabilization is achieved through imposition of regulations which cover all financial institutions performing depository-like functions. In addition, the regulations are designed to both limit competition and restrict the behavior of these institutions. This approach agrees with the side of the debate favoring a new approach to regulation for financial intermediaries.

One example of how differing assumptions result in opposing viewpoints regarding financial regulation is illustrated in how each side models the DFF. The Deregulationists' model of the DFF, in a stark form, can appropriately be depicted as a passively adaptive profit maximizer operating against a portfolio-centered risk constraint. Under this model, the Deregulationists see increased DFF soundness and stability best accomplished by policies which strengthen the limits on portfolio risk-taking imposed by the constraint. These limits are strengthened by more fully exposing the DFF, through deregulation, to the discipline, the risks and rigors, of the market.

Under the alternative approach, the DFF is depicted as entrepreneurial and growth oriented, operating against a security constraint. The security constraint is composed of a balance between portfolio risk and competitive risk, wherein an increase (decrease) in one can usually be offset by a decrease (increase) in the other. This means that deregulatory measures which open up markets through deregulation will decrease DFF soundness and stability. This happens because competitive risk has risen and can most effectively be countered by accepting greater portfolio risk to ease growth. Instead, DFF soundness and stability is achieved by imposing regulations which limit competition and restrict behavior. This reduces competitive risk and therefore any pressure for DFFs to ease growth by assuming destabilizing portfolio risk.

ANALYTICAL APPROACH TO THE TOPIC

Following the introductory chapter, the study will be divided into seven additional chapters. Chapter 2 will review a prominent, coherent and well-supported program of financial system deregulation. At the outset, this chapter will first establish that there is a cohesive group of economists exhibiting similar thinking that can appropriately be called Deregulationists. These economists include George J. Benston, Robert A. Eisenbeis, Paul M. Horvitz, Edward J. Kane, George G. Kaufman, Allan H. Meltzer, Franklin R. Edwards, Anna J. Schwartz and others. The common anchor for all these economists, Deregulationists, is the philosophical approach underlying the SFRC. Following this, the chapter will review, point by point, the deregulatory program of the Deregulationists and how they think greater exposure to discipline promotes greater aversion to portfolio risk, making both depository firms and financial markets more robust and stable. This review will include both earlier and later proposals because the arguments advocating each succeeding proposal help reveal the theoretical foundations of the Deregulationists' thinking.

Chapter 3 will examine the Deregulationists' assumptions and spell out their shortcomings. This will be accomplished by first bringing out into the open the assumptions, concerning both depository firms and financial markets, which are implied by the supporting arguments of the Deregulationists. Some explicit assumptions adopted in a model of the DFF developed by Lewis J. Spellman, an economist closely associated with the Deregulationists, will also be included. The chapter will then show how these assumptions led the Deregulationists to their conclusion that extensive deregulation will enhance both soundness and stability. The assumptions are found to be a blending of those from both conventional marginalist analysis and monetarist theory proffered by Milton Friedman.[3]

Chapters 4 and 5 will propose a set of alternative assumptions about the behavior of both DFFs and financial markets which more closely reflect behavior observed in the real world. The assumptions regarding DFFs, which are developed in Chapter 4, will primarily be derived from Alfred D. Chandler, Jr's, extensive historical analysis of the development and behavior of the modern business enterprise.[4] The proposed alternative model of the firm will also incorporate theories of the firm developed by a few economists who have sought to take into account how firm behavior is shaped by institutional structures. Lastly, Chapter 4 includes an analysis of short-termism, studying what has caused it and how it influences firms in general, and DFFs specifically.

The assumptions regarding financial markets, which are developed in Chapter 5, will be gleaned from works which have extended or built upon the theoretical foundations laid by Keynes in his writings on financial markets. The focus will be on the works of Hyman Minsky, but will also include others with a similar approach such as James Crotty, Don Goldstein, Randall Wray, Martin Wolfson, Jane D'Arista, Robert Pollin and Gary Dymski.[5]

Chapter 6 will suggest the most likely outcomes that will result when the Deregulationist program is applied under the alternative assumptions proposed in Chapters 4 and 5. A core result of extensive deregulation is heightened 'competitive risk' for depository firms, and the acquisition of greater portfolio risk to counter it to meet changed security parameters. This depository firm behavior, along with other factors, generates interactive conditions making both depository firms and financial markets more fragile and unstable under deregulation. It appears that, under the alternative assumptions, regulators have been correct in trying to achieve robustness and stability through regulations which limited competition and restricted depository firm behavior.

Chapter 7 provides a couple of historical examples to test the arguments developed in Chapter 6 that deregulation under the alternative assumptions is destabilizing. The two examples that are examined are the Penn Square Bank failure and its repercussions on Continental Illinois and Seafirst, and the near government takeover of the Financial Corporation of America. The examination strongly indicates that both DFFs and financial markets behave in close accordance with the alternative assumptions, thus making deregulation destabilizing, not stabilizing as the Deregulationists claim.

Chapter 8 concludes by proposing a new approach to financial regulation guided by the alternative set of assumptions. This program maintains, resurrects or extends, in altered form, some of the regulations developed in response to the banking crisis of the 1930s. The major additions or changes are nationwide banking, the shifting of deposit insurance from institutions to individuals, the imposition of floating deposit interest-rate ceilings tied to interest rates allowed or imposed by the Federal Reserve, the allowance of financial conglomerates/full-service banking under strict regulations, a greater provision of reserves through the discount window to encourage lending for productive investment, and a single national financial services regulator housed in the Federal Reserve. Also emphasized are the advantages of both enforcing higher capital standards and developing procedures expediting the reorganization or closure of troubled institutions to minimize the use of forbearance.

A surprising overlap is found to exist between the alternative and Deregulationist programs. It is discovered, however, that this area of overlap only provides apparent, or superficial, and not actual points of agreement. Even in this area, when one gets to the fundamentals of policy implementation, the disagreement between the two approaches is quite severe. It becomes more drastic beyond the range of overlap. The question then becomes, which program should be adopted? The deciding argument is that the program providing a new approach to regulation has more credibility because it employs the alternative assumptions. These assumptions more fully incorporate, or reflect, the motives and behavior observed in reality, than do those of the Deregulationists. This provides the alternative framework with a better ability to correctly anticipate responses to proposed policies. This characteristic of the alternative assumptions should make its predictions concerning both outcomes and behavior more accurate than those claimed by the Deregulationists. For this reason of enhanced understanding, it is concluded that the alternative regulatory approach ought to be adopted over that advocated by the Deregulationists.

NOTES

1. This concept of 'competitive risk' is fully developed in Chapter 4.
2. A good source of information on this debate and how it was driven forward by the S&L crisis is *The Future of the Thrift Industry*, Federal Home Loan Bank of San Francisco: Proceedings of the Fourteenth Annual Conference, 8–9 December 1988.
3. The core references for Chapters 2 and 3, which contain works from all of the mentioned Deregulationists, are: George J. Benston, Robert A. Eisenbeis, Paul M. Horvitz, Edward J. Kane and George G. Kaufman (1986), *Perspectives on Safe and Sound Banking: Past, Present, and Future*, Cambridge, MA: MIT Press; William S. Haraf and Rose Marie Kushmeider (eds) (1988b), *Restructuring Banking and Financial Services in America*, Washington, DC: American Enterprise Institute; Catherine England and Thomas Huertas (eds) (1988), *The Financial Services Revolution: Policy Directions for the Future*, Boston: Kluwer Academic Publishers; George G. Kaufman (ed.) (1990), *Restructuring the American Financial System*, Boston: Kluwer Academic Publishers; and Lewis J. Spellman (1982), *The Depository Firm and Industry: Theory, History, and Regulation*, New York: Academic Press.
4. Alfred D. Chandler, Jr's three main works are: (1962), *Strategy and Structure: Chapters in the History of Industrial Enterprise*, Cambridge, MA: MIT Press; (1977), *The Visible Hand: The Managerial Revolution in American Business*, Cambridge, MA: Belknap; and (1990), *Scale and Scope: The Dynamics of Industrial Capitalism*, Cambridge, MA: Belknap. A comprehensive collection of Chandler's essays is Thomas K. McCraw (ed.) (1988), *The Essential Alfred Chandler: Essays Toward a Historical Theory of Big Business*, Boston: Harvard Business School.
5. The primary references in this area are: Hyman P. Minsky (1982), *Can 'It' Happen Again: Essays on Instability and Finance*, Armonk: M.E. Sharpe, Inc.; Hyman P. Minsky (1977), 'A Theory of Systemic Fragility', in Edward I. Altman and Arnold W. Sametz (eds), *Financial Crises: Institutions and Markets in a Fragile Environment*, New York: John Wiley & Sons, pp. 138–52; Steven Fazzari and Dimitri B. Papadimitriou (eds) (1992), *Financial Conditions and Macroeconomic Performance: Essays in Honor of Hyman P. Minsky*, Armonk: M.E. Sharpe, Inc.; Gary Dymski and Robert Pollin (eds) (1994), *New Perspectives in Monetary Macroeconomics: Explorations in the Tradition of Hyman P. Minsky*, Ann Arbor: University of Michigan Press; Gary Dymski, Gerald Epstein, and Robert Pollin (eds) (1993b), *Transforming the U.S. Financial System: Equity and Efficiency in the 21st Century*, Armonk: M.E. Sharpe, Inc.; and Jane W. D'Arista (1994),

The Evolution of U.S. Finance, Volume II: Restructuring Institutions and Markets, Armonk: M.E. Sharpe, Inc.

2. The Deregulationist Program

REPRESENTATIVE DOCUMENTARY SOURCES

This chapter will summarize both the reasoning and policy recommendations of some of the more prominent economists advocating extensive deregulation of the US depository financial system. I refer to these economists as Deregulationists. The summary will mainly focus on the type of work published by five of the more active (measured by their published output) Deregulationists. They are George G. Kaufman,[1] Edward J. Kane,[2] George J. Benston,[3] Robert J. Eisenbeis[4] and Paul M. Horvitz.[5] All five are members of the Shadow Financial Regulatory Committee (SFRC), which meets on a quarterly basis and issues statements on financial policy and legislation.[6] Kaufman has long served as a co-chair of the SFRC. Additionally, all five of these economists were co-authors of *Perspectives on Safe and Sound Banking* (Benston et al., 1986), a study commissioned by the American Bankers Association and published in cooperation with MIT Press in 1986. This is an important publication, even though it is a bit dated, because it is the first volume which brings together, in an organized and comprehensive manner, mainstream Deregulationist thinking. Lastly, *Safe and Sound Banking*, along with Kane's, *The Gathering Crisis in Federal Deposit Insurance* (1985), are two earlier Deregulationist works which are still commonly cited in current Deregulationist books and articles.

Another center of focus is a study sponsored and published by the American Enterprise Institute, *Restructuring Banking and Financial Services in America*, edited by William S. Haraf and Rose Marie Kushmeider, and published in 1988. This study, like *Safe and Sound Banking*, is important because it, too, pulls together the dominant core of Deregulationist thinking. All five of the economists noted above contributed to this study. Another contributor, Allan H. Meltzer,[7] is a past member of the SFRC, and served as a co-chair of the committee, while yet another contributor, Franklin R. Edwards,[8] is still a member of the SFRC. The well-known monetary economist, Anna J. Schwartz,[9] also wrote an article for the American Enterprise Institute study.

I shall also include material from Lewis J. Spellman's[10] book, *The Depository Firm and Industry: Theory, History, and Regulation* (1982). Spellman has not served on the SFRC but his book and articles clearly indicate that he associates himself with the Deregulationists. It is helpful to refer to the material in his book because he develops detailed models of the banking firm.

The last area of focus, from which summary material will be gleaned, will be the statements on financial legislation and policy adopted and published by the SFRC. Beginning in May 1991 (with statement numbers 70 and 71) the statements of the SFRC have been published in the next feasible quarterly issue of the *Journal of Financial Services Research*. The SFRC statements through number 69 were published in a special issue of the *Journal of Financial Services Research* in 1992.

The SFRC, organized in 1985, is a self-appointed group which 'consists of 12 independent banking experts from the academic and practitioner worlds that meet quarterly to analyze current developments in the financial services industry and to make recommendations for improvements that would be in the public interest' (Kaufman (ed.), 1990, p. xi). The SFRC sees itself performing an ongoing function which raises the level of debate on financial issues and has the intention of pushing public policy in a direction it advocates (Kaufman (ed.), 1990, pp. 1–7 and 149–50).[11] According to the SFRC's *Statement of Purpose and Membership* 'the only common denominators of the [SFRC] members are their public recognition as experts on the industry, and their preferences for market solutions to problems and the minimum degree of government regulation consistent with efficiency and safety' (Kaufman (ed.), 1990, p. 150).

It should be recognized that all five of the more active Deregulationists listed above and Franklin R. Edwards, also noted above, are not only charter members of the SFRC but are also co-editors of the *Journal of Financial Services Research* in which the committee's statements are published. In addition, members of the SFRC, through Kluwer Academic Publishers (which also publishes the *Journal of Financial Services Research*) published, in 1990, a collection of their essays, *Restructuring the American Financial System*, edited by George G. Kaufman.

This publication history, the establishment, purpose and success of the SFRC, and the many articles written independently as individuals and in pairs (from which summary material will also be obtained) clearly indicates a long-term cohesiveness in thinking among this group. It is appropriate to label this approach 'Deregulationist' because it is the central and most influential work advocating extensive deregulation of the financial system in the United States. It is the policy proposals of these Deregulationists which will be summarized point by point.

DEREGULATIONIST DEVELOPMENT

The policy proposals put forth by the Deregulationists have changed over time. During the early to middle 1980s, the focus was on the moral hazard created by flat-rate deposit insurance premiums. This encouraged DFFs to acquire greater risks than they otherwise would since such risks presented greater profit opportunities absent any increased costs. The solution was to impose risk-related deposit insurance premiums. In conjunction with this, they also suggested that risk-related capital standards would have similar disciplinary effects.

Over the next couple of years, in discussions among themselves, triggered by risk-related capital standards proposed by the regulatory agencies, the Deregulationists abandoned both risk-related deposit insurance and capital standards. They did so because they realized that under regulatory supervision risk exposure would not be determined by the market but risk would instead be ranked according to type of asset. This subjective ranking of risk would not only lead to an administrative quagmire, but it would also result in an arbitrariness in measuring risk which would provide banks with the incentive to take on inappropriate risks, exactly what the Deregulationists' risk-related proposals were intended to prevent. An additional problem with risk-related deposit insurance was that it would require such a dramatic escalation in rates that the insurance agency would suffer an adverse selection problem, thus increasing, not decreasing, its risk exposure.[12]

Given these implementation problems, the Deregulationists responded with a much better-developed proposal – prompt closure (Kaufman (ed.), 1990, pp. 23–34 and 163–8).[13] The idea behind this proposal is that if all depository firms can be shut down before net worth falls below zero there would never be losses to the deposit insurance fund. Given that there would be no losses to the insurance fund, there is no longer any need to restrict depository firm behavior. The Deregulationists ensure closure, before net worth becomes negative, by escalating regulatory oversight as capital declines.

Throughout these developments the Deregulationists have stressed the need for substantial capital requirements, the merits of subordinated debt, and the disciplinary benefits of market value accounting. This indicates a theoretical continuity in their thinking. Therefore, in spite of the developments in Deregulationist thinking which have markedly changed the focus of their work, I shall review all of their major proposals because they reveal the theoretical foundations upon which they have built their arguments.

MARKET DISCIPLINE

The Deregulationists think that the basic cause of instability among DFFs is excessive portfolio risk resulting from insufficient market discipline (Benston et al., 1986, pp. 173–201).[14] Market discipline was much reduced with the passage of the 1930s' banking legislation which sought to protect banks by insulating them from the rigors of the market. With the passage of time, market discipline became further impaired because DFFs, through market-driven financial innovations which at first eroded, and then resulted in the elimination of interest-rate ceilings on deposits, learned to play the regulatory structure to their advantage.

According to the Deregulationists, many DFFs, as deposit rates became uncapped, came to realize that they had a strong incentive to attract funds to invest in higher-risk and higher-profit portfolios because deposit insurance would override depositors' incentives to withdraw funds. In fact, these more profitable but higher-risk DFFs could rapidly attract high levels of deposits, and fuel high rates of firm growth, by simply offering greater returns to depositors.[15]

In addition, the Deregulationists think managerial loss of control and/or failure of the DFF is not a substantial threat due to Federal Deposit Insurance Corporation (FDIC) forbearance policies and liberality at the Federal Reserve's discount window. Both agencies, they say, adopted these policies to prevent instability. Both agencies feared that doing otherwise might result in the instability becoming a contagion spreading through the system. It appears, to the Deregulationists, that the regulatory agencies have traditionally operated on the assumption that financial system stability and DFF failure are almost mutually exclusive (Kaufman, 1988, pp. 9–40; Benston et al., 1986, pp. 1–80).

In essence, the Deregulationists see the DFF operating in an atmosphere where the rewards of its practices are exclusively enjoyed by the firm, but its losses are largely borne by others. This creates a condition which the Deregulationists refer to as moral hazard. This condition of moral hazard is created when DFF regulatory agencies adopt policies giving DFFs incentives to expose themselves to levels of risk that they would otherwise find it in their interest to avoid (Benston et al., 1986, p. 247).[16]

The Deregulationists desire to create a greater level of market discipline by adopting policies which will reduce the level of incentive incompatibility in the system.   The goal is to develop policies to give individual DFFs the incentive to work with, rather than against, the stability objectives given the regulatory agencies.   The Deregulationists, in the main, do this by more fully exposing DFFs to the risks and rigors of the market.

It is important to note that much of the market discipline the Deregulationists want to re-establish is generated through regulatory action.   This means that much of the market discipline the Deregulationists strive to restore is actually an outgrowth of regulatory discipline.   This distinction between market and regulatory discipline is not very important because the Deregulationists' regulatory discipline is designed to emulate the market discipline they think would occur in free financial markets.   Examples of regulatory discipline are risk-related deposit insurance and capital standards, stricter capital standards, the imposition of market value accounting and the prompt closure of failing DFFs. The Deregulationists claim that if financial markets were free, then markets would naturally impose the same standards and modes of operation upon DFFs through private channels.   Therefore, regulatory discipline is not much different from market discipline because it mimics the market discipline spontaneously generated by free financial markets.   Given this, the following discussions of proposed Deregulationist policies will not consistently make note of the distinction which can be made between regulatory and market discipline.

DEPOSIT INSURANCE

A major theme running through earlier Deregulationist thinking is the need to re-establish market discipline by abandoning flat-rate deposit insurance premiums in favor of risk-related premiums.   The Deregulationists argue that flat-rate premiums encourage inappropriate portfolio risks by DFFs because the costs of such risks are covered by the insuring agency, while all the benefits flow to the DFF and maybe its depositors.   According to the Deregulationists, this creates a problem of moral hazard, an incentive incompatibility between insured and insurer. This occurs for two reasons.

One is that there are no increased costs from deposit insurance to constrain DFFs from taking on profitable, but excessive, portfolio risks because the insurance premium remains constant.   The profits from such risk-taking flow solely to the DFF and possibly its depositors. None of it is transferred into the insurance agency fund to cover the increased losses which will likely occur. When some DFFs become insolvent, and losses occur, the insurance agency must cover them with an insufficiently financed fund. In the end, the taxpayer covers the losses. Therefore, DFFs, as an industry, do not fully pay their insurance costs, yet they fully enjoy, along with their depositors, any profits they may earn. The result is a disappearance of market discipline and a reckless striving for profits and growth by DFFs (Benston and Kaufman, 1988b, pp. 23–5; Benston et al., 1986, p. 137).

A second reason is that depositors have little reason to be concerned about the riskiness of their DFF's portfolio. Depositors, given how DFF failures have historically been handled, see little chance of deposit loss. Therefore, they see little, if any, difference in safety among DFFs. In this atmosphere, their primary concern is what is the best return they can obtain on their deposited funds. DFFs can pay higher returns on deposits they hold only if they earn higher returns on their portfolio. DFFs, to earn these higher returns, must invest in riskier assets. The result is that because deposit insurance makes all deposits equally safe, depositors see it in their interest to place their funds in higher-risk and higher-profit DFFs. In other words, market discipline from depositors becomes nonexistent. The DFF is encouraged to fuel high rates of growth by attracting deposits, through high interest rates, to finance investments in riskier and more profitable assets (Benston et al., 1986, pp. 227–33; Tobin, 1987, p. 171; Benston and Kaufman, 1988b, pp. 34–8).

The Deregulationists argue that the above two difficulties can be overcome by adopting a system of risk-related deposit insurance premiums. Under risk-related premiums the DFF's cost of insurance will rise along with the level of portfolio risk. This will inhibit inappropriate risk-taking and supply the insurance agency with sufficient funds to cover losses. DFFs fully pay for the risks they take on and are no longer subsidized. Therefore excessive risk-taking is no longer encouraged and some degree of market discipline is restored.

Additionally, if the imposition of increased premiums for greater DFF riskiness is made public knowledge, depositors will perceive a difference in safety among DFFs and demand higher returns to compensate for the greater risk exposure. DFFs will also likely lose more risk-averse depositors. Therefore, each DFF's investment in riskier assets is deterred by the threat of losing current depositors and/or by the higher costs associated with keeping them or attracting new ones. The depositors, through informed, self-interested, disciplinary action, persuade DFFs, out of their own interest, to behave in a more risk-averse and conservative manner.

COMPANION POLICIES FOR RISK-RELATED PREMIUMS

The Deregulationists acknowledge that market discipline from risk-related deposit insurance premiums will only be fully effective when two other policies are adopted.

Limited Deposit Insurance

The Deregulationists point out that the prevailing insurance agency policy of fully covering all depositor funds removes from depositors any incentive to monitor their DFF(s) for safety. In fact, as already noted, the prevailing policy gives many depositors an incentive to seek out the most reckless of DFFs, because at these firms they will obtain significantly higher returns on their deposited funds, yet still enjoy the benefits of being fully insured. (An industry of deposit brokers developed to assist depositors in finding DFFs offering the best returns.) Incentives to monitor can only be brought into play if deposit insurance coverage is clearly limited, both *de jure* and *de facto*, so that depositors know they are exposed to fairly large potential losses.

The Deregulationists note that a relatively simple way to limit deposit insurance is to shift coverage from a per deposit to a per depositor basis. Under this scheme, depositors with large (above the maximum coverage) and/or multiple deposits will be subject to substantial potential loss and thus be driven to monitor their DFFs for safety. Another scheme is to limit coverage by requiring the depositor to supply some form of coinsurance. This can be done by having some fairly substantive percentage of each deposit dollar left uninsured by the insuring agency. This will generate market discipline because depositors, to protect themselves, will only place funds with riskier institutions when the greater risk of loss is sufficiently offset by higher returns.

This more substantial rise in the cost of funds to finance riskier portfolios will, say the Deregulationists, through competitive pressure, compel DFFs to evaluate closely the overall riskiness of their holdings. In order to maximize the attractiveness of their deposit offerings, DFFs will find it necessary to minimize their portfolios' risk exposure at any given level of expected return. The profit motive under this magnified discipline, claim the Deregulationists, will drive DFF management to minimize such risk so that costs are minimized and earnings maximized. The result is that when depositors find it important to evaluate the safety of their DFF(s), the DFFs find it in their own interest to behave in a more conservative and risk-averse manner. This, for the Deregulationists, in their initial thinking, would go quite far in reducing the instability that has plagued the American depository financial system (Benston et al., 1986, pp. 89–90 and 186–90; Benston and Kaufman, 1988b, pp. 32–4; Benston and Kaufman, 1988a, pp. 66–8).

Adequate Capital

The Deregulationists repeatedly note that the lower the amount of capital at risk the greater are the incentives for DFF management (and its owners) to take on highly risky investments with potentially large payoffs. If the managers gamble by taking on excessive risk they may reap returns sufficient to restore the firm to financial health. On the other hand, losing such a gamble only entails the loss of a capital base insufficiently large to guarantee the firm continued operation under strictly enforced guidelines. Thus, when little or no capital is at stake, the rising costs of risk-related deposit insurance are largely rendered ineffective in inducing risk avoidance on the part of the DFF.

Because of these incentives, the Deregulationists quite forcefully make the point that capital standards must be strictly enforced so that DFFs are exposed to substantial potential losses. They especially decry that policies of forbearance, wherein regulators allow DFFs that do not meet capital standards (or may even be insolvent[17]) to continue in business in the hope that they will eventually recover and meet the standard, do violence to efforts to enhance market discipline. Market discipline, the Deregulationists argue, especially in their later work, is only enhanced in such situations when the regulators force the reorganization of DFFs (Kane, 1989, pp. 4–7; Kane, 1988, pp. 49–50; Kane, 1990, pp. 119–20; Benston and Kaufman, 1988b, pp. 43–4; Benston et al., 1986, pp. 104–5).

DFF CAPITAL AND ACCOUNTING

Another series of proposals centers around the amount of capital, as a percentage of assets, which regulators should require DFFs to hold and how the value of this capital is best measured. The Deregulationists make two major points in their proposals in this area. One is that we want clear and accurate signals sent to shareholders, management, regulators and depositors concerning the health of the DFF. The other is that by having sufficient amounts of capital at stake and, if this is not the case (as with troubled institutions), by having sufficient supervisory control, to ensure that DFFs steer clear of undue risk-taking.

Market Value Accounting

The Deregulationists repeatedly make the argument that capital is best measured by market value accounting. They state again and again that the true value of any asset, at any point in time, is what it can currently capture in the market, that is, its going market price. The asset's proper value is certainly not measured by its book value or historical cost, the price at which the depository firm acquired it, because this price, in all likelihood, will be very different from the current market price.

Thus, if book value or historical cost accounting is used to measure capital, a true measure of its value will not be obtained. Market value accounting arrives at the best measure of capital because it comes closest to estimating the capital that would be obtained if the DFF were liquidated. Presently, the Deregulationists point out, the standard practice is to use some form of book value or historical cost accounting to measure the capital of depository firms. This results in unclear and inaccurate signals being sent to shareholders, managers, regulators and depositors.

Unclear and inaccurate signals regarding capital dangerously weaken both the regulatory and market discipline these signals should at times generate. The Deregulationists insist that desirable increases in both regulatory and market discipline will be achieved (and will enhance the safety/stability of both firms and markets) if some form of market value accounting is adopted and phased into use. The essence of the argument is that both discipline and stability are generated because market value accounting clearly exposes DFFs to market reversals which may deplete their capital. This prompts a DFF to operate more conservatively and to hold greater capital.

The Deregulationists claim that market value accounting is achievable because markets in assets, typically held by DFFs, through developments such as securitization, are sophisticated, numerous, large and deep. Therefore, essentially similar and commonly traded assets can be found to estimate accurately the market value of almost any asset. When it comes to nonmarketed investments, goodwill and other intangibles, the Deregulationists assert, without spelling them out, that accounting standards can be developed which are acceptable at least from the point of view of the regulatory agencies (Benston and Kaufman, 1988b, pp. 47–53; Kaufman, 1988, pp. 29 and 33–4; Benston and Kaufman, 1988a, pp. 78–82 and 93; Morris and Sellon, 1991, pp. 5–

19; Kaufman, 1990 (ed.), pp. 35–55; Benston et al., 1986, pp. 203–25).

Capital Standards

The Deregulationists repeatedly push for increased capital standards. They give several reasons as to why this would increase not only market discipline, but also the safety/stability of both DFFs and the financial markets in which they operate.

The first and most significant reason they give is that both the owners of a DFF and its management will operate in an increasingly more risk-averse manner the greater the amount of capital at stake. Risk aversion rises with capital size because the potential loss from failure rises dollar for dollar with capital. This will prompt increased owner monitoring of the firm's investments and therefore generate heightened market discipline.

Second, they point out that higher capital standards also enhance safety/stability by increasing the depth of the cushion on which the DFF can absorb unexpected economic shocks before becoming insolvent.

Third, they note that the higher capital standards give regulators a longer time frame with which to work with troubled DFFs. This should reduce the incidence of failure and better ensure that those that do fail are liquidated, or reorganized, before net worth becomes negative. Fewer failures and reduced insurance losses both raise the level of safety/stability.

Fourth, they claim that higher capital standards should increase the level of safety/stability by reducing the likelihood of depositor runs. The greater the amount of capital held by a DFF, the greater the perceived distress the DFF must face before depositors think deposit safety is sufficiently imperiled to run.

Fifth and last, the Deregulationists encourage the use of subordinated debt as a part of capital. The holders of subordinated debt have claims which fall behind or are 'subordinated' to the claims of the deposit insurance agency on the assets of the depository firm. The Deregulationists claim that allowing the use of subordinated debt has three advantages. It allows the DFF to exploit, through the deduction of interest as a business expense, the tax advantage which debt funding can have over equity funding, reducing the cost of capital, and thereby encouraging its use. Second, it is easier and cheaper for smaller firms to sell subordinated debentures than equities (since they are basically selling explicitly uninsured time deposits). This puts smaller DFFs on a more equal footing with larger ones in raising capital. Third, as portions of the subordinated debt are rolled over the firm must pass the test of the market. The yields will serve as signals to regulators, depositors and bondholders about the risks undertaken by the DFF. This will generate both market and regulatory discipline which will reduce the likelihood that the firm's operators will undertake inappropriately risky investments (Benston and Kaufman, 1988b, pp. 57–60; Benston and Kaufman, 1988a, pp. 85–8; Benston et al., 1986, pp. 176–84; Kaufman (ed.), 1990, pp. 163–8).

RISK-RELATED CAPITAL STANDARDS

In conjunction with risk-related deposit insurance, the Deregulationists have also advocated risk-related capital standards. As with risk-related deposit insurance, risk-related capital standards increase the incentives toward risk avoidance in the DFF's portfolio holdings. Both programs discourage higher-risk portfolios by directly confronting the firm with explicitly higher costs to finance riskier portfolio holdings.

In the case of risk-related capital standards, the cost of additional risk-taking arises out of the additional costs of obtaining and holding greater amounts of capital as risk exposure rises. The capital standards are imposed by the regulatory authorities, and in this sense is regulatory-, and not market-, generated discipline. However, the capital funds must be raised and maintained through the market, wherein market discipline is imposed.

The Capital Market Imposes a Two-tiered Test

The Deregulationists point out that, under a program of risk-related capital standards, when a DFF takes on additional risk it can only do so if it can meet the test of the market and raise the required additional capital. This market test for potential investors is two tiered. One is that a sufficient number of market participants must have good reason to think that the expected returns they calculate from the DFF's riskier portfolio are sufficiently large to compensate for the greater likelihood of loss. The second is that investors must have sufficient confidence in the abilities of DFF management to not only avoid pitfalls leading to losses but also possess and use judgement which will maximize the potential earnings from the portfolio. If the DFF can pass this two-tiered market test with a sufficient number of investors, it will be able to attract the additional capital it needs to finance its riskier portfolio holdings.

Subordinated Debt as Capital

The Deregulationists, while discussing risk-related capital, make an additional case for the use of subordinated debt as capital. They claim that capital, in the form of subordinated debt, provides greater market discipline than does equity capital, because the DFF's credit rating, and ability to borrow, is directly affected by its record in meeting contracted payments. This provides investors with a detailed track record reflecting on the health of the DFF which is missing in equity capital transactions. Additionally, each time the subordinated debt is rolled over, the same two-tiered market test for capital funding, described above, must also be passed. Thus, for Deregulationists, the great merit in the use of subordinated debt as capital is that it heightens the intensity of market discipline and thereby increases the DFF's incentive to avoid undue portfolio risk.

Market Value Accounting and Proper Risk Measurement

The Deregulationists have argued that risk-related capital standards will only result in the desired risk-avoidance incentives if capital is correctly measured and if its standard is clearly linked to actual/real market assessment of risk, and not some arbitrary risk ranking. In their criticisms of the risk-related capital schemes proposed by the regulatory agencies, the Deregulationists have compiled a few requirements for a properly functioning risk-related capital standards program. (These same requirements also apply to a well-designed system of risk-related deposit insurance premiums.)

One, in order to properly monitor and effectively enforce risk-related capital standards, some form of market value accounting must be adopted. The proper measure of capital, for both regulatory and market evaluation purposes, is the market value of assets minus the market value of nonsubordinated liabilities. Remember, the Deregulationists regard subordinated liabilities as a part of capital.

Two, the risk-level asset classes used in determining capital requirements must not be arbitrary. The level of risk associated with assets of various classes must be supported by evidence from market valuations of risk or historical loss experience. To the extent that the risk weighting of assets is arbitrary, incentives are created to avoid capital constraints and increase actual risk exposure.

Three, both credit and interest-rate risk must be taken into account when evaluating the level of risk.

Four and last, the weighting scheme for risk must take into account how diversification can change the risk borne by a financial institution.

A proper look at diversification must include off-balance sheet items and how associations with subsidiaries and affiliates influence riskiness (Benston and Kaufman, 1988b, pp. 38–42 and 57–60; Benston and Kaufman, 1988a, pp. 71–4 and 85–8; Benston et al., 1986, pp. 192–5; Benston and Kaufman, 1986, pp. 70–73).[18]

TIMELY REORGANIZATION

In their later studies, the Deregulationists have focused on an assertion that the largest losses to the federal insurance agencies are the result of their forbearance policies. Under these policies the resolution of failures has been delayed until after DFF net worth has fallen below zero. Timely reorganization (either through takeover and recapitalization, assumption and merger, or liquidation before net worth becomes negative), claim the Deregulationists, is the most important, and essential, aspect in a successful restructuring of the DFF regulatory apparatus.

The Costs of Forbearance

The Deregulationists argue forcefully that allowing both insolvent and nearly insolvent DFFs to continue in operation is costly to the insurance agencies. These costs arise because only the funds of others are now at risk and this gives DFF management (and owners) a powerful incentive to place large and risky bets in an effort to restore solvency. The Deregulationists note that raising funds to place these bets requires the insolvent DFFs making them to offer depositors highly attractive rates of return. These high rates of return, through competition for funds, spill over into the general market for deposits, increasing the costs of funds for all other DFFs. Under these conditions, if deposit rates are pushed high enough, weaker DFFs may be pulled toward insolvency. This results in a greater number of DFFs having a strong incentive to bid up deposit rates, thus putting even greater pressure on fully solvent DFFs. This running up of deposit rates, say the Deregulationists, forces solvent DFFs to invest in riskier and more lucrative assets in order to cover the costs of their more expensive deposits.

In addition, according to the Deregulationists, policies of forbearance send out a signal that the penalties of failure are not as great as they were once thought, because, even with the DFF technically in failure, the authorities appear likely to allow it to continue to operate. This reduction in the penalties from failure will encourage greater risk-taking by all DFFs.   Thus, for the Deregulationists, policies of forbearance through pervasive spillover effects, increase risk-taking incentives not only for insolvent, but also for wholly solvent DFFs.

Incentive Compatibility Restored Under Timely Reorganization

The Deregulationists claim, regardless of how deposit insurance premiums or capital standards are structured, that unless failures are resolved in timely fashion, the depository financial structure will impose unnecessary risks and costs on the economy.   Their point is that if DFFs are subject to increased scrutiny as capital adequacy erodes and are reorganized before the market value of their capital falls to zero, incentives and abilities for risk-taking on the part of owners and managers will be reduced, thus removing any subsidies derived from deposit insurance.   Timely reorganization replaces incentive incompatibility between DFFs and their regulators with incentive compatibility, simply because the DFF is only free to operate without excessive regulatory interference if it maintains adequate capital.   DFFs will, according to the Deregulationists, find that the best way to have sufficient and growing capital (and the freedom to operate as desired) is by operating in a more cautious/conservative manner, wherein inappropriate or undue portfolio risk is avoided.

Under the Deregulationists' proposal, timely reorganization is achieved by escalating regulatory supervision as capital falls through a series of specified ranges.   This increasing oversight as capital becomes more and more inadequate gives regulators the information they need to liquidate or recapitalize the institution before net worth falls below zero and imposes losses on the insurance fund.   Additionally, creditors of ailing DFFs, through regulatory suspension of dividends and payments of interest on subordinated debt, have an incentive to both correct poor performance and inject new capital to prevent takeover by the insurance agency.

Deregulationists occasionally argue that timely reorganization, in conjunction with increasingly close supervisory monitoring of individual DFFs as their capital adequacy declines, is sufficient, as a stand-alone reform, to restore the financial system to health.   It is thought that the market and regulatory discipline created by such a reform will be so substantial that discipline gained through risk-related deposit insurance premiums and capital standards will be redundant and/or unnecessary.

Timely Reorganization Also Enhances Discipline and Stability

Timely reorganization, according to the Deregulationists, also has the benefit of enhancing discipline in two ways. First, subordinated debt holders and shareholders would subject the firm to greater discipline because they will not get a second chance to recoup their losses. Second, there will also be greater discipline from managers who will quickly lose their positions if the DFF becomes insolvent. In both cases there is increased incentive to keep risk in check to preserve capital.

Stability is also strengthened in two ways. Since prompt closure minimizes losses to the insurance fund, the public's confidence in the solvency of the fund will increase. Also, closure before capital is negative will reduce the tendency of DFFs to make reckless last ditch efforts to restore solvency. Each of these will reduce the number of both bank runs and bank failures and therefore enhance stability.

Additional Benefits

The Deregulationists list four additional benefits of timely reorganization which they reason should encourage its adoption:

1. Except in cases of major fraud, timely reorganization would effectively eliminate losses from DFF failure. With these losses eliminated, the insurance premiums need only cover the operating expenses of the insurance agencies. For the Deregulationists, the elemental operations include improved and more frequent monitoring of the insured institutions and the development and deployment of an effective market value accounting system. In addition, quick and certain reorganization of DFFs, by reducing the time frame for recognition and response, will save the insurance agencies additional funds by reducing the number of uninsured depositors who are able to transform unsecured claims into secured ones. This will simultaneously improve both discipline and stability. Discipline is improved because uninsured depositors are given a greater incentive to monitor the health of their DFF(s). Stability is improved because the reduction in losses to the insurance fund bolsters its solvency and thereby the public's confidence in it.

2. With the passage of time, experience will be gained with timely reorganization of DFFs. Insured depositors will learn that they suffer very small, if any, losses under reorganization, since

reorganization is now quick and takes place before net worth becomes negative. This will make insured depositors less likely to run when they hear that their DFF may be in trouble. This greater confidence in the security of insured deposits, will strengthen the stability of the depository financial system while imposing greater discipline.

3. The Deregulationists claim that under a system with vigilant regulatory monitoring of capital adequacy and enforcement of timely reorganization, regulations concerned with the riskiness associated with various DFF activities become unnecessary. Guidelines, restricting the range of products and services on the basis of risk, become unnecessary because insurance fund losses from risk no longer occur. Losses are eliminated from DFF failure, because of excessive risk-taking or not, because DFFs are more intensely monitored as capital adequacy declines, and because of such monitoring, they are reorganized before capital falls below zero.

Under this sort of regime, DFF owners and managers will come to realize that they will only be free to take on desired risks and activities when they are deemed to have adequate capital. In essence, well-capitalized DFFs buy themselves freedom from excessive monitoring and supervisory interference. This freedom allows well-capitalized DFFs to assume those risks and offer those products and services which are in the best interests of the firm. This unencumbered pursuit of self-interest, due to timely reorganization, does not jeopardize the solvency of the insurance fund. This is the case because incentive compatibility is achieved between the DFF and its deposit insuring agency. DFFs know they are only fully free to operate as they think is best when they have adequate capital, and this is exactly what the insuring agency wants DFFs to maintain. (DFFs also know that the penalties of inadequate capital are swift and sure and thus something to strive to avoid.)

Since regulatory restrictions on product and service offerings on the basis of risk are no longer necessary under timely reorganization, the focus of regulators can shift to other areas. Restrictions on DFF activities, according to the Deregulationists, become appropriate only when issues about concentration, competition and conflict of interest arise.

4. Under a program of timely reorganization no DFF will be too large to fail because the insuring agency, through diligent monitoring of troubled firms, will know when to act to avoid losses to depositors. With resolution taking place before any significant

losses occur, the regulatory authorities need not fear that reorganization of a large DFF will touch off contagious runs and financial disruption. This means that depositors at large DFFs will no longer enjoy an historically lower rate of loss than those at smaller firms undergoing reorganization. This will make the competition between large and small DFFs more equitable and intense by eliminating the advantage once held by large DFFs (Benston and Kaufman, 1988b, pp. 43–7 and 68–9; Benston and Kaufman, 1988a, pp. 75–8 and 94–5; Horvitz, 1988, pp. 102–3; Eisenbeis, 1990, pp. 23–34; Kaufman (ed.), 1990, pp. 163–8).

FREEDOM OF FINANCIAL FIRM ACTIVITIES

The Deregulationists strongly favor allowing all financial firms (FFs) full freedom in determining the type and range of both liabilities and assets in which they will do business. The Deregulationists argue that their program of timely reorganization, along with their other market discipline-amplifying measures, will produce an incentive compatibility between insured and insurer. This incentive compatibility renders it unnecessary to restrict FF holdings on the basis of risk, according to the Deregulationists. They reason that the FF's management, since they now face the full costs of their risk-taking and are the most knowledgeable concerning the firm, its activities and its environment, are in the best position to determine what sorts of diversification, synergies and risks are in the best interest of the firm. The key is that Deregulationist proposals produce incentive compatibility, so that actions, such as extensive diversification, which are in the best interest of the FF, are also in the best interest of the insuring agency. In addition, the Deregulationists' prompt closure provision serves as a backstop by shutting down any mismanaged or ailing FFs before losses occur.

Risk and Cost Minimization

The Deregulationists extol the benefits which flow from allowing FF management the freedom to diversify as they think best. They argue that full diversification freedoms will enable FFs to fully minimize risk at each level of expected return, and fully maximize efficiency. This happens because the FF will not be hindered in adopting a structural organization, and offering a range of products and services (on both the liability and asset side), which will minimize both overall costs and total risk exposure.

It is also noted by the Deregulationists that allowing extensive diversification may strengthen financial firms through increased profitability. Diversification into additional lines of business will allow the exploitation of synergies in areas such as management, production and marketing. This should increase the profitability of financial firms and, thereby, their stability, in two ways. The first is that greater profits will better enable financial firms to add to capital. The second is that greater profits through the exploitation of synergies reduce both the need and the incentive to pursue profits through the acquisition of risky portfolios.

Therefore, the Deregulationists think that it is best that the market, through competition, determines what kind of financial service companies are best. This requires the dropping of various regulatory restrictions which impede the establishment of full line financial service companies which offer insurance, commercial banking and investment banking services. Under a free financial market, or one with minimal restrictions, the Deregulationists foresee full line financial service companies and specialty financial service companies in heated competition with one another.

Commercial Holdings

The Deregulationists associated with the SFRC and its positions have such faith in the market's ability to determine what is best that they also support the removal of restrictions on nonfinancial or commercial holdings by FFs. They say that if the acquisition of commercial holdings by financial companies is determined by the market to produce profits, cost savings and/or risk exposure reductions, then such acquisitions ought to be allowed. In fact, if the noted benefits do flow from commercial holdings, then a free market will foster and encourage commercial acquisitions by financial companies. On the other hand, they argue, if commercial holdings cause problems, instead of benefits, the market, by meting out discipline through the competitive process, will discourage financial companies from acquiring or maintaining commercial holdings. The market alone will prevent a blending of the financial and the commercial within a single firm if it is found to generate unacceptable costs or risks. In essence, the market is best at determining what is optimal, and therefore should be free, and not restricted, from doing so (Edwards, 1988, pp. 113–35; Saunders, 1988, pp. 156–93; Huertas, 1987, pp. 139–65; Huertas, 1988, pp. 289–307; Benston et al., 1986, 137–8).

Conflict of Interest

Deregulationists, as a whole, are in agreement that allowing the full conglomeration of financial and nonfinancial activities will not create any serious or insurmountable conflict of interest problem. They claim that the conflict of interest problems traditionally thought to arise with the combining of commercial banking, investment banking and commercial business are historically misunderstood, not very serious and easily dispelled. In fact, they think that the extensive synergistic benefits they see arising by ending these separations give ample cause to be open to some degree of conflict of interest – especially since they see a minimally restricted financial market doling out ample doses of competitively generated discipline which will limit, to an acceptable level, all kinds of risky behavior. The Deregulationists believe that the current firewall protections, which are now applied to bank holding companies and limit the activities that can take place among affiliates, are more than adequate regulatory controls, with some modification, to prevent dangerous conflicts of interest, under a program of functional regulation. Benston, in his book, *The Separation of Commercial and Investment Banking* (1990) argues that self-interest and competitive market pressures alone are sufficient to prevent full-service FFs from getting involved with customer-damaging conflicts of interest (Litan, 1988, pp. 269–87; Benston et al., 1986, pp. 150–52; Benston, 1990, pp. 43–122 and 205–11). In the unlikely event that firewalls fail, prompt closure again serves as a backstop and prevents any dangerous exploitations of conflicts of interest from being disruptive.

In addition, the Deregulationists note that an alternative to firewall protections and functional regulation, to prevent conflicts of interest, is regulating the banking organization as a consolidated entity. Under the consolidated entity approach the banking organization (holding company) is viewed for regulatory purposes as analogous to a branch system, with its subsidiaries representing ways for the firm to organize its internal control and accounting systems. This, under a deregulated environment, say the Deregulationists, makes such organizations evolve into the functional equivalent of a bank. Alternatively, banks could be given powers making them functionally the same as holding companies. According to the Deregulationists, this more thorough integration of both banking stuctures and regulatory supervision eliminates any conflict of interest or safety and soundness concerns regarding the relationships among subsidiaries and whether or not these subsidiaries can stand and function on their own.

This, claim the Deregulationists, has two advantages over firewall protections between sudsidiaries under functional regulation. One, since the firm strives for maximization of profits for the consolidated entity, the firm will strive to do so by shifting activities from more- to less-regulated subsidiaries. This game of regulatory circumvention leads to complex organizational structures, making conflict of interest difficult to monitor and detect for both the firm's managers and the regulators. Second, the rescue of a troubled subsidiary, exposing regulatory agencies to unexpected risks, will not occur under consolidated regulation because subsidiaries are both organized and regulated as part of the bank; they are not expected to stand independently (Benston et al., 1986, pp. 142–3, 152–3 and 155–7).

Policy Proposals

Some of the policy changes the Deregulationists propose to lift restrictions and promote FF diversification are:

1. Overturn the Glass–Steagall Act to remove the unwarranted barriers which separate commercial and investment banking activities. Again, the conflict of interest problem is not as serious as has typically been thought. This will increase the intensity of competition, which not only creates risk-reducing discipline, but also enhances efficiency and the ability to compete at the international level.
2. Eliminate any regulatory imposed restrictions on portfolio holdings which are based on riskiness. This is not an appropriate or effective way to deal with inappropriate risk-taking because arbitrary risk ranking, generated by regulations, enters the picture. These arbitrary rankings encourage FF manipulation of regulatory rules to discreetly take on inappropriate risks. The Deregulationists claim that risk-taking will only be minimized when unrestricted diversification, the best way to fully exploit risk-reducing strategies, is allowed under a regime imposing ample market discipline.
3. Establish nationwide banking by eliminating unit banking laws and any restrictions on interstate branching. They claim that nationwide banking will promote stability because the greater geographic diversification will enable DFFs to better insulate themselves from the economic downturns or crises suffered in local and regional economies. They argue that competition on the local level will increase because the lifting of unit banking laws and branching restrictions will destroy the monopoly power many DFFs have enjoyed. The Deregulationists also claim that competition on the national level will probably increase, and will

definitely not suffer, because of the entrance of traditionally nondeposit financial firms into the depository financial service industry. Of course, for the Deregulationists, any intensification of competition also produces disciplinary forces which both increase efficiency and strengthen limits on risky behaviors and portfolio holdings (Mengle, 1990, pp. 3–17; Benston et al., 1986, pp. 138–9).

DISCLOSURE

The Deregulationists recognize that the successful implementation of both regulatory and market discipline requires that there be full and honest disclosure on the part of FFs. Agents in the market can only forcefully impose market discipline if they have full and accurate information on the condition of FFs. The same is true for regulatory agencies. They can effectively impose regulatory discipline only if they have complete and accurate information on the status of DFFs. The Deregulationists think that disclosure laws may help in the initial implementation of disclosure, but argue that competitive market pressures, introduced under their market-oriented proposals, will enforce full and honest disclosure.

The Deregulationist argument is that there will always be conservatively run FFs that will find it to their competitive advantage to use market value accounting and fully disclose all information pertinent to their financial health. Less conservative FFs which may not initially find disclosure advantageous will, say the Deregulationists, quickly find it essential to their success as they come under competitive pressure to release such information to attract needed capital, subordinated liabilities and deposits. Deregulationists see highly competitive financial markets eventually requiring all FFs to disclose truthful and accurate information to compete effectively. They must all do this to establish and maintain the reputation and trustworthiness they will need to win business on an equal footing with their competitors. In essence, the Deregulationists claim that the market, through competition, will spontaneously generate an environment wherein agents will not conduct business with an FF unless they have good reason to believe they have been provided with truthful and accurate information on the health of the firm.

Conversely, argue the Deregulationists, FFs operating in this competitive environment will find it highly disadvantageous to disclose less than truthful or accurate information. They argue that any false or inaccurate disclosure will end up being detected by the market since it is in the interest of too many players to know the truth. The result is that any firm that either carelessly or deliberately foists discrepancies and/or deceptions on the market will pay a hefty price in the loss of client trust that will not easily or quickly be re-established. The Deregulationists see these carrot and stick incentives, automatically produced by a free market, as being more than sufficient to obtain the full disclosure that is often sought after through law (Benston et al., 1986, pp. 195–201 and 205; England, 1988, pp. 323–5).

CONCLUDING COMMENTS

It is clear, from the above proposals, that the Deregulationists thoroughly believe in the efficacy of free markets to optimize both institutional structures and the outcomes which flow therefrom. Their position is that US financial markets are unstable because markets are restricted and are prevented from operating as they naturally would. FFs behave in a reckless manner and take on excessive portfolio risk because they are insulated from the true, free market costs of such risk-taking. The Deregulationists argue repeatedly that exposing FFs to the full discipline of a free market will compel them to assume only those risks which are appropriate. Thus, free markets minimize the portfolio risks which FFs may acquire and still succeed, which in turn maximizes the stability of the overall financial structure. The free market also bolsters stability by enabling FFs to diversify in a manner which not only minimizes risk but also enables FFs to capitalize on a full range of synergies which both minimize costs and maximize profitability.

Given this trust in the efficacy of markets, the Deregulationists remove all regulatory structures except those in the following areas:

1. The maintenance of, and slight modification to, firewall restrictions to limit conflicts of interest.
2. The maintenance of deposit insurance in a more limited form to induce greater monitoring by, and discipline from, depositors.
3. Stricter regulatory enforcement of more substantial capital standards.
4. Creation of an extensive monitoring and supervisory apparatus to ensure the prompt closure of ailing DFFs.

It is the fourth provision, however, which the Deregulationists repeatedly focus on in their arguments extolling the virtues of free financial markets. The prompt closure provisions serve as the Deregulationists' safety net. If trouble of any kind arises, it will rapidly be isolated and resolved with some form of reorganization before losses occur. Therefore, FFs can take on any sort of risks and not, in the end, disrupt financial markets. Prompt closure is the saving grace of Deregulationist doctrine.

In closing it should be noted that the maintenance of the above four regulatory structures is, for the Deregulationists, not indicative of market failure. One gets the impression, even though it is never explicitly stated, that the Deregulationists maintain these four regulatory structures because it is not politically feasible to abolish the entire regulatory apparatus (Benston and Kaufman, 1988b, pp. 55–6).[19] In addition, the maintenance of these regulations makes their program more palatable since, even though it closely emulates what would happen in a free market, it leaves intact some rather extensive regulatory supervision.

It is clear that Benston, in his book *The Separation of Commercial and Investment Banking* (1990), thinks that conflict of interest has not been and is not a problem. In fact, according to Benston, market competition prohibits banks, out of self-interest, from exploiting customer-damaging conflicts of interest. In addition, the Deregulationists' alternative proposal to regulate bank holding companies as a consolidated entity is claimed to eliminate any conflict of interest problems (Benston, 1990, pp. 43–122 and 205–11; Benston et al., 1986, pp. 142–3, 152–3 and 155–7). One gets the impression that the Deregulationists are willing to accept firewall restrictions as the political price that must be paid to buy greater freedoms for DFFs. Thus firewalls are kept in place not because of market system failure but because of political system failure.

Kaufman, in his article 'The Truth About Bank Runs' (1988), makes it clear that deposit insurance is maintained to serve as a stabilizing counterweight to possible destabilizing mistakes of the Federal Reserve. The Deregulationists also point out that in the absence of a central bank, banks form private clearinghouses which, because of both market incentives and self-interest, will not undertake the destabilizing actions occasionally followed by central banks (Kaufman, 1988, pp. 19–21, 24 and 32; Benston and Kaufman, 1988a, pp. 64–5; Benston and Kaufman, 1988b, p. 55). Again the market is not failing; instead, an institutional structure, which cannot be removed for political reasons, is failing.

The imposition of stricter capital standards and the prompt closure of failing DFFs by regulators flow from the inability to eliminate both deposit insurance and the Federal Reserve. In the absence of these institutions, the Deregulationists argue that markets would require greater capital and would not allow insolvent DFFs to operate, thus forcing their prompt closure (Benston and Kaufman, 1988b, pp. 29 and 38–9). The Deregulationists advocate imposing strict capital standards and the prompt closing of DFFs by regulators because it is a way to emulate what would take place under free markets given the current institutional structure. (With the Deregulationists, as discussed earlier, there is no significant distinction between regulatory and market discipline.) Once again, the problem is not market failure, but institutional and political failure.

Lastly, in this chapter I have not discussed any of the empirical evidence which the Deregulationists use in crafting their policies. This evidence is primarily obtained from a fresh look at banking history. Examples of this are Benston's book, *The Separation of Commercial and Investment Banking*, Rolnick and Weber's articles on the free banking era,[20] and Calamoris's work on early deposit insurance schemes, branch banking and clearinghouse-like regulatory mechanisms.[21] Some of this empirical evidence will be presented in the following chapter.

NOTES

1. The John F. Smith, Jr. Professor of Finance and Economics at Loyola University of Chicago.
2. Formerly the Everett D. Reese Professor of Banking and Monetary Economics at Ohio State University and a research associate in the National Bureau of Economic Research. Currently a professor at Boston College.
3. The John H. Harland Professor of Finance, Accounting and Economics and Associate Dean for Research and Faculty Development in the School of Business at Emory University.
4. The Wachovia Professor of Banking and Associate Dean for Research at the School for Business Administration of the University of North Carolina.
5. The Judge James A. Elkins Professor of Banking and Finance at the University of Houston.
6. A discussion of the origin and purpose of the SFRC is contained in George G. Kaufman (ed.) (1990), *Restructuring the American Financial System*, Boston: Kluwer Academic Publishers, pp. 1–7.
7. The John M. Olin Professor of Political Economy and Public Policy at Carnegie–Mellon University.
8. The Arthur F. Burns Professor of Free and Competitive Enterprise and Director of the Center for the Study of Futures Markets at Columbia University.
9. A research associate with the National Bureau of Economic Research and the 1987–88 president of the Western Economic Association.

10. Professor of Finance at the University of Texas.
11. On these pages is described the purpose and operation of the SFRC.
12. For this transition in thinking compare George J. Benston, Robert A. Eisenbeis, Paul M. Horvitz, Edward J. Kane and George G. Kaufman (1986), *Perspectives on Safe and Sound Banking*, Cambridge, MA: MIT Press, pp. 227–43, an analysis of risk-related premiums, with that in George J. Benston and George G. Kaufman (1988b), *Risk and Solvency Regulation of Depository Institutions: Past Policies and Current Options*, New York University: Salomon Brothers Center for the Study of Financial Institutions (Monograph Series in Finance and Economics, No. 1), pp. 34–56; George J. Benston and George G. Kaufman (1988a), 'Regulating Bank Safety and Performance', in William S. Haraf and Rose Marie Kushmeider (eds), *Restructuring Banking and Financial Services in America*, Washington, DC: American Enterprise Institute, pp. 69–96.
13. This gives both the initial policy statement (no. 41) of the SFRC and a fuller development of the prompt closure proposal. This proposal is also discussed in the second and third citations in the previous note.
14. This is an excellent chapter on market discipline and the role that Deregulationists think it can play.
15. The definitive work on this historical process is a short book by Edward J. Kane (1985), *The Gathering Crisis in Federal Deposit Insurance*, Cambridge, MA: MIT Press. A thoughtful article on this is Roger W. Garrison, Eugenie D. Short and Gerald P. O'Driscoll, Jr. (1988), 'Financial Stability and FDIC Insurance', in Catherine England and Thomas Huertas (eds), *The Financial Services Revolution: Policy Directions for the Future*, Boston: Kluwer Academic Publishers, pp. 187–207.
16. Here the term moral hazard is used in passing, the problem is described in detail, without using this term, in the preceding chapter, 'Risk-Related Premiums'. The term is clearly used in Kenneth E. Scott (1990), 'Never Again: the S&L Bailout', in George G. Kaufman (ed.) (1990), *Restructuring the American Financial System*, Boston: Kluwer Academic Publishers, pp. 74–5. The term is sprinkled throughout the Deregulatory literature.
17. Kane aptly refers to these insolvent DFFs as 'zombies'.
18. In addition, see Shadow Financial Regulatory Committee Statements on risk-related capital from 9 June 1986, 9 February 1987, 18 May 1987, 8 February 1988 and 4 December 1989. These are found in the special 1992 edition of the *Journal of Financial Services Research*, which contains the first 69 statements of the SFRC.
19. This is a good example of a concern with what is politically feasible.
20. Arthur I. Rolnick and Warren E. Weber (1983), 'The Free Banking Era: New Evidence on Laissez-Faire Banking', *The American Economic Review*, December, 1080–91. Arthur I. Rolnick and Warren E. Weber (1984), 'The Causes of Free Bank Failures', *Journal of Monetary Economics*, October, 267–91.

21. Charles W. Calamoris (1989b), 'Deposit Insurance: Lessons from the Record', *Economic Perspectives*, Federal Reserve Bank of Chicago, **XII** (3), May/June, 10–30. Charles W. Calamoris (1989a), 'Do "Vulnerable" Economies Need Deposit Insurance? Lessons from the U.S. Agricultural Boom and Bust of the 1920s', Federal Reserve Bank of Chicago, Working Paper Series, **WP–89** (18), October.

3. The Deregulationist Assumptions

INTRODUCTION

This chapter will focus on the assumptions which underlie the arguments that the Deregulationists wage in support of their policy recommendations. These assumptions require a little digging to unearth because they are usually made in an implicit rather than an explicit manner. Fortunately, they are fairly clearly implied through the theoretical underpinnings that the Deregulationists repeatedly employ in crafting their supporting arguments.

It is important that these assumptions be discerned. They provide the road map which leads the Deregulationists to advocate the replacement of regulatory restrictions and supervisory monitoring, to maintain a safe and sound financial system, with market and regulatory (which is market imitating) discipline based on free market principles. Virtually fully free financial markets are the end result, with DFFs essentially unencumbered by restrictions and operating as they think best.

This is a radical departure from the consensus, which formed after the banking collapse of the 1930s, on the need to regulate the behavior of both financial firms and markets. This drastic change in policy, which some wrenching historical experience has brought us, requires that a careful study be made of the Deregulationist assumptions so that it can be determined how well they reflect the behavior taking place in the real world. The use of assumptions which do not adequately reflect or take into account real-world (historical) experience may very well lead to the adoption of policies which will not result in the desired outcome.

Chapter Approach

The Deregulationist assumptions will be brought out by looking at what lies behind the arguments that are made in three broad, but basic, areas. First will be a review of how the Deregulationists model the nature and behavior of DFFs. Second will be a review of how they model the nature and behavior of financial markets. Third, and last, will be a look at how they think that runs on DFFs, through a redepositing of funds, will not destabilize the money supply and, in turn, not destabilize the level of economic activity.

THE NATURE AND BEHAVIOR OF DFFS

It is clear that the Deregulationists use a solid neoclassical model of the firm in their arguments. In fact, the use of a neoclassical model to depict DFF behavior is explicitly stated by Lewis J. Spellman in his book, *The Depository Firm and Industry*, published in 1982. Spellman is closely allied with the Deregulationists and employs the same modes of thought in his work. He frequently cites the Deregulationists in a positive light in both his book and his articles. In the introduction to his book Spellman writes:

> This volume has a point of view. Commercial banks, savings and loan associations, mutual savings banks, and credit unions are dealt with much like firms in any other industry. They purchase resources, produce a product, and price that product. The firms operate in an environment constrained by competition and regulation. ... Treating profit as a motive allows one to understand the depository firms' actions as market-induced, regulatory-constrained responses; decisions are not based on tradition or custom. ...
> The analysis of the depository firm acting as a private entity, operating only under restrictions imposed by the marketplace, is developed first. The neoclassical devices of firm cost and revenue curves and market supply and demand curves provide the structure for establishing an optimum deposit rate and the resulting rate spread, deposit and asset size, and the levels of cost and profit. The depository firm is treated like any other microproducing unit. (Spellman, 1982, p. 1)

It is obvious from this statement that well-established neoclassical microeconomics is being used to depict the nature and behavior of the DFF.

The Deregulationists' depiction of the DFF is analogous to a well-designed, well-oiled machine. It has no memory, no 'tradition or custom', to affect current action. It simply responds, much as a machine would, to outside demands it was designed to fulfill. A DFF's actions are 'market induced' and 'regulatory constrained'. Its scale is determined by marginal revenue and marginal cost curves, the shape and position of which are determined by market conditions and technical endowments. This makes the DFF essentially adaptive in behavior and, therefore, primarily passive in nature. The DFF is primarily passive because most of its efforts are spent on defensive operations; it adjusts, as best it can, to changes in its environment. Less effort is spent on offensive operations to change the environment in its favor. The DFF is adaptive in behavior, because its design automatically prompts profit-maintaining adjustments, in a mechanical way, to environmental changes which touch upon its operations. Those DFFs which more readily adapt to market trends will be more successful than those which lag behind. I shall refer to this DFF characteristic as being passively adaptive.

The Deregulationists' Model of the DFF

As Spellman points out, the Deregulationists do not see the DFF as different from other firms in any essential way. Therefore, they find it effective to model DFFs after the manufacturing concern frequently analyzed by traditional microeconomics. This firm has a goal of maximizing profits. It does this by doing three things. First, it chooses the most profitable goods to produce. Second, it adopts the least costly method of production. And third, it produces at that level of output where the marginal revenue is equal to the marginal cost of production.

The Deregulationists see the DFF operating much as does such a manufacturing concern, with only minor modifications. Thomas M. Havrilesky in his article 'Theory-of-the-Firm Models of Bank Behavior' describes the behavior of the DFF in a succinct manner. He writes:

'Banks' have profitable opportunities for meeting customer loan demands while maintaining adequate liquidity. In order to meet customer loan demands and satisfy liquidity needs, a bank can attract funds from a wide variety of sources.

A useful way to view this process is to see the bank attracting funds from deposits and other sources until the marginal cost of attracting those funds (marginal cost includes interest costs and resource [production] costs borne by the bank) is equal to the marginal return on investments. This marginal return is adjusted downward to reflect legal reserve requirements, if any, on each source of funds. Having determined the total level of funds and the optimal scale of bank operations, management would allocate funds across alternative investments until their respective marginal returns, adjusted for any risk aversion on the part of bank management, are equal. (Havrilesky, 1985, pp. 7–8)

Spellman, in his book, *The Depository Firm and Industry*, uses a virtually identical model (Spellman, 1982, pp. 56–61 and 130).

Under this model, both maximum profit and optimal scale for the DFF are determined at that point where marginal cost equals marginal revenue. Liquidity, credit, interest rate and other risks are incorporated into the model by making appropriate adjustments to either costs or revenues. Basically, the DFF, according to the Deregulationists, functions as a profit-maximizing, risk-averse portfolio manager. The Deregulationists see DFFs simply supplying what the market demands. The market demands deposits which carry the highest possible returns in conjunction with a very high level of safety. The Deregulationists think that the discipline produced under deregulation will induce DFFs to either provide what the market demands or suffer reduced success.

DFF Nature, Behavior and Goals

In summary, the Deregulationists' DFF has three major characteristics in common with the perfectly, or atomistically,[1] competitive neoclassical firm. They are:

1. The well-run DFF prefers long-term over short-term planning horizons. It is clear that the Deregulationists think that DFFs will be induced to adopt this preference when there is ample market discipline. In any discussion of market discipline (that is, monitoring of safety by depositors and others) the Deregulationists point out how it will coax the DFF to operate in a conservative manner in order to satisfy the interests of depositors, shareholders and other creditors. This requires the DFF to opt to finance productive investment projects over speculative ones. Productive investments are safer to finance because their expected returns are more predictable since such projects provide more certain analytical data (examples are engineering and consumer preference studies) than do the anticipated market changes upon which speculative investments are based. Productive investment is also longer term because its profitability requires consistent investment over time in captial, personnel, marketing and distribution, and/or research and development. Speculative investment, on the other hand, is shorter term because its profitability depends on proper prediction of changes in market valuations which are fast paced and can only be foreseen, with sufficient confidence, over the near term. This longer-term operations horizon is analogous to how the manufacturing concern must operate to be successful. For the Deregulationists, the discipline which generates this conservative behavior is at its maximum when the freedom of markets is maximized, that is, when they come closest to the perfectly competitive ideal. Therefore, in a 'state of nature', wherein there

are no restrictive regulations, the DFF operates with an induced conservatism favoring the finance of safer and longer-term, productive investment.[2]

2. The DFF has a single goal of profit maximization and the DFF's management works as a unified team toward that goal. Havrilesky, in his model of the DFF, openly adopts these characteristics (Havrilesky, 1985, pp. 5 and 8). The authors of *Perspectives on Safe and Sound Banking* also clearly see DFFs holding these characteristics when they discuss how managements may operate their bank subsidiaries and affiliates as consolidated entities seeking a single profit objective. This makes it difficult for regulators to insulate some subsidiaries from the risks undertaken by others because the goal of management is to maximize profits for the institution as a whole (Benston et al., 1986, pp. 143 and 152–3). Spellman, through a succession of increasingly complex models of the DFF, in his book, *The Depository Firm and Industry*, maintains the single goal of profit maximization. In one section of the book he discusses alternative objectives but concludes that profit maximization is the best objective to use for modeling DFF behavior (Spellman, 1982, pp. 56–61, 85–94, 130, 145 and 344).

3. The DFF is characterized as being passively adaptive. The DFF's passivity comes from its primary efforts being expended on defensive operations. Its best defense is adaptation; it adjusts to environmental changes as quickly as possible in ways best calculated to maintain a maximization of profits. This sort of behavior is implied through the profit-maximization models which the Deregulationists use to describe the DFF. Passively adaptive behavior is implied because the DFF's optimal scale is determined at that point where profit is maximized. It was noted earlier that both the Havrilesky and Spellman models of the DFF have this characteristic (Havrilesky, 1985, pp. 7 and 17–18; Spellman, 1982, 56–61). This precludes the DFF from aggressively pursuing growth or increases in market share. These active efforts require accepting less than maximum profits to hopefully gain a better competitive position and better profitability in the future. Instead, the DFF simply accepts its environment, and, when that environment changes, it makes those adaptations which will keep profits at their maximum.

Havrilesky, when describing what DFFs do in reality, says that their 'balance sheet undergoes a dynamic adjustment to shocks' (Havrilesky, 1985, p. 10). This clearly indicates that a DFF's mode of operation is to respond to outside forces which touch upon it. This premise that DFFs are passively adaptive is sprinkled throughout Deregulationist literature in their descriptions concerning change in financial markets and institutions. Financial innovations, the introduction of new products, and DFF expansion in both scale and scope are all seen as changes that result when DFFs adapt to changes in the environment. These changes, since around 1960, arise, for the Deregulationists, from three main areas. One, is changes in what is demanded by the nonfinancial sector. Another, is financial market changes which make regulations binding and necessitate the finding of loopholes. The third is the availability of advanced technologies (Haraf and Kushmeider, 1988a, pp. 2 and 7–10; Schwartz, 1988, p. 37; Kaufman et al., 1983, pp. 102–3; Eisenbeis, 1983, p. 154; Greenbaum and Higgins, 1983, pp. 208 and 230–32). Spellman, in his DFF models, supports this scenario of adaptive change because the optimal scale of the DFF is determined by the positions and shapes of both the cost and revenue curves which the DFF sees as a given (Spellman, 1982, pp. 56–61, 70 and 75).

Free Markets, Competition, Discipline, and DFF Behavior

The Deregulationists' discussions of how free markets reduce DFF risk-taking also imply the assumption of a passively adaptive, profit-maximizing DFF. The argument is basically twofold and is used in discussing the merits of market discipline and deregulation, and how free financial markets really operate. On the one hand, greater competition, which is created under freer markets, generates greater market discipline which gives DFFs the incentive to operate in a more risk-averse manner. On the other hand, freer markets present DFFs with the opportunities they need to reduce their risk exposure. For the Deregulationists, these two forces operate hand in hand upon the DFF. The DFF responds to the new market discipline incentives to reduce risk by taking advantage of those new opportunities which reduce risk (Benston et al., 1986, pp. 138–9 and 173–9; Kaufman, 1988, pp. 17–21; Spellman, 1982, p. 17; Kaufman et al., 1983, pp. 113–17; Benston, 1990, pp. 106–7 and 179–214; Edwards, 1987, pp. 12–13).[3] This describes exactly how a passively adaptive, profit-maximizing firm would react. Since this sort of reaction from the DFF is essential to the Deregulationists' argumentation, it is a more than reasonable conjecture that the passively adaptive, profit-maximizing DFF described above is what the Deregulationists work with, or assume, in their writings.[4] Again, for the Deregulationists, the DFF is analogous to a well-oiled machine designed to respond to market signals.

THE NATURE AND BEHAVIOR OF FINANCIAL MARKETS

It appears that the Deregulationists also turn to well-established neoclassical analysis when it comes to the functioning of financial markets. This comes out quite clearly in Thomas F. Huertas's article, 'Can Banking and Commerce Mix?', when he describes the benefits of allowing such a mixing. He notes that allowing banks to enter commerce, and commercial firms to enter banking will promote more intense competition. He lists the standard benefits attributed to competition. The consumer benefits from lower prices, greater variety and greater convenience. The society benefits through increased efficiency and productivity, and greater output (Huertas, 1988, pp. 291–3). These are the benefits of competitive markets taught in any mainstream microeconomics course.

Basically, the Deregulationists' view of markets is in line with that espoused by Milton Friedman. According to Friedman, the voluntary exchanges, which take place under free markets, provide both the cooperation of agents and the coordination of market activities because the resulting market prices of such exchanges serve as signals which create both the incentive and the information needed to act (Friedman, 1962, pp. 13–14; Friedman and Friedman, 1979, pp. 11–20). Under these conditions, allowing all agents (individuals and institutions) a free pursuit of their own interest will optimize the institutional structures of society and maximize social welfare. With such a view of markets, it is natural for the Deregulationists to argue that free financial markets, through heightened market discipline, will deliver what is in both the individual and public interest – a safe and sound financial structure.

This view of markets can be seen in the Deregulationists' discussion of free markets and the efficiencies and discipline they generate. They note that free markets increase competition. This prompts DFFs to minimize costs through greater efficiencies and exploitation of scale and scope economies, to diversify to decrease risk, and to take advantage of production, marketing and management synergies (reducing both costs and risks) presented by diversification into new activities. The Deregulationists also equate increased competition of freer markets with increased discipline because the DFF is more fully exposed to the risks and rigors of the market. The DFF adapts to this exposure by operating in a more cautious and conservative manner, in that market competition forces it to minimize risk at each level of expected return. Also, they see highly competitive markets causing a DFF to find full and accurate disclosure of essential information regarding its health to be in its own best interest. This incentive for disclosure automatically supplies a free financial market with the information it needs to function effectively (Benston et al., 1986, pp. 138–9, 173–9, 195–200 and 205–12). Given this, the Deregulationists are, in essence, focusing on Adam Smith's view of markets, while setting aside his concerns about externalities. Free markets maximize social welfare because the pursuit of self-interest by individuals is best accomplished by fulfilling the needs (demands) of others.

Historical Analysis Reveals a Complementary Monetarist Viewpoint

The Deregulationists' analysis of US financial history indicates the use of a monetarist framework in their thinking concerning financial markets. In addition to adopting Friedman's description of market mechanisms, the Deregulationists also adopt the influential monetarist school of thought which Friedman developed with Anna Schwartz. Under Friedman's monetarism, good financial and economic performance over a sustained period depends on price-level stability. It argues that because of slowly changing institutional structures, the velocity of money is relatively constant and, when it is subject to change, the magnitude of that change is predictable. Given this, the central bank, through its control over bank reserves, has clear control over the money supply. To maintain price stability, and therefore economic stability, the central bank should provide monetary growth which closely tracks the sustained growth rate of the economy. Out of this logic falls the contention that bank runs which result in a redepositing of funds are not destabilizing because the money supply remains intact. A further extension is that private clearinghouse systems can be as or more successful than central banks at maintaining stability because they have stronger incentives for both monitoring members and taking action that stabilizes the money supply.

The Deregulationists' historical observations lead one to conclude that they think financial markets, when left to their own devices, left free to develop naturally, are inherently robust and stable. The Deregulationists think financial markets possess endogenous forces which maintain stability and quickly re-establish it when it is disrupted. Given these endogenous forces, periods of instability are short-lived and are the result of exogenous shocks to the system. These exogenous shocks include erroneous policies and inappropriate action or inaction by the regulatory authorities.

The Deregulationists' study of US financial history is grounded in two tenets of Friedman's monetarist doctrine. One is that noncontagious or limited contagious bank failures do not carry negative externalities which are any greater than those associated with the failure of a nonfinancial firm of equal size and relative importance. The other is that systemwide contagious bank failures are very rare because their occurrence requires a systemwide flight to cash by the banking public (Benston et al., 1986, p. 53). There will be more on these tenets later. Keeping these two tenets in mind will help shed some light on Deregulationist thinking regarding financial markets.

A note on deregulationist statistics

The Deregulationists, in the second chapter of their book, *Perspectives on Safe and Sound Banking*, have compiled an impressive set of historical statistical data. In table form, for each year from 1864 to 1940, they give the number of commercial banks, the number of failures, the commercial bank failure rate, the currency, the total commercial bank deposits, the currency-to-deposit ratio, the industrial production, the Standard and Poor's Index of common stocks, the long-term interest rate and the business failure rate. In another table they aggregate the data for bank failures and business failures across several useful year groupings. All of these statistics, except for those regarding industrial production, are taken from various series of the Bureau of the Census, *Historical Statistics of the United States Through 1970*. The data on industrial production come from the Bureau of the Census, *Long Term Economic Growth, 1860–1965*. The data on currency and total commercial bank deposits are included because the Deregulationists hold that sytemwide contagious bank failures should occur only in periods where there is a net currency outflow. They say this condition exists when both currency increases relative to total bank deposits and total bank deposits decrease. A look at the data shows that this only happened three times prior to the Great Depression – in 1878, 1893, and 1908. However, they doubt the contagiousness of the 1908 episode since the rate of bank failure remained below one percent (Benston et al., 1986, pp. 53–60).[5]

Of the only overlapping period which can be compared, the Deregulationists' numbers regarding both bank and business failure rates are nearly indentical to those of Pollin and Dymski in their article, 'The Costs and Benefits of Financial Stability'. For the period from 1875 through 1929 the Deregulationists calculate the bank failure rate as 1.02 percent. For the same period, the rate of bank failure calculated by Pollin and Dymski is 1.05 percent. The Deregulationists calculate the business failure rate for the same period at 1.00 percent. For Pollin and Dymski it is also 1.00 percent. Pollin and Dymski gather their statistics from sources similar to the Deregulationists, but their sources are more wide ranging and therefore likely to be more accurate (Pollin and Dymski, 1994, pp.375–83 and 392–8).

The Deregulationist data on bank and business failure is accurate. However, it is interesting to note the data they exclude. The data series begins in 1864 with the establishment of the national banking system. It excludes the free banking era which ran from 1837 to 1863. Rolnick and Weber, in their article, 'The Free Banking Era: New Evidence on Laissez-Faire Banking', compile data from four different states with wide-ranging free bank experience and the availability of state auditor reports. These states were New York, Wisconsin, Indiana and Minnesota. For the four states, they calculate the rate of bank failure as 15 percent. They define failure rather narrowly as banks which closed and redeemed their notes below par. Any bank which closed and redeemed its notes at par is deemed to have not failed. They do not include losses to shareholders and depositors as a sign of failure. Rolnick and Weber give the rate of closure for the four states as 48 percent (Rolnick and Weber, 1983, pp. 1080–91). Since most banks will not close unless there is some sort of trouble, it is likely that most of the bank closures resulted in losses to depositors and/or shareholders. Therefore, if we include losses to depositors and/or shareholders as a sign of failure, then the failure rate would be much greater than 15 percent.

This is obviously an unacceptable rate of bank failure. Rolnick and Weber's low estimate of 15 percent is nearly three times higher than the year of the highest rate of failure prior to 1930 which the Deregulationists compiled in *Perspectives on Safe and Sound Banking.* That was the 5.80 percent rate in 1893. A 15 percent bank failure rate is only exceeded once in the Deregulationists' data series and that is in 1933 when the failure rate peaked at 28.16 percent. It is troubling that data from the free banking era are excluded from the Deregulationists' historical analysis for two reasons. One is that this era most closely resembles the deregulated banking system that the Deregulationists advocate. The other is that the free banking era's rates of bank failure are similar to those which existed from 1930–33 and which the Deregulationists blame, not on bank behavior, but on the shortcomings of the Federal Reserve.

The Deregulationists also exclude data on bank failure after the 1930 banking legislation was imposed. As was noted earlier, the bank failure rates compiled by Pollin and Dymski are comparable to those compiled by the Deregulationists. For the period from 1947 to 1989, which excludes the favorable data from World War Two and includes the unfavorable data from the 1980s, Pollin and Dymski calculate the bank failure rate to be 0.2 percent. This means that the bank failure rate, when banks were operating under the 1930s legislation which the Deregulationists regard as misguided, was a fifth of what it was, according to the Deregulationists, from 1875 to 1929. This is a serious omission because a 1 percent bank failure rate looks pretty good until one realizes that a failure rate a fifth that size is achievable.

It is clear that by eliminating periods preceding and succeeding their data series, the Deregulationists have skewed the presentation of statistical data in a manner which bolsters their advocacy of extensive bank deregulation. It is important to keep this skewing in mind to understand why the Deregulationists' historical analysis departs sharply from the consensus. In the summaries of the Deregulationists' historical presentations which follow, I am striving to give the flavor of their analysis so that some of the theoretical foundations from which they work may be discerned. All the data referred to come from the two tables referred to earlier in *Perspectives on Safe and Sound Banking*.

The pre-1920s

The Deregulationists claim that the rate of bank failure prior to 1920 average around 1 percent. The rate of failure exceeded 2 percent in only three years prior to 1920. Their point is that 'large-scale bank failures do not appear to have been a normal part of the American banking scene' (Benston et al., 1986, p. 58). The Deregulationists go on to point out that systemwide contagious bank failures appear to have occurred only three times before the Great Depression. This condition, which requires a net currency drain from the banking system, occurred in 1878, 1893 and 1908. The Deregulationists note that there is doubt about the 1908 episode being one of systemwide contagion because the rate of bank failure remained below 1 percent. Their conclusion is that 'systemwide contagious bank runs have not occurred frequently' (Benston et al., 1986, pp. 59–60). Therefore, to the Deregulationists, bank failures and their possible contagion have no need of being a major concern. Bank failure alone is not destabilizing. Destabilizing disruptions only occur when there is a substantial external shock resulting in a generalized flight to currency. Such shocks, they claim with statistical validation, are rare.

The 1920s

The Deregulationists do admit that during the 1920s the number of bank failures rose substantially. It was ten times the average up to then, rising from an average of 60 per year to about 600 per year. But they go on to note that:

Throughout the 1920s, total bank deposits increased and the ratio of currency to deposits decreased. Thus, it appears that the large number of bank failures neither caused economic or financial hardship at the national level nor ignited ripple effects that toppled other banks outside the same market area. The failures primarily reflected depressed local agricultural prices. Most of the small banks were unit banks and were apparently not sufficiently diversified to withstand default on farm loans, which was their major loan category. (Benston et al., 1986, p. 61)[6]

This quotation indicates, in another way, that, for the Deregulationists, bank failure alone is not contagious. Contagion requires an external shock substantial enough to result in a generalized currency drain from banks. The bank failures that did occur were due to poor local economic conditions and these failures were exacerbated by unit banking laws which prevented diversification adequate enough to survive downturns (Benston et al., 1986, p. 61).[7] Again, instability is due to exogenous shocks. In this case the instability is exacerbated by poor regulatory restrictions. The implication is that if the market had been left free to develop naturally, then DFFs would have been more diversified and would have failed in such small numbers that there would be no or insignificantly small destabilizing effects. The Deregulationists are claiming that free, undisrupted markets naturally create endogenous structures and forces which maintain stability.

The 1930s
When it comes to the banking crisis of the 1930s, wherein bank failures rose to 13 percent, almost triple the already high 1920s rate, the Deregulationists hold to the same line of thinking they used to describe the increased rate of bank failures during the 1920s. They assert that, as with the 1920s, the banks which failed during the 1930s were quite small. They conclude that 'many banks continued to fail primarily because of adverse local business conditions rather than because of spillover from other failed banks outside their market areas' (Benston et al. 1986, p. 62). They also note that many of these were small nonmember banks which could not be assisted by the Federal Reserve (Benston et al., 1986, p. 32).[8] The Deregulationists go on to conclude that the 1930s are 'unique in U.S. history, and the lessons drawn from it are probably not very applicable to other periods, even those of other economic and financial crises, and they should not be used to make decisions about financial structure' (Benston et al., 1986, p. 62). Therefore, not even the Great Depression jars the Deregulationists from their belief that free financial markets are inherently stable and can only be upset by a significant external shock.

For the Deregulationists, what makes the 1930s unique is the great depth and length of the downturn. They claim that most bank runs, including the 1908 episode which spawned the Federal Reserve, 'have been contained by appropriate action, with only minimal and short-lived adverse effects on national financial stability and economic activity. Generally, the instability of individual banks or groups of banks has not translated into instability in the banking system as a whole' (Benston et al., 1986, pp. 60 and 77). The 1930s, they note, is a traumatic exception to this for there was a run on all banks in late 1932 and early 1933. This 'caused the banking system to grind to almost a complete halt and substantially reinforced the economic crisis at the time' (Benston et al., 1986, p. 77). Again, the Deregulationists claim that this event is an exception and that it has unduly 'colored the analysis of bank runs and failures ever since' (Benston et al., 1986, p. 77). They conclude that 'it is time to discard the fears of bank runs based on the experiences of the Great Depression and to adopt more realistic attitudes and policies based on both the long sweep of U.S. history and the new institutions and arrangements now in place' (Benston et al., 1986, p. 77).

The Deregulationists also claim that the 1930s' banking collapse was not due to the kind of excessive risk-taking by banks which the Banking Act of 1933 addressed. They claim that the payment of higher rates of interest on deposits did not cause banks to make riskier investments and fail at a higher rate. Such banks, they claim, had lower rates of failure. Also, speculation in securities did not result in failed banks. According to the Deregulationists 'no bank that traded or underwrote substantial amounts of securities failed' (Benston and Kaufman, 1988b, p. 6). Instead, according to the Deregulationists, the collapse became extensive because of poor policies and mismanagement by the authorities. There was a one-third decrease in the money supply caused by bank failures but exacerbated by state-imposed bank holidays which encouraged the public to withdraw funds and hold cash. The hoarding of gold, prior to Roosevelt taking office, due to anticipation that the authorities would devalue the dollar in terms of gold, led to the conditions which caused the president to declare a bank holiday upon taking office. This deepened the crisis (Ely, 1988, pp. 55–61; Benston et al., 1986, pp. 31–2 and 61–3). Lastly, the unit banking system, by fostering inadequate diversification, magnified the crisis by increasing the number of bank failures. From this it is clear that, for the Deregulationists, the elements which precipitated and deepened the collapse were not bank behaviors but erroneous regulatory restrictions and mismanagement.

Federal Reserve failure

The Deregulationists, however, go on to state that the primary cause of the severity of the Great Depression was inappropriate inaction by the Federal Reserve. The Deregulationists note that, before the creation of the Federal Reserve, banks, through market incentives, had created an extensive private clearinghouse network. These private clearinghouses, by serving as lenders of last resort, or by suspending the conversion of deposits into specie and issuing certificates, effectively contained bank runs, claim the Deregulationists. Such clearinghouses performed well but there were imperfections and concerns about technical illegalities occasionally committed under tacit approval of the authorities. This led, according to the Deregulationists, to the formation of the Federal Reserve, which was intended to be an improvement by serving as a legally sanctioned, national clearinghouse. The Federal Reserve, however, did not have the same direct incentives as did the private clearinghouses, say the Deregulationists, to maintain the solvency of their member banks. Thus, the Federal Reserve, unlike the private clearinghouses in earlier panics, failed to perform as it should when faced with its first banking panic, the panic of 1929–33 (Kaufman, 1988, pp. 19–21; Benston and Kaufman, 1988a, pp. 64–5). In conjunction, Charles W. Calomoris, in his studies of state-run deposit insurance systems, concludes that the most successful were mutual guarantee systems which took advantage of the same self-regulation and incentive compatibilities developed under private clearinghouse systems (Calomoris, 1989b, pp. 10-30; Calomoris, 1989a).

This Deregulationist reading of history indicates once more their beliefs concerning the efficacy and stability of free financial markets. One is that markets, when they are free and left to their own devices, develop institutional structures, such as the clearinghouse, to maintain stability. Another is that instability is the result of some external shock. In this case the shock was unexpected inaction by the Federal Reserve. The inaction was unexpected because of the aggressive action that clearinghouses undertook in response to panics before their replacement by the Federal Reserve. This belief that banking instability is the result of an external shock is consistently adhered to because the Deregulationists take pains to argue that the direction of causation runs from economic difficulties to bank panics. Banking panics do not start economic downturns (Benston et al., 1986, pp. 53 and 66; Kaufman, 1988, p. 17; Benston and Kaufman, 1986, p. 70).

Benston and Kaufman's vivid description of how the Federal Reserve failed its mission during the late 1920s and early 1930s lucidly demonstrates how they use Friedman's monetary analysis to erect their arguments.

The general banking collapse and much if not all of the depression of the 1930s could have been prevented by the Federal Reserve, which could have stemmed the decline in the money supply with open market operations and reductions in the required reserve ratio. Indeed the central bank can always offset a multiple contraction of the money supply. Hence a financial panic and collapse of the banking system as a whole are entirely preventable. Individual banks or groups of banks may fail [for various reasons]. ... But none of these situations need start a chain reaction that affects other banks not directly subject to the same shocks, thereby causing a systemic collapse. That can both be prevented and caused by the central bank. (Benston and Kaufman, 1988b, p. 7)[9]

Basically, for the Deregulationists, major financial collapses, even those before 1930, are the fault of government action or inaction (Benston et al., 1986 pp. 30–35). In fact, the Deregulationists state that any extensive last resort lending by a central bank is evidence of poor monetary control (Benston et al., 1986, pp. 116–17).

One gets the strong impression from Deregulationist writings, that if the Federal Reserve had never been established, and if the natural, free market developments of a money supply tied to gold, in conjunction with the private clearinghouse system, had been allowed to remain and improve, then there never would have been a Great Depression. With such an impression, combined with their blending of well-established neoclassical and monetarist frameworks, one can only conclude that the Deregulationists think that free financial markets are robust and stable; that optimal structures naturally develop; that there are endogenous forces which maintain a stable state and quickly re-establish it when disrupted; and that periods of instability, which are few and short-lived, are the result of external shocks.

Other Positions Signifying Confidence in Free Financial Markets

The Deregulationists also adopt specific theoretical and policy positions which signify confidence in the efficacy of free financial markets. These positions take us beyond that established through Deregulationist historical analysis where financial markets are inherently self-equilibrating and develop optimal structures. These positions also require financial markets to predict well and generate prices which are informative, sending participants clear signals. These added characteristics are most clearly implied in the Deregulationists' discussion of how risk is best evaluated and managed. But they are also implied in their discussions of what makes an asset liquid and what makes market value accounting useful.

Before going into these specific areas it is valuable to look briefly at some of the terminology used by the Deregulationists. They frequently speak of the equilibrium market value of assets, of the equilibrium market interest rate, of equilibrium market levels, of competitive equilibrium, and of financial equilibrium (Benston et al., 1986, pp. 114, 117, 125, 228 and 229). All of these terms indicate that they think markets operate effectively and smoothly. Also, the Deregulationists' definition of financial equilibrium indicates that the famous rule of one price for any specific item is followed. Financial equilibrium is defined as 'reached when the market price for bearing every relevant type of undiversifiable risk is the same for every asset to which this type of risk applies' (Benston et al., 1986, p. 229). It appears, from this terminology, that well-established neoclassical market theory is a basis for Deregulationist thinking.

Risk

In the Deregulationists' discussion of risk, uncertainty is referred to but not in the Keynesian sense wherein uncertainty is the unknowable or unpredictable future. In the Keynesian world, according to James Crotty, the

> central thesis is that the future is *unknowable in principle.* Keynes theorized human decision making in a nonergodic, ever-changing economic and social environment. The economic outcomes we observe over time, he argued, are generated by an ever-changing system of agents, agent preferences, expectations, and economic, political, and social institutions, a system of 'originative' choice in which future states of the world are in part created by the current agent choice process itself. ... Thus, each observation is drawn from a unique generating mechanism whose structure depends on current and future agent choice as well as the future pattern of institutional change, both of which are inherently unpredictable. There can be no pregiven center of gravity to anchor the expectations of Keynesian agents; they never have complete knowledge of the future. (Crotty, 1994, pp. 111–12)

Instead, for the Deregulationists, uncertainty is a measurable element of risk. According to them, an assumption of risk exposes one to an uncertain outcome whose expected value is measured by a probability and variance distribution. That with the greater variance has greater risk (Benston et al., 1986, pp. 18 and 25; Benston and Kaufman, 1988b, pp. 34 and 37; Spellman, 1982, pp. 121–2 and 124; Kaufman et al., 1983, pp. 113–14). In this world

> theories of agent choice use the probability calculus, a statistical theory developed for repetitive and mechanistic games of chance such as

roulette or dice. The statistical properties of the probability distributions used in these theories are based on the assumption of at least potentially infinitely repeatable experiments in an unchanged structure. (Crotty, 1994, p. 108)

This process is an ergodic one wherein the averages calculated from past observations cannot be persistently different from the averages of future outcomes.

This means that the risk of an investment can be measured in what are essentially actuarial terms, just like life or homeowners' insurance (Crotty, 1994, p. 112).[10] The riskiness associated with an asset is measured by its past performance, its past variance and probability. Life and homeowners' insurers can successfully measure risk in this way because the law of large numbers gives them a relatively stable and unchanging structure upon which to gather statistics and make projections.

If the Deregulationists think that investment risk can be measured in the same way, they must think that financial markets are inherently stable. Inherent stability requires that financial markets be endowed with powerful endogenous forces which constantly pull the market toward a state of equilibrium. This means that financial markets must lack destabilizing endogenous forces powerful enough to derail the equilibrating ones. The presence of such forces, by generating bouts of instability, makes market behavior unpredictable, rendering past performance an unreliable guide for the future. In other words, if financial markets did contain destabilizing endogenous forces, investment risk would be more akin to the risk associated with earthquake insurance, a Keynesian form of uncertainty, than the risk associated with life or homeowners' insurance.

When discussing the setting of risk-related deposit insurance premiums, the Deregulationists note that it is a problem solvable not by bureaucrats but by financial markets. They claim that financial technology is sufficiently advanced that free financial markets would supply the information necessary for observers to assess and price risk (Benston et al., 1986, pp. 236–7). In addition, Huertas claims that advances in financial theory have allowed the development of new financial instruments which

liquify what were once illiquid assets, and make it possible to separate the credit risk, interest-rate risk, and exchange-rate risk that were traditionally bundled into single financial instruments, such as bank loans or corporate bonds. Thus, these new instruments permit portfolio managers to manage and price risk more precisely. (Huertas, 1987, p. 144)

In order to be able to precisely price risk in this way, financial markets must not only be inherently stable, but also sober, for they must also supply participants with accurate and informative signals which predict well. If market signals were volatile, because of a lack of stability, or contradictory, because of a lack of sobriety, any effort to precisely price risk would fail. Given this, the Deregulationists must believe that financial markets behave as does the basic neoclassical model of markets.

Lastly, the Deregulationists also repeatedly note how portfolio diversification can decrease overall risk exposure through the acquisition of assets whose variance patterns offset one another. Risk is reduced because the offsetting variance patterns, in effect, cancel out, to a significant extent, different risks (Benston et al., 1986, pp. 25 and 139; Benston and Kaufman, 1986, pp. 61 and 63). For risks to be precisely offset in this way requires variance patterns to be consistent which, in turn, as with the precise pricing of risk, requires financial markets to be inherently stable and sober. If financial markets were subject to endogenous forces which occasionally produced less than sober cycles of boom and bust, then the variance patterns of all assets would be overwhelmed by less than sober forces pulling them all in the same direction. This would quickly erase any pattern of offsetting variances used in a diversification strategy to reduce risk exposure. Thus, if financial markets are unstable and/or less than sober, the Deregulationists are incorrect, and diversification is not a reliable and precise method of risk reduction simply because offsetting variance patterns will not be consistent.

Liquidity
The Deregulationists equate marketability with liquidity. The more marketable an asset is, according to the Deregulationists, the more liquid it is and the better money substitute it becomes. Eisenbeis, in his article, 'Eroding Market Imperfections', claims that new, more highly marketable financial instruments, along with advanced computer technology, will make the use of money (transaction accounts) unnecessary. Eisenbeis's basic argument here is that the wide marketability and divisibility of almost all financial assets will make the exchange of assets through electronic financial barter a simpler process than converting assets into a transaction account to accomplish exchanges. In essence, money becomes obsolete because of a wealth of highly marketable financial assets which serve as close money substitutes (Eisenbeis, 1987, pp. 38–41).

This reasoning ignores the second aspect which has traditionally made money the most liquid of financial assets. This second aspect is the soundness of the value of money. Absent rampant inflation, money is the most sound of assets because, unlike other financial assets, its value tends to rise during periods of financial market distress. To ignore this soundness aspect of liquidity implies that the Deregulationists believe that episodes of financial market distress are not the result of the normal functioning of the market. To equate marketability with liquidity requires that one think financial markets are stable. If financial markets are held to be occasionally unstable, liquidity (or moneyness) unavoidably has two characteristics: marketability and soundness. Additionally, for money to lose the role it has long played not only requires financial markets to be stable, but also requires that they consistently send participants accurate and reliable signals. If financial markets failed to send trustworthy signals, participants would not have sufficient confidence in highly marketable assets for them to displace money by serving as close money substitutes.

Market value accounting
The Deregulationists repeatedly claim that market value accounting will strengthen the stability of financial markets by imposing greater discipline on DFFs. This argument carries weight when markets are stable and market prices serve as accurate and trustworthy signals. In financial markets which fall short of this ideal, market value accounting may foster increased instability.

If financial markets suffer episodes of instability, market value accounting would increase the amplitude of boom and bust by mandating supporting asset revaluations. During expansions, when asset values rise, the upward revaluation of DFF assets would increase capital and allow them to expand more than they could without such revaluations. During contractions, the opposite occurs and DFFs, due to decreased capital, are forced to contract more than they would without market value accounting. Thus, if financial markets suffer occasional instability, market value accounting will result in DFF behaviors which amplify, instead of subdue, those periods of instability.

Lastly, if market prices are erratic, and fail to serve as trustworthy signals, then the revaluation of assets to market value will be destabilizing on account of both the frequency of the changes and the sandy foundation for them. Thus, the Deregulationists' advocacy of market value accounting arises out of their belief that financial markets possess those characteristics ascribed to ideal markets in neoclassical theory.

DFF TROUBLE, THE MONEY SUPPLY AND ECONOMIC ACTIVITY

The Deregulationists' analysis of bank runs, through the use of money mechanics, is a further indication of their monetarism. It explains why they believe depository financial markets are free of any serious contagion problems and therefore can function best when they are essentially free of binding regulations.

This analysis of bank runs is bound up with the Deregulationists' assumptions about markets, discussed in the previous section. The Deregulationists' work on bank runs relies strongly on the existence of rational market participants. This rationality assumption falls directly from the Deregulationists' belief that markets generate accurate signals which participants have confidence in and therefore act upon. These accurate signals will only be produced by markets if players are rational.

Rational participants are essential to the Deregulationists' analysis of bank runs. Rational observers will evaluate the soundness of each DFF's portfolio on an independent basis. Under such rational DFF evaluation, the confidence in any DFF known to be sound will not be swayed by the distress or failure of surrounding DFFs. Thus, for the Deregulationists, rationality limits and contains the contagion that has traditionally been feared in depository financial markets. This element of rationality, in which funds are typically redeposited in safe banks, will become clear in the following review of the Deregulationists' analysis of bank runs.

Bank Runs: A Bogey Man

The Deregulationists claim that the traditional fear of bank runs is based on an unjustifiable reasoning that bank runs are highly contagious in a sequential manner. The Deregulationists say that this belief that bank runs are highly contagious is due to the widespread notion that a run on one bank will generate suspicions and fears about nearby and similar banks which are likely to result in runs upon them and so on. They claim that it is believed that with each succeeding wave of runs the degree of financial distress rises, making it more likely that individual banks will experience failure. As failures occur, suspicions and fears, it is commonly thought, will grow into panic which increases the rate at which bank runs and failures spread. If the panic is not somehow arrested, and it is believed a force outside the market is required, the result will be the collapse of the financial system (Kaufman, 1988, pp. 9–10).

The Deregulationists assert that the argument, given above, of sequential contagion is wrong. They use the following reasoning, based on money mechanics, to explain why.

When an individual withdraws funds from a DFF he/she deems to be unsafe he/she has three options: (1) He/she can shift his/her deposit to a bank he/she thinks is safe. This is a direct redeposit. (2) If he/she does not think any bank in his/her market area is sufficiently safe he/she can purchase safe nonbank securities such as treasury securities. The sellers of the securities will deposit the proceeds in their banks, which they must think are safe or they would not have sold the securities. This is an indirect redeposit. (3) No banks are deemed to be safe and direct and indirect deposits do not take place. Instead, individuals choose to hold cash. This represents a flight to currency.

The Deregulationists claim that under the first two scenarios there is very little, if any, threat of sequential contagion, because reserves and deposits are not lost to the banking system as a whole. They note that if a solvent bank endures a run, then banks not suffering runs, because of the deposits they gain, will be able to extend it loans so that it will have the liquidity it needs to cover withdrawals and thereby avoid any erosion of solvency. Therefore, say the Deregulationists, bank runs, in and of themselves, are not a cause of bank insolvency.

The Deregulationists point out that when runs occur on insolvent banks it is simply a symptom of that bank's failure and does not in any significant way weaken the system as a whole, because, through redeposits, both reserves and deposits are preserved and contagion is contained. The Deregulationists admit that there may be regional contagion, wherein funds are withdrawn from firms in similar circumstances. However, they claim that the contagion will be contained within the region as funds are redeposited in safe institutions outside the region.

Simultaneous, not sequential, contagion

According to the Deregulationists, it is only under the third scenario, a flight to currency, that the traditional fear of bank runs has any validity. As this scenario unfolds, all banks, at the same time, are striving to meet deposit outflows. Under these conditions, fire sale losses will occur and liquidity problems will expand into solvency problems. This happens because both deposits and reserves are being pulled out of the banking system. The feared contagion has become a reality. Solvent banks become insolvent because of severe and unresolvable liquidity problems caused by massive withdrawals of deposits.

These events, the Deregulationists point out, may appear to be the traditionally feared banking panic where healthy banks come to fail solely because of a shattering of depositor confidence. The above case, the Deregulationists note, is quite different from the traditional description of a banking panic because the contagion is not sequential, it is simultaneous or instantaneous. In the traditional description of a banking panic, the crisis, represented by bank runs, spreads from bank to bank in a sequential manner. In the third scenario, the contagion is not sequential but is simultaneous because it is a flight to currency which is not a run on an individual bank but is a run on the entire banking system.[11]

Historical evidence

As was extensively discussed in the preceding section on markets, the Deregulationists claim that historical studies of financial crises indicate that the times when a flight to currency may have occurred are very rare, and that the Great Depression of the 1930s, the worst of all, was a unique experience which will not recur, because of the stabilizing presence of deposit insurance (Kaufman, 1988, pp. 25 and 32). Therefore, according to the Deregulationists, episodes of dangerous contagion, a flight to currency, need not be feared. In addition, as was also noted in the preceding section, the Deregulationists further dismiss the danger of banking panics because they are not endogenously generated but are the result of exogenous shocks because their studies, they claim, show that nationwide runs are more likely the result than the cause of their concurrent economic depressions.

The Deregulationists, however, give three additional conditions, new to modern financial markets, which make contagious flights to currency less likely in the future than their rare occurrences in the past. These three conditions are:

1. The Federal Reserve is better, more sophisticated and more experienced at managing financial markets. Remember, the Deregulationists have adopted Friedman's monetarism and they think that the Federal Reserve is fully capable of maintaining stability by keeping reserves, and in turn the money supply, steady. (See note 9 for references.)
2. Financial markets and financial players are more sophisticated and are equipped with far better and far greater information than was obtainable in the past. Also, the domination of large units with many varied and sophisticated financial transactions prevents any major sustained flight to cash. Only simple units, with very small financial dealings, can function on a cash basis. The larger and more sophisticated units, which compose the bulk of the economy,

cannot function on a cash basis and therefore must remain 'plugged in' to the financial system.

3. Federal deposit insurance and its success at protecting depositors from loss, have given the public much trust and confidence in the safety of the banking system. Therefore, currently, it will take much more banking distress to spark runs than it did in the past.

Lastly, the Deregulationists note a fourth condition, the adoption of their reforms, which will virtually eliminate the likelihood of nationwide runs since powerful market discipline will be produced which will induce DFFs to operate in a cautious and conservative manner, making banks more robust and better able to withstand external shocks and maintain the public's confidence in them (Benston et al., 1986, pp. 53–72 and 74–8; Benston and Kaufman, 1986, pp. 64–70; Kaufman, 1986, pp. 1–4; Kaufman, 1988, pp. 9–40; Benston and Kaufman, 1988b, pp. 13–14).

Banks are not special

Thus, for the Deregulationists, banks are not special. They do not carry any externalities which make their distress or failure any more harmful than that of a comparably sized nonfinancial firm. Losses to the surrounding community, according to the Deregulationists, only become more severe than those from the failure of a nonbank firm when a bank is allowed to operate after it becomes insolvent. To prevent such losses banks approaching insolvency should be reorganized in some way or closed and liquidated. This is analogous to the bankruptcy process nonbank firms use to contain losses. In addition, bank failure may be less harmful than the failure of nonbank firms, claim the Deregulationists, because bank services and products are more homogeneous and more easily and quickly replaced than nonbank products and services. They also point out that advances in computer and telecommunications technology further ease the quick replacement of lost bank services (Benston and Kaufman, 1988b, pp. 14–22; Kaufman, 1988, pp. 30–32; Benston and Kaufman, 1986, pp. 64–7).

Summary of bank run argument

To summarize, the Deregulationists claim that banks are not special because bank failures and the runs which cause them are not costly and are not to be feared for the following reasons:

1. Banks are not special. They do not possess any externalities which are significantly different from those possessed by nonbank firms.

In fact, bank services are claimed to be more easily replaced than nonbank services.

2. Runs on individual banks, which are most common, are not contagious and, therefore, not dangerous. Such runs are contained because withdrawn funds are redeposited. This maintains both banking system reserves and the money supply. The result is that there is very little, if any, impact on the level of economic activity. This same process also contains runs on groups of banks or regions.

3. Runs on the banking system have been very rare, and, except in the case of the 1930s, have been effectively contained, with only short-term negative fallout, through the clearinghouse actions sponsored by the banks themselves. In addition, nationwide runs will be even more rare in the future. This is due to the existence of deposit insurance, a central bank which (having learned from the past) will fulfill its lender-of-last-resort function, more sophisticated markets which provide better information, and more sophisticated participants which cannot operate on a cash basis. Lastly, the Deregulationists' reforms, if adopted, would make the banking system more robust, enabling it to absorb shocks which would otherwise be destabilizing.

Assumptions implied by bank run argument

This Deregulationist argument concerning the innocuous nature of bank runs and failures is obviously drawn from assumptions developed in well-established monetarist and neoclassical frameworks. The argument that a churning of funds among DFFs will not cause disruptions because bank reserves and the money supply are preserved arises out of a monetarist viewpoint. It essentially ignores or discounts into insignificance the disruptions of broken credit relationships and interlinkages caused by any churning of funds among DFFs. The Deregulationists' use of that framework is also indicated by their position that the Federal Reserve is fully capable of maintaining reserves and the money supply and therefore banking system stability. This makes the central bank one of the external shocks which can disrupt the inherent stability of the banking system.

Lastly, the calculated and rational manner in which depositors are believed to respond to individual and group bank runs, by not panicking and redepositing their funds, brings out front their use of neoclassical assumptions regarding both markets and their participants. Markets are stable and provide accurate and reliable information because, even during periods of distress, the health of each DFF, through market signals, can be evaluated independently of others. Participants are rational because they do not allow distress in other sectors to color their judgements about their own investments. Instead, evaluations are performed independently and logically on a case-by-case basis.

LIST OF ASSUMPTIONS

In closing I shall simply list the assumptions behind Deregulationist thought which have been discussed.

1. DFFs do not have extensive externalities.
2. The DFF is primarily passively adaptive in nature.
3. Well-run DFFs operate with longer-run planning horizons.
4. The DFF has a single goal of profit maximization.
5. DFF management works as a unified team toward profit maximization.
6. DFFs only allocate credit, they do not create it.
7. Financial markets are robust and stable. They possess endogenous forces which either maintain or quickly re-establish a state of equilibrium. Disruptions are caused by shocks to the system.
8. Market signals are accurate and trustworthy.
9. Market participants have adequate information. They behave rationally and are capable of processing and putting to advantageous use available information.
10. Market risks are insurable because they can be evaluated objectively through probability and variance distributions obtained through reliable actuarial-like analysis.
11. The financial system will remain stable, excluding major shocks, as long as the money supply remains stable. Therefore, a churning of funds among DFFs is not destabilizing. Also, as long as the money supply is stable the system will quickly recover from disruptive shocks.
12. The Federal Reserve is fully capable of maintaining a stable money supply.

NOTES

1. Spellman, in his model of the DFF, has it operating in an atomistically competitive environment. Only the local market for deposits is imperfectly competitive. All the asset markets (those for loans and securities) and all other deposit markets are modeled as perfectly competitive. See Lewis J. Spellman (1982), *The Depository Firm and Industry: Theory, History, and Regulation*, New York: Academic Press, pp. 53–5.

2. The most extensive discussion of market discipline that I have seen is in George J. Benston et al. (1986), *Perspectives on Safe and Sound Banking: Past, Present, and Future,* Cambridge, MA: MIT Press, pp. 173–201.

3. This series of citations provides a quick observation of this pattern of thought.

4. A helpful way to shed greater light on this Deregulationist reasoning is to make use of a crude model of the Deregulationist DFF presented in the introductory chapter and used again in the concluding chapter. This model depicts the DFF as a passively adaptive profit maximizer operating against a portfolio-centered risk constraint. The goal of deregulation is to generate market discipline which makes the risk constraint more prominent in the DFF's behavioral calculations. This prompts the DFF to avoid portfolio risks, thereby enhancing financial system soundness and stability.

5. These pages include the two data tables, an accounting of where the data came from and some cursory analysis of the data.

6. Also see Bert Ely (1988), 'The Big Bust: The 1930–33 Banking Collapse – Its Causes, Its Lessons', in Catherine England and Thomas Huertas (eds), *The Financial Services Revolution: Policy Directions for the Future,* Boston: Kluwer Academic Publishers, pp. 51–5 and 66.

7. The Deregulationists base this claim on data from E. A. Goldenweiser (193X), *Bank Suspensions in the United States, 1892–1931,* material prepared by the Federal Reserve Committee on Branch, Group and Chain Banking, 5.

8. This is either a rather logical assertion or it may be based on material from Clark Warburton (1963), *Depression, Inflation, and Monetary Policy: Selected Papers, 1945–1953,* Baltimore: Johns Hopkins University Press.

9. This claim about the Federal Reserve is repeatedly made. See: George J. Benston et al. (1986), *Perspectives on Safe and Sound Banking: Past, Present, and Future,* Cambridge, MA: MIT Press, pp. 28, 32–5, 37–49, 109–12, 114, 116–17 and 292; Anna J. Schwartz (1988), 'Financial Stability and the Federal Safety Net', in William S. Haraf and Rose Marie Kushmeider (eds), *Restructuring Banking and Financial Services in America,* Washington, DC: American Enterprise Institute, pp. 37, 41–3 and 49-52; George J. Benston and George G. Kaufman (1988a),'Regulating Bank Safety and Performance', in William S. Haraf and Rose Marie Kushmeider (eds), *Restructuring Banking and Financial Services in America,* Washington, DC: American Enterprise Institute, pp. 54–64; George G. Kaufman (1988), 'The Truth About Bank Runs', in Catherine England and Thomas Huertas (eds), *The Financial Services Revolution: Policy Direction for the Future,* Boston: Kluwer Academic Publishers, pp. 19, 25 and 35; George J. Benston and George G. Kaufman (1988b), *Risk and Solvency Regulation of Depository Institutions: Past Policies and Current Options,* New York University: Salomon Brothers Center for the Study of Financial Institutions; Monograph Series in Finance and

Economics, No. 1. pp. 6–7, 27 and 30; Franklin R. Edwards (1987), 'Can Regulatory Reform Prevent the Impending Disaster in Financial Markets?', in *Restructuring the Financial System: A Symposium Sponsored By The Federal Reserve Bank of Kansas City*, August, pp. 9–11.

10. Here Crotty quotes from J.M. Keynes (1937), 'The General Theory of Employment', *Quarterly Journal of Economics*, 51, 209-33. In this article Keynes speaks of risk incorrectly thought to be measurable in actuarial terms.

11. All the preceding material on bank runs comes from the following: George G. Kaufman (1988), 'The Truth About Bank Runs', in Catherine England and Thomas Huertas (eds), *The Financial Services Revolution: Policy Direction for the Future*, Boston: Kluwer Academic Publishers, pp. 10–15; Benston et al. (1986), *Perspectives on Safe and Sound Banking: Past, Present, and Future,* Cambridge, MA: MIT Press, pp. 42–52; George J. Benston and George G. Kaufman (1986), 'Risks and Failures in Banking: Overview, History, and Evaluation', in George G. Kaufman and Roger C. Kormendi (eds), *Deregulating Financial Services: Public Policy in Flux*, Cambridge, MA: Ballinger Publishing Company, pp. 64–7.

4. Six Alternative Assumptions for Firms

AN ALTERNATIVE VIEWPOINT

This chapter, and the one following, will propose a set of twelve alternative assumptions concerning both DFFs and financial markets to replace the Deregulationist assumptions which were discerned and analyzed in Chapter 3. These alternative assumptions are proposed because they more closely reflect observed behavior. Over the years, a number of economists such as Adolph A. Bearle and Gardiner C. Means,[1] P.W.S. Andrews,[2] Robin Marris,[3] Edith T. Penrose,[4] Gordon Donaldson and Jay W. Lorsch,[5] William Lazonick,[6] G.B. Richardson,[7] Charles P. Kindleberger,[8] Hyman P. Minsky[9] and Martin Wolfson[10] have analyzed, or developed studies which indicate, how the assumptions associated with established microeconomic theory fail to correspond with what is believed to occur in reality. Bearle and Means, Andrews, Marris, Penrose, Donaldson and Lorsch, and Lazonick focus on the firm and either how the setting of prices or how the behavior and goal setting by the firm differ markedly from the typical marginalist model of the firm. Richardson, Kindleberger, Minsky and Wolfson focus on financial markets and institutions and how their actual behavior differs from that depicted in mainstream economics. Some, such as Marris and Richardson, have even strived to develop alternative frameworks. Marris, in the introduction to his book, *The Economic Theory of 'Managerial' Capitalism*, said it was 'inspired by a growing sense of frustration at the divorce between the motivational axioms employed in the established micro-economic theories and the type of behaviour most believe to be real' (Marris, 1964, p. xi). A set of alternative assumptions will be offered in this chapter, and the following one, out of a similar frustration with the assumptions employed by the Deregulationists.

Given the radical policy changes proposed by the Deregulationists, the lack of realism exhibited by their assumptions becomes a concern. How close actual, end results come to desired results depends on how accurately we anticipate, through theoretical reasoning, the responses of participants to the changed policy environment. With motivational and behavioral assumptions which abstract markedly from reality, the danger is that the world is not made more intelligible to us and a great deal of explanatory power is lost. To anticipate behavior with accuracy, assumptions which strive to mirror reality are necessary in order to explain how, not just predict how, participants will react to policy shifts.

For example, the real-world behavior, motivations and constraints of DFF managements are not analyzed in the Deregulationist literature. Instead, management is made an inexplicable black box, with the assumption of profit maximization, and it is predicted how this pursuit of profits will be favorably altered through the imposition of greater market discipline. However, when the real-world behavior, motivations and constraints on managers are observed it is quickly realized that managements have multiple and, at times, conflicting goals which are most readily accomplished and resolved when the firm is increasing in size, usually at the expense of profits. By being more realistic, and bringing management discretion to the forefront of analysis, one is much better equipped to explain how DFF managers will respond to the opportunities presented by deregulation. With this greater explanatory power, it is more likely that the anticipated results, according to theoretical reasoning, will closely correspond to reality (Hay and Morris, 1979, pp. 231–8).[11] For this reason a more realistic set of alternative assumptions is presented in both this chapter and the one succeeding.

Primary Sources and Approach

These alternative assumptions will be gleaned from two primary sets of literature corresponding to the two chapters. One, covering the development of firms in general, is analyzed in this chapter. The other, covering financial institutions and markets in particular, is analyzed in the next chapter. For firms, the behavioral and motivational assumptions are mainly derived from the work of Alfred D. Chandler, Jr. who has written a series of long and detailed studies on the origin, development and growth of the modern industrial corporation. Chandler's work is given considerable support by the similar conclusions of some economists working within the concern that economic theories need to be more realistic. For financial markets, the assumptions will be derived from the works of the Keynesian economist Hyman P. Minsky, similar thinking Keynesians, and those who have incorporated Minsky's theories into historical studies of financial crises. Both areas will occasionally be supplemented by

observations made by market analysts, such as the less systematic
Albert M. Wojnilower. The remainder of this chapter will focus on firms. After a quick
review of Chandler's work on firms, six alternative assumptions
regarding firms will be offered. These six alternative assumptions
correspond directly with the first six of the twelve Deregulationist
assumptions outlined at the end of Chapter 3. The chapter will end
with a discussion of each of these alternative assumptions regarding
firms. The following chapter, Chapter 5, will focus on a set of six
alternative assumptions concerning financial markets which correspond
with the second six of the twelve Deregulationist assumptions listed at
the end of Chapter 3. Chapter 5 will follow the analytical structure
used in Chapter 4.

Chandler on firms[12]

Chandler defines the modern business enterprise as a multidivisional
enterprise. Each division is overseen by its own salaried management,
often referred to as middle managers, who focus on operational
concerns. These divisions could theoretically be operated as independent
business enterprises. In turn, the contingent of divisions which
compose a multidivisional enterprise are overseen by an upper level of
management which focus its concerns on strategic decisions.

According to Chandler, prior to the emergence of the modern
business enterprise, the typical American business was composed of a
single division, operated out of a single office, performed a single
economic function, dealt in a single product line, and operated in one
geographic area. Interactions among these firms were coordinated and
monitored by market and price mechanisms. The multidivisional
structure, in contrast, operates over a wide geographic area, performs
multiple economic functions, and handles several product lines or
services. Under this structure, many transactions which were
previously coordinated by markets became internalized within the firm.

Chandler contends that the rise of the multidivisional business
structure led to two basic changes. One is the replacement of market
coordination of transactions with the administrative coordination of
transactions. This shift from market to administrative coordination
took place because the increased speed and higher levels of output
associated with the emergence of new technologies and expanded
markets made administrative coordination more certain and efficient than
market coordination. The second change is the rise of a salaried
managerial hierarchy, composed of upper, middle and lower managers,
to monitor and coordinate the various transactions taking place within a
multidivisional structure. It is Chandler's position that we need to

focus on the behavior of this new business institution, and the professional, salaried management class which came to administer it, to understand how modern firms function and why they have succeeded. Chandler develops five propositions which help explain why the modern business enterprise has prospered and grown. (Today's DFFs, with their multidivisional structures and professional management hierarchies, certainly fit within Chandler's definition of the modern business enterprise.) First, once a managerial hierarchy is established and successfully achieves its administrative function, the hierarchy itself becomes a source of permanence, power and continued growth. Traditional enterprises were short-lived because they were almost always partnerships which were reconstituted or dissolved upon the death or retirement of one of the partners. When a managerial hierarchy is in place there are lower-level managers who are trained and ready to take the place of upper-level managers who leave office for any reason. The management hierarchy provides an institutional structure which endures beyond the life of any individual or group of individuals.

Second, salaried managers tended to become increasingly technical and professional. With the modern business enterprise a manager could conceive of a lifetime career moving up the corporate hierarchy. This resulted in the increased length and formalization of management training. They came to receive similar schooling, read the same journals and joined the same associations. In short, salaried managers quickly became a professional class, akin to doctors and lawyers, possessing greater expertise than the owners who founded the businesses they worked for.

Third, as the multidivisional firm grew in size and diversity, and managers became more expert, the management of the enterprise increasingly became separated from its ownership. Under this separation, management came to dominate the firm's operational and strategic decisions because owners, who no longer managed, lacked the experience, knowledge and commitment necessary to seriously challenge management. This led to a divergence in the interests of owners and managers. Managers saw their success, their career, directly tied to the long-term growth and prosperity of their firm. Owners, on the other hand, saw the firm solely as a source of income. Thus, owners came to focus on the firm's financial condition and dividend policy, and how this affected the market's valuation of their shares.

Fourth, career managers, when they made administrative decisions, preferred those policies which favored the long-term growth and stability of their organization over those which maximized current profits.

[Managers] were far more willing than were the owners (the stockholders) to reduce or even forego current dividends in order to maintain the long-term viability of their organizations. They sought to protect their sources of supplies and their outlets. They took on new products and services in order to make more complete use of existing facilities and personnel. Such expansion, in turn, led to the addition of still more workers and equipment. If profits were high, they preferred to reinvest them in the enterprise rather than pay them out in dividends. In this way the desire of the managers to keep the organization fully employed became a continuing force for its further growth. (Chandler, 1977, p. 10)

Fifth and last, as these modern business enterprises grew, becoming large and dominant, their actions began to alter the market, the production process and the institutional landscape in which they operated. In short, the modern business enterprise does not see the environment (including technology) as a given which it is essentially powerless to change. Instead, modern business enterprises realize they have a capacity to at least foster, if not implement, change. Therefore, they develop an activist nature wherein they undertake actions designed and intended to reshape the environment to their competitive advantage.

From these foundational propositions Chandler comes to conclude that the American business enterprise became more, not less entrepreneurial as professional, career managers came to dominance and replaced the founding owner–managers. He comes to this conclusion in spite of his assertion that the founders of American big business were the driving force behind new products, new production processes, new marketing and distribution networks, and to some extent new organizational structures, which generated their success.

Chandler bases this conclusion on his argument that the most important innovations, in determining the success of the founders of big business, were not in the technical arena, but in organization and in marketing. It is precisely in these areas in which professional career managers have excelled, enabling modern US firms to be more entrepreneurial than those from which they descend. According to Chandler, professional, career managers developed the multidivisional structure. This not only made the enterprise more entrepreneurial by better enabling it to grow through diversification, but also freed top management from operational responsibilities so that it could work full-time on strategic, or entrepreneurial, plans and decisions. These decisions make top management highly entrepreneurial in function because their job is to focus on the determination of goals and how to allocate resources to best meet those goals, leaving operational decisions to middle- and lower-level management.

In addition, an organization run by career managers who are employees of the organization also magnifies entrepreneurial strivings after growth in two other ways, according to Chandler. One is that the returns to upper-level managers are directly tied to the performance of the organization which they oversee. This tie disciplines upper management to pursue what Lazonick calls innovative investment and growth strategies. Another entrepreneurial incentive which upper management has to pursue growth is the need to motivate lower-level managers to pursue the goals they set. Innovative investment and robust growth accomplish this by creating and opening up new opportunities for advancement (Chandler, 1988b, p. 73; Chandler, 1988e, pp. 128 and 137–9; Chandler, 1988g, pp. 392–7; Chandler, 1988f, 496–502; Chandler, 1994, p. 16).[13]

It is clear from Chandler's extensive writing that he develops a detailed perspective in which firm managements have considerable discretionary power, in which they have multiple goals centered around growth and profitability, and in which much business behavior is concerned with changing the structures faced by firms to their advantage. A number of economists have also advanced similar perspectives regarding the firm, its organization and its behavior. Some of these economists, whose arguments will be considered later, are Penrose,[14] Marris,[15] and Donaldson and Lorsch.[16]

A List of the First Six Alternative Assumptions

At this point it is helpful to provide a list of the six alternative assumptions which are primarily derived from Chandler's perspective on firms. This list corresponds directly with the first six of the list of twelve Deregulationist assumptions given at the end of Chapter 3. These six assumptions deal DFFs. The second six concern financial markets and will be the focus of Chapter 5.

The proposed first six alternative assumptions are:

1. DFFs have extensive externalities.
2. The DFF is primarily actively entrepreneurial in nature.
3. Because of competitive pressures, DFFs adopt shorter-run planning horizons to succeed.
4. The DFF has multiple goals entailing a balance between profit and growth goals (involving size, scope and market share) under a security constraint, which itself is composed of a balance between portfolio risk and competitive risk.
5. DFF management is often disunited because of independent empire building within the firm. Disputes over resource allocation are

more easily resolved when growth is given precedence over profitability.

6. DFFs allocate credit *and* create credit.

The remainder of this chapter will center around this list of six alternative assumptions concerning DFFs. Each of them will be discussed in the order that they appear in the list. The discussions will strive to provide a rough foundation for each assumption.

ASSUMPTION ONE DEPOSITORY FINANCIAL FIRMS AND EXTERNALITIES

DFFs are special, and differ from nonfinancial firms (NFFs), simply because their operations carry more externalities than those of NFFs. The failure or closure of a DFF has far more ripple effects on the surrounding economy than the failure or closure of an NFF of similar size and importance (Dymski, 1993, pp. 119–20). This difference in externalities is due to five basic reasons. They are:

1. *DFFs operate the payments system* DFFs are responsible for the smooth functioning of the payments system. Any disruption in payments due to default by a DFF will result in a widening circle of losses as other payments are interrupted down the line. This happens because participants depend upon payments to others to make payments to them. An example of this externality is the failure of a DFF which prevents an employer from meeting its payroll. This will result in the employees being unable to pay many, if not most, of their financial obligations. This will result in widespread disruptions and losses. If the default occurring in the payments system is due to the difficulties or failure of regional or money center banks which have large customers and hold clearing balances for other financial institutions, the disruptions and losses will be even more widespread. This potential for high levels of loss when the payments system is disrupted is why Jane W. D'Arista advocates unlimited insurance coverage for transaction balances (D'Arista, 1993, pp. 214–17).

2. *DFFs provide essential credit* In addition to operating the payments system, DFFs oversee, allocate and create a very large portion of available credit. The successful functioning of production and trade requires convenient and reliable access not only to the payments system but also to credit. The extension of credit by DFFs has externalities which are similar to those of the

payments system, because of similar problems with contagion. Through the normal course of business, as DFFs extend credit, intricate, interlocking webs of credit relationships develop around them. Trouble in any one DFF is likely to spread quickly to other DFFs. The complex chains of credit interlinkages which join DFFs together make the successful functioning of each DFF's credit operations dependent upon payments made to them to make payments to others. Therefore, just as with the payments system, any breakdown in the chain of credit payments negatively affects many others in domino-like fashion.

It is this dual dependence which the nonfinancial sector has on DFF operations which gives DFFs extensive externalities. These externalities can be positive or negative in nature, having positive or negative effects on the level of economic activity. They will remain positive as long as the public has confidence in the safety of their funds deposited with DFFs, as long as they believe DFFs are meeting their fiduciary responsibilities. For this reason DFFs, unlike NFFs, have traditionally been burdened with regulations which limit competition and contain their entrepreneurial drive so that they can better meet their fiduciary responsibilities (Corrigan, 1985, pp. 207–9; Corrigan, 1986, pp. 11–21; D'Arista, 1994, pp. 115, 153–4, 345 and 377).

3. *DFFs provide needed liquidity for other institutions and markets* DFFs also provide the liquidity which enables other financial institutions and markets to operate. D'Arista's analysis of the parallel banking system serves as an example which vividly illustrates this characteristic. Access to the payments system operated by banks and the provision of guarantees, or back-up lines of credit, issued by banks provide money market mutual funds, finance companies and commercial paper markets (the three sectors composing D'Arista's parallel bank system) with the liquidity they need to function. This enhances the externalities of DFFs because such actions on their part foster the creation of extensive credit networks with intricate interlinkages and high levels of contagion (Corrigan, 1985, pp. 209–12; D'Arista, 1994, pp. 418–33; D'Arista and Schlesinger, 1993, pp. 172–3).

4. *DFFs serve as the conduit for monetary and credit policy* These externalities associated with operating the credit and payments system are shaped by the central bank's use of DFFs as the conduit through which monetary and credit policies are made effective. Externalities from DFFs are not only generated through the conduct of DFFs themselves but are also generated through the conduct of the central bank as it implements policy. According to D'Arista,

securitization and the parallel banking system have weakened traditional DFFs. It is by manipulating the reserves of these traditional DFFs that the Federal Reserve implements policy. The erosion of traditional DFFs dilutes reserves as a policy tool which forces the Federal Reserve to take more drastic and forceful steps for each desired level of effect. This will tend to make Federal Reserve actions more destabilizing which means that Federal Reserve policy implementation currently carries greater externalities through DFFs than it did in the past (Corrigan, 1985, pp. 212–13; D'Arista, 1994, pp. 274–5 and 442–3; D'Arista and Schlesinger, 1993, pp. 159 and 184–5).

5. *DFFs are evaluated on a comparative basis* The health of any single DFF, because it depends on both portfolio risk and competitive risk (threats to market share and the capabilities of maintaining or expanding it),[17] is not strongly independent of the health of neighboring DFFs. When DFFs are entrepreneurial and growth oriented (note assumptions 2 and 4), the evaluation of a DFF must be expanded to include comparisons with competing DFFs. Therefore several factors determine the strength of a DFF. Only one of these is the soundness and liquidity of its portfolio taken as a whole, or the level of portfolio risk. There are three other factors indicating how well a DFF is coping with, or overcoming, competitive risk which must also be taken into account. They are: (a) expectations about the growth potential and level of competition in the markets wherein the DFF does the bulk of its business; (b) the level of confidence evaluating parties have in the talents and abilities of DFF management in comparison to those of competing DFFs; and (c) how well a DFF's strategic plan measures up against those of its competition, and thereby how likely its growth will keep pace with, or exceed, that of the competition. Therefore, it is through comparative, not stand-alone evaluations, that the relative strength of each DFF is determined. This means that the health of any one DFF is going to reflect on the health of similar and neighboring DFFs because of characteristics which are common among them. The commonality of characteristics may be extensive because competitive strivings after growth cause each DFF to extend loans and make investments in those sectors of the economy which are most prosperous. This helps magnify the level of contagion, intensifying the extensive externalities associated with DFFs.

Financial Fragility, Contagion and Externalities

Lastly, any tendency toward increased financial fragility amplifies the above five sources of DFF externalities. This amplification occurs because greater financial fragility results in heightened contagion. There are two reasons for this. One, it increases the likelihood that any single DFF will fall into default because it operates with tighter, more fragile financial structures. Second, the disruption others suffer through the chain of credit interlinkages is more likely to result in further difficulties and additional contagious disruptions. This happens because other DFFs are also operating with fragile financial structures which are not capable of absorbing interruptions in expected payments without manifesting difficulties which will affect other DFFs. Intensified competition exacerbates this problem with contagion because it prompts DFFs to grow by assuming more risky portfolios – a form of escalated financial fragility.

ASSUMPTION TWO DFFs ARE ACTIVELY ENTREPRENEURIAL

Economists concerned about developing a more realistic model of the firm, such as Penrose, Marris, and Donaldson and Lorsch, have followed a line of thinking similar to that developed by Chandler in his historical studies. A theme common to each of the three economic models of the firm is that they agree with Chandler's contention that the professionally managed firm is as entrepreneurial as, if not more entrepreneurial than, the owner-managed firm. These models of NFFs are reviewed because they help lay the groundwork for a model of the DFF.

Penrose argues that at all times unused productive services exist within every firm. These unused services, together with the changing knowledge of management, present each firm with unique productive opportunities. The challenge for each firm is to successfully exploit these opportunities in a manner which innovates, expands the enterprise and builds some degree of competitive advantage. Penrose, in a rather roundabout way, explains that this challenge can only be met effectively when the enterprise has at its disposal well-developed entrepreneurial services, a managerial approach, or way of thinking, which is imaginative, creative, ingenious, versatile and ambitious (Penrose, 1968, pp. 411–12; Penrose, 1959/1980, pp. 31–42). Chandler, as already noted, expounds on this pressure to keep resources fully employed, how it drives growth, and how this process is successfully accomplished only when top management meets its entrepreneurial responsibilities (Chandler, 1988c, pp. 349–51).

Donaldson and Lorsch,[18] in their study of management decision making, build on the prior work of Marris.[19] Donaldson and Lorsch find that the primary goal of top corporate management is not the maximization of shareholder wealth, as commonly believed. Instead,

> their primary goal is the survival of the corporation in which they have invested so much of themselves psychologically and professionally. Therefore, they are committed, first and foremost, to the enhancement of corporate wealth, which includes not only the firm's financial assets reflected on the balance sheet but also its important human assets and its competitive positions in the various markets in which it operates. (Donaldson and Lorsch, 1983, p. 7)

In summary, Donaldson and Lorsch argue that corporate managements strive to maximize their discretion by minimizing their dependence on, or potential domination by, three different but interdependent constituencies. These are the capital market, the product market and the organizational market. Management limits its links to the capital market by balancing two sectors. It minimizes its use of debt by funding investment projects as much as possible through retained earnings. This, however, conflicts with the demands of shareholders who want high earnings per share and so desire earnings to be distributed through dividends, not retained. In the end, management realizes that low dividends can to some extent be offset by stock-price appreciation through growth. The dependence on any one product market is best alleviated through diversification – one form of growth. The demands of the organizational structure, the need to attract and retain necessary talent, are best accomplished through growth which provides new opportunities and room for advancement.

Therefore, according to Donaldson and Lorsch, managements, through a hierarchy of goals (the target growth rate; the target return on investment; the target earnings retention ratio; and the target debt/equity ratio), strive to balance growth and profits. Growth must be sufficient to avoid potential dominance by both the product and organizational markets. Yet profits must be ample enough to fund the investment projects needed to meet target growth rates, while minimizing debt and releasing that proportion of earnings just sufficient to satisfy shareholders to avoid dependence on or dominance by capital markets. In short, the job for management in accomplishing self-sustaining growth is to balance the supply of funds with the demand for funds (Donaldson and Lorsch, 1983, pp. 6–10, 34–40, 43–8, 50–57, 66–78 and 162–9). This is what Chandler refers to as the goal determination and allocation of funds role, the entrepreneurial role, played by top management.

Marris previously presented a simpler but similar corporate model. He says that under managerial capitalism managers have wide discretion and the organizations they lead are capable of moulding environments in directions convenient to themselves. Thus, management strives to maximize growth under a security constraint. Managements strive for high levels of corporate growth because their ambitions, prestige and earnings are tied to the size of the organizations they lead. This striving after growth is constrained by managements' need to be secure in retaining their positions. This security is eroded with exposure to both excessive debt and disgruntled shareholders. Therefore, managements must balance growth against profits. Profits must be ample enough to fund investment projects required for desired growth, to avoid undue debt and to provide shareholders with sufficient earnings (Marris, 1964, pp. 1–5, 42–56, 61–6, 106–7, 206–7 and 224). Once again management is playing an entrepreneurial function by determining goals and allocating resources.

DFFs, Growth and Portfolio Risk

Chandler's depiction of the firm, and the economic models of the firm just summarized, which share a kinship with Chandler, describe NFFs. We now consider the common elements of these models of the firm as they apply specifically to the DFF.

To begin with, an entrepreneurial striving after growth becomes clear, making DFFs more prone to acquire portfolio risks than to avoid them. Under both the Marris, and Donaldson and Lorsch models of the firm, the firm balances growth and profit against a self-sufficiency or security constraint. A part of this constraint is keeping shareholders satisfied. The more binding portion of the constraint is the avoidance of debt because the firm can use more debt to finance faster rates of growth. Since debt has this characteristic, the constraint on its use may ebb and flow as competitive needs to grow rise and fall.

Goldstein addresses this particular point in depth (Goldstein, 1991, pp. 65–7). He explains how the security constraint disciplines management's decision making in the direction of self-sustaining growth. This generates a conservative use of debt. However, he argues that this conservative use of debt may be altered in favor of more liberal uses of debt when a gap needs to be filled between internal funds and desired expenditures. Goldstein argues that such funding gaps arise 'if technological change or other competitive forces generate a perceived need to (say) invest heavily or risk the firm's survival. It is the source of the chief threat to security that has changed' (Goldstein, 1991, p. 67). This means that for security reasons, constraints on the use of debt will change as competitive conditions change. Constraints on debt will be significantly relaxed as demands for investment funds rise, be it to fund a new product line, update technology or simply increase the rate of growth. The security constraint is no longer primarily composed of borrowers' risk alone. It now also entails what I call competitive risk. Under Goldstein's modification, the security constraint becomes a balancing between borrowers' risk and competitors' risk. When severe competitive pressures arise, firms will opt to acquire more debt, more borrowers' risk, to reduce competitive risk, market conditions which threaten its survival. Security here is being enhanced because the borrowers' risk assumed is much less than the competitive risk, which the borrowed funds are used to combat and reduce.

An adaptation for DFFs

How does this new security constraint for NFFs apply to DFFs? DFFs as intermediaries are in the business of borrowing funds from depositors and then lending those borrowed funds to others. Given this, debt and concern about borrowers' risk cannot be a part of a DFF's security constraint even though competitive risk definitely is. I propose that instead of borrowers' risk, DFFs are concerned with portfolio risk as a part of their security constraint.

Under this proposition, a DFF's security constraint is composed of a balance between portfolio risk and competitors' risk. The Deregulationists correctly speak of how excessive portfolio risk can threaten a DFF's security. A DFF needs to avoid nonperforming loans and investments in its portfolio because they threaten to deplete capital and pull the firm into insolvency. On the other hand, a DFF must counter threatening moves made by rivals in order to secure the firm's survival and keep competitive risk in check. When a DFF's exposure to competitive risk rises, it can pare down that exposure by boosting growth through the assumption of greater portfolio risk. This will enhance security when the greater portfolio risk assumed is less than the decrease in competitive risk.

For example, a DFF's competitive risk rises when it lags behind its rivals in introducing successful innovations, when its marketing campaign lacks the know-how of others, when others have developed a more lucrative geographic dispersion of branches, when others have adopted narrower spreads or margins, or when others have found it advantageous to lower credit standards and/or make more speculative investments. A DFF suffering any of these ailments is not growing as fast as its rivals. If a DFF fails to grow as fast as its rivals, it loses market share and its size relative to its rivals shrinks. Any DFF in such a circumstance is at heightened competitive risk, and this competitive risk will grow the longer its growth rate lags behind its rivals, eroding its competitive position. The quickest way that any DFF can boost its growth rate is to assume greater portfolio risk by narrowing margins, by reducing credit standards, and by making more speculative investments.

Other methods of expansion, especially when entered into quickly, also tend to increase portfolio risk. Expansion through merger and acquisition frequently results in the assumption of assets of unknown and disappointing quality. Expansion through diversification or scope brings the DFF into new fields where it often lacks the expertise to adequately assess new and unfamiliar risks. Lastly, expansion through scale (or scope) brings the DFF in contact with new rivals with abilities it has not yet tested itself against.

Competitive risk is immediate; portfolio risk is not

It is clear that DFFs can reduce competitive risk by accepting more portfolio risk to hasten growth. In highly competitive environments, reducing competitive risk in this way will tend to enhance a DFF's security. This is the case simply because the threat from competitive risk is immediate, while that from increased portfolio risk is not.

Losses in market share automatically weaken a firm's competitive position because they stifle current and potential earnings. This makes it more difficult for the firm to retain and attract workers with needed skills and talents. This is exacerbated by a lagging growth rate which presents employees with fewer opportunities for advancement than are available elsewhere. Also, the firm loses market status and prestige. This results in a loss of depositors. Clients requiring credit and other financial services also tend to abandon the DFF since its sophistication and expertise have been tarnished. Because of this snowballing effect, competitive risk presents the DFF with a powerful and immediate threat to its survival.

On the other hand, increased portfolio risk is not an immediate threat to the DFF because the risks assumed are only potential ones whose possible negative outcomes are further into the future than are those from competitive risk. The following section on assumption three includes a discussion of how human tendencies toward optimism and gambling contribute toward short-termism. Under this tendency, managements will think that they have the skill and foresight necessary to reduce substantially both the likelihood and the size of any potential loss. In addition, more risky loans and investments will not be assumed if they present an immediate risk of loss. The potential for loss arises sometime in the future. This future need not be very distant for increased portfolio risk to enhance present security since competitive risk is so instantaneous.

An example of this process is the extensive less developed country, energy and real estate loans made by DFFs during the 1980s. These loans were initially quite lucrative and did not run into difficulties until a number of years after they were made. At the time these loans were made, each DFF thought it was enhancing its security simply because the perceived increase in portfolio risk was less than the reduction in competitive risk that such an increase purchased. This was the perception because the threat from competitive risk was immediate and required an immediate response of more rapid growth. On the other hand, those increased portfolio risks assumed to speed up growth were less than immediate and were thought to be capable of significant reduction through skillful management.

The more the rivalry, the more the portfolio risk

Under this process, it follows logically that the more entrepreneurial are DFFs, the more prone they will be to assume higher levels of portfolio risk. DFFs become more entrepreneurial the more intense becomes the competitive environment in which they operate. This happens because increased competitive intensity compels DFFs to quicken and lengthen their strides in pursuit of growth. Once started, this process becomes self-sustaining and self-reinforcing. This is the case because each DFF's striving after growth to reduce its own competitive risk increases the competitive risk within the system as a whole. This spawns yet another need to grow to reduce competitive risk and so on. The result is an increasing acceptance by DFFs of a persistently rising level of portfolio risk as DFFs are channelled into an endless pursuit of growth. This pursuit of growth, in a hotly competitive environment, opens up a route for increasing financial fragility (through increased portfolio risk) during expansions; a process aptly illustrated by Hyman Minsky, and discussed in the following chapter.

Entrepreneurial Factors Specific to DFFs

Chandler notes that

> where specialized skills of the managers and workers were involved in the exploitation of a particular technology or market know-how, diversification into new areas came relatively easily. Where the resources were concentrated instead on the mass production of a single line of goods in which the technology was fairly simple and yet required

much capital, diversification proved to be more difficult. (Chandler, 1988c, p. 350)

Therefore, for example, in the process industries, entrepreneurial innovation and growth through diversification is less costly and risky because the introduction of new products only requires a change in raw material or a new ingredient mix. In the mechanical industries, on the other hand, such introductions require heavy capital outlays for machinery and tools (Chandler, 1988d, pp. 114–15).

DFFs are analogous to Chandler's process industries and therefore will tend to be more entrepreneurial than NFFs in general. DFFs have very little, if any, capital tied up in production and so the introduction of new products or services does not entail heavy capital costs. New financial products are the result of specialized managerial skills involving imagination, creativity, ingenuity, versatility and ambition. After these products are thought up they are spontaneously created as they pass through the financial firm's marketing and distribution unit. Their creation does not require passage through a production unit. Without need for a production unit outside of management, the capital costs of introducing a new financial product are negligible in comparison to manufactured products, which require factories for their production. Therefore financial firms (FFs), even more than process industries, will tend to be more entrepreneurial than NFFs in general.

In addition, Wojnilower, in an extension of a theme running throughout his article, 'The Central Role of Credit Crunches in Recent Financial History',[20] argues that FFs operate under hyper-competitive conditions which require them to be more entrepreneurial than NFFs to be successful. He says that

> from the standpoint of the individual depository institution, the recent abolition of interest rate controls on consumer deposits has made more rapid expansion a matter of necessity as well as choice. An earnings squeeze has been created from which 'growing your way out by lending more' seems the only hope of escape. ... So long as interest rate ceilings held deposit rates at below market levels, depository insitutions had an easier way out. The cushion provided by a reliable stock of cheap deposit 'raw material' gave them the option of building up earnings and capital by means of a 'play safe' policy of investing only in relatively low yield safe loans and government securities. But in the new environment, safety is a luxury most lenders cannot afford. (Wojnilower, 1985b, p. 353)[21]

Given this atmosphere, Wojnilower claims that the essence of banking is overcoming in imaginative ways constraints on growth and profitability, especially those imposed by the Federal Reserve to control inflation by limiting monetary growth. What he describes is pure entrepreneurship:

> To escape the profit ceiling imposed by limits on monetary growth, financial institutions have shown great ingenuity in inventing new instruments and mechanisms that enhance earnings by accelerating the turnover of official money. That is what banking enterprise is all about. On occasion ... the innovations are so successful as to force themselves within the official monetary definition. (Wojnilower, 1991, p. 4)

Thus, it appears that conditions faced by FFs require them to have a high entrepreneurial drive. Wojnilower hints that such a drive is pervasive among FFs when he writes that 'changes in what central bankers blandly label "velocity" are often (possibly always) caused by the ebb and flow of the financial sector's efforts to overcome the close-to-zero-sum game to which it is condemned' (Wojnilower, 1991, p. 4). The result is almost unlimited growth prospects for each DFF through innovations which spawn inflation and/or speculative excess. This overcoming of the constraints of real growth by DFFs generates an atmosphere of hyper-competition among them. Therefore, in the end, each DFF's success depends on a highly developed entrepreneurial drive.

Entrepreneurial Drive Brings Activist Nature

The DFF that has been described thus far is what Hay and Morris refer to as the active firm as opposed to the passive, or traditional depiction of the firm. In the previous chapter it was noted that the Deregulationists adopted the traditional, or passive, depiction of the firm with regard to expected DFF behavior. According to Hay and Morris, the active firm model is the result of efforts to be more realistic by encompassing many commonly observed characteristics of existing companies not included in the traditional approach. From works by Chandler, Penrose, Marris, and Donaldson and Lorsch we have seen the importance of managerial motivation and organizational structure and how this promotes entrepreneurial behavior and a striving after growth to balance conflicting desires and demands under a constraint of self-sufficiency or security. Part of this package is that such firms do not simply passively adapt to their competitive environments. Instead, the firm, as an organization, is able to manipulate to some extent the competitive environment in which it finds itself (Hay and Morris, 1979, pp. 20–25, 238–43 and 277–8).

Chandler, throughout his work, has repeatedly documented how firms have found it advantageous to alter their environment by internalizing transactions so that they could be coordinated administratively, instead of through market mechanisms. This was accomplished by integrating backwards to secure inputs, be they raw, partially processed or intermediate finished goods, and by integrating forward, developing sales and distribution networks to get the final product directly to the ultimate consumer. According to Chandler, all this was done to smooth and coordinate the flow of material through the organization so that economies of speed, not size, could be exploited. The goal is to keep all units continuously operating at optimal capacity. Chandler's historical analysis of corporations such as US Steel, International Harvester, Kodak, DuPont, General Motors, Singer, Standard Oil, Firestone and others illustrates how each strived to grow in a manner that would alter its environment in ways which would better enable them to exploit Chandler's economies of speed; what economists typically refer to as economies of scale. Chandler also points out how this competitive need to keep resources fully employed leads to environment-altering diversification into related areas to exploit economies of scope.[22]

With regard to DFFs, Wojnilower's depiction of the plight faced by FFs illustrates best why such firms must be active in nature to survive. It has already been discussed that one of Wojnilower's themes is that FFs are at a competitive disadvantage because unlike NFFs their growth and profitability are capped by limits on monetary growth. Therefore, needed growth is attained by 'inventing new instruments and mechanisms that enhance earnings by accelerating the turnover of official money' (Wojnilower, 1991, p. 4). This is a highly entrepreneurial activity and it naturally leads to growth in another manner which Wojnilower touches on. This is growth through the expansion of market share.

This necessitates that the market shares of rivals be encroached upon. Growth of this sort is often accomplished through innovations which threaten the survival of institutions tied to more traditional assets and liabilities. These sorts of innovations succeed because they either circumvent or take advantage of the existing sets of rules, be they written or unwritten. Because of these innovations, the rules are subject to constant revision. This means that 'every [financial] firm takes for granted that seeking to have the rules altered in its favor (or preserved, as the case may be) must be an important part of its business strategy' (Wojnilower, 1991, p. 5). Thus, DFFs strive to alter their environment not only by altering the composition of both the money supply and the competitive environment, but also by having rules and regulations altered in their favor.

ASSUMPTION THREE DFFs AND THE NEED OF SHORT-TERMISM FOR SUCCESS

Many authors (such as Jane D'Arista,[23] Michael Porter,[24] James M. Poterba and Lawrence H. Summers,[25] Don Goldstein[26] and William Lazonick[27]) have described how recent financial market developments generate substantial pressures which promote short-term planning on the part of NFFs. FFs will participate with NFFs in this short-termism because they are subject to the same competitive market forces evaluating performance. These evaluative pressures will also force FFs, including DFFs, to bolster near-term returns to attract capital, appease stockholders and maintain stock price. In fact, since short-termism is promoted by financial markets, the FFs operating in and driving these markets probably need to put greater emphasis on near-term results than do NFFs. In short, it is mainly quantitatively and financially centered competitive market pressures evaluating performance which foster the use of short-term planning over long-term planning.

This development of short-termism presents a concern because a firm's time horizon determines its willingness to forgo earnings today to earn returns and increase performance in the future. In the non-financial sector it has been described in many places how shortened time horizons can reduce competitiveness and, in turn, robustness and stability. This happens because reduced expenditures on plant, equipment and R&D, reduce capacity and flexibility, reduce productivity and morale, and hinder innovation and new product development. The US has experienced these shortcomings since the 1970s in areas such as automobiles, aviation and, especially, consumer electronics. In the depository financial sector, short-termism may well be displayed in a more striking and destabilizing way. Longer-term, more conservative, productive investments with good, solid, moderate, returns will be abandoned in favor of shorter-term, more speculative investments with potentially quick and lucrative rates of return.

Short-termism and Institutional Structures

Poterba and Summers, in their survey of US, Japanese and European chief executive officers (CEOs), indicate that US CEOs think that their time horizons are shorter than those of their counterparts in Europe and Japan. The US CEOs attribute this difference from intense evaluative pressures from financial markets which they contend tend to undervalue longer-term investments. The survey also shows that US firms operate with hurdle rates – rates of expected return at which investment would be considered – which are substantially higher in the US than in Japan or Europe. In fact, the hurdle rate in the US is significantly higher than cost of capital analysis suggests it should be (Poterba and Summers, 1992). A standard of this sort cuts from consideration many longer-term investment projects.

Porter's research substantiates the findings of Poterba and Summers. He reports that the differences in time frames and hurdle rates result in a striking difference in managerial goals. In the US, corporate goals center around earning high returns on investment and maximizing current stock price. On the other hand, in Japan and Europe, top goals are focused on securing the competitive position of the corporation through product development and in ensuring the company's continuity by securing market share. Information flow is more diversified and wide ranging, lacking any marked focus on financial criteria. The result is that there is greater tolerance of the financial costs of investment.

Porter notes that in the US managers must justify investments on a quantitative basis. The result is that expenditures on things such as R&D and market entry are not viewed as investments but as costs which harm profitability. In Japan and Europe, the justification of investment is centered around technological leadership, product development and the maintenance/expansion of market share. Therefore, expenditures on R&D and efforts to enter markets are viewed as investments likely to enhance profitability. Porter notes that statistical data support these findings. US corporate expenditures on R&D, intangibles (especially training and human resources), and plant and equipment lag behind those of corporations in Europe and Japan (Porter, 1992b, pp. 71–2; also see Porter, 1992a).

Capital market-based vs. bank-based systems

A review of the literature on short-termism indicates that this difference in behavior is due to institutional differences. This institutional difference was first clarified in Gerschenkron's noted study comparing the financial development of Britain and Germany.[28] Britain's financial system developed into what can be called a capital market-based system. Germany's financial system developed into what can be called a bank-based system.

In general a capital market-based system is characterized by NFFs which operate and finance long-term investment in a manner largely independent of financial firms. This arm's-length relation between the nonfinancial and financial sectors leads to the development of a highly sophisticated and independent capital market. Here, capital markets are large and intricate, the ownership of equity and debt instruments is widely dispersed and frequently traded. In addition, the large banks have relatively little involvement in the allocation of funds and the ownership of finanical assets. Opposing this is the bank-based system. Here the capital markets are dominated by fairly few large universal banks. These banks are actively involved in the long-term financing of investment projects undertaken by NFFs. They provide managerial direction and serve as coordinators of investments made by groups of firms. They are the primary source of long-term funds and they maintain ownership of their debt instruments (including shares) over the long term. Under this system, capital markets are closely linked to the nonfinancial sector. This results in relatively little secondary trading of financial assets.[29]

The separation of ownership and management
The bank-based system is better able to keep short-termism in check because it is better able to overcome the divergence in interests which exists when management of firms and their ownership becomes separated. This divergence in interests, now called a principal–agent problem, was first noted by Bearle and Means,[30] and has been expanded by Chandler and Lazonick.[31] The basic crux of the problem is that owners remain focused on profits while managers see their interests best served by focusing on growth and increased firm size. The conflict lies in the fact that efforts to grow detract from current profits.

This divergence in interests is related to problems of asymmetric information between owners and managers. Bank-based systems overcome these asymmetries better than capital market-based systems. Under capital market-based systems, ownership is obtained through trading in uncertain financial markets. Therefore, owners lack inside information on firm strategies and base their analysis of firms on relatively simple, short-term financial indicators provided through financial markets. Shareholders will receive straightforward cost-cutting programs favorably because they directly increase profits. However, programs which increase a firm's long-term viability, such as enhancing technical expertise or employee capabilities, will not be rewarded or will be held in disdain because they represent expenditures which detract from current profits. If a stock fails to perform well in the short term, shareholders find it easier to get what they want by trading for those stocks which do perform as desired. This trading pressures firms to adopt short-term strategies which boost current profitability at the expense of competitiveness over the long term.

On the other hand, under bank-based systems, ownership is not obtained through trading but is instead obtained through long-term relationships. Banks provide NFFs with advice and counsel; they are essentially investment partners and permanent owners of shares. Here, shareholders are privy to extensive inside information and come to understand the investments necessary for maintaining a firm's long-term viability. Under these conditions, shareholders encourage, instead of discourage, expenditures on technological and worker improvements which enhance long-term viability. The bank-based system enables lenders to be committed and adopt longer grace periods before financed investment projects must produce competitive returns (Pollin, 1996).

Fluid Capital vs. Dedicated or Committed Capital

Porter, in 'Capital Disadvantage: America's Failing Capital Investment System', describes this institutional problem in a succinct way when he compares the US capital market to that in both Germany and Japan. He says that in the United States, 'attributes combine to create a system distinguished by fluid capital: funds supplied by external capital providers move rapidly from company to company, usually based on perceptions of opportunities for near-term appreciation' (Porter, 1992b, p. 69). In this system the owners are primarily agents rather than principals and they hold fragmented stakes. In contrast, the Japanese and German systems are 'defined by dedicated capital. The dominant owners are principals rather than agents; they hold significant stakes, rather than small, fragmented positions. These owners are virtually permanent, they seek long-term appreciation of their shares, which they hold in perpetuity' (Porter, 1992b, p. 70). With US corporate goals centered partially on the maximization of stock prices, the behavior of US shareholders, in addition to that of lenders, brings pressure on US corporate management to focus on actions which improve near-term results (Porter, 1992b, pp. 69–71).

From an industrial organization perspective, Lazonick, in 'The Organizational Capabilities in American Industry: The Rise and Decline of Managerial Capitalism', describes how the financial revolution has drained managerial talent away from the industrial sector. This dominance of the financial interests over industrial interests has, according to Lazonick, eroded the organizational capabilities of firms through the loss of needed financial commitment, wherein claims to revenues are not enforced in ways which undermine the utility and development of a firm's organizational capabilities. Lazonick also describes how mobile capital has reduced corporate control over retained earnings, further eroding organizational capabilities. He also notes that mobile capital is 'impatient' and more costly than committed capital (Lazonick, 1990, pp. 51–2; Lazonick, 1992, pp. 457–60). Both the erosion in organizational capabilities and the increased mobility of capital have fostered greater short-termism.

It is apparent from Poterba and Summers to Porter and Lazonick that the statistical and institutional evidence of the prevalence of short-termism in the American economy is significant. The problems of short-termism are further magnified by two other recent institutional changes. These are the institutionalization of the savings function and changes in corporate organization. In addition, two other sections will describe two other causes of short-termism. These are the interactions among increased competition, evaluative pressures and financial fragility, and the methods by which managers are evaluated and compensated. Lastly, a section reviewing short-term pressures specific to DFFs will be included.

The institutionalization of the savings function

Porter and others have observed how institutional investors have come to dominate the equity market. Porter notes that in 1950 institutional owners accounted for 8 percent of the equity market; in 1990 they held 60 percent (Porter, 1992b, p. 69). Chandler in his article, 'The Competitive Performance of U.S. Industrial Enterprise Since the Second World War', cites similar figures. Chandler notes that as late as 1952, most securities were held by wealthy individuals and families and, since they faced a 70 percent tax on income, they preferred long-term capital gains to short-term income. In contrast, Chandler says that the success of institutional fund managers

> was measured by the ability of their portfolios to out-perform Standard and Poor's index of the value (dividends and appreciation) of five hundred blue-chip corporate stocks. To meet their portfolio objectives, fund managers were obliged to buy and sell securities continuously in transactions made far more for short-term performance than for long-term potential. (Chandler, 1994, p. 21)

Porter also notes several factors pushing institutional fund managers to focus on short-term performance. He says that the goals of American institutional investors are purely financial and focus on the quarterly or annual appreciation of their investment portfolios compared to stock indices. Since fund managers are evaluated on their short-term performance, it is understandable that their goals focus on the near-term appreciation of shares.

In addition, Porter argues that investors' desire for liquidity, in conjunction with constraints on concentrated ownership and fiduciary requirements, compels institutional agents to hold highly diversified portfolios with many small stakes. With widely spread fragmented stakes, short holding periods and lack of access to inside information, fund managers base their investment choices on limited outside information oriented toward predicting near-term stock price movements. Operating in such an environment, fund managers have no substantive ownership role and little influence on corporate management. This is another reason why fund managers find it more lucrative to trade stocks frequently rather than hold them. (Porter, 1992b, pp. 69–70).[32]

The changes in the organization of corporations

In his analysis of post-World War Two American industry, Chandler explains how the emergence of intensified competition during the 1960s resulted in excess capacity and a corresponding reduction in return on investment (ROI). For the first time American firms began to expand by entering into unrelated businesses. The primary motive for such amalgamations 'was the desire of managers to ensure continuing growth of their enterprises by entering industries that promised higher ROIs and less competition than their own' (Chandler, 1994, p. 17).

This freewheeling diversification led to a separation between top management, those responsible for coordinating and monitoring current operations and allocating resources for the future, and middle management, those responsible for maintaining the competitive capabilities of the operating divisions in the battle for market share. The cause of this separation was twofold, according to Chandler. First, top managers had little technical knowledge of many of the businesses they acquired. Second, the acquisitions created an extraordinary demand for decision making which overloaded the corporate office.

Lacking the training or experience to evaluate proposals and monitor performance of so many divisions, senior management came to rely on statistics for decision making. Chandler notes that the problems of such data are that in a rapidly changing competitive environment they are 'increasingly less pertinent to controlling costs and to understanding the complexities of competitive battles' (Chandler, 1994, p. 19).

Chandler argues that this use of statistics on which to base decisions hurt competitiveness and encouraged short-termism in two ways. First, for upper-level management, statistical ROI data about performance, profit and long-term planning became a reality, not just a starting-point for discussion, but 'a target sent down from the corporate office for division managers to meet. Since managers' compensation and promotion prospects depended on the ability to meet targets, these middle managers had a strong incentive to adjust their data accordingly' (Chandler, 1994, p. 19). Second, this use of statistics made it appear that one could determine more precisely that rate at which a project would become profitable, taking into account the cost of time and the risk involved. If management accepts these estimates literally, which require a higher threshold of return for longer-term projects to be profitable, managers' time horizons could be shortened.

According to Chandler, such capital-budgeting processes fail to take into account

> complex nonquantifiable data[33] about the nature of particular product markets, factory methods, competitors' activities, and organizational settings. ... Top management was basing decisions on numbers, not on knowledge, a practice that made it all the more difficult to carry out the basic function of monitoring current operations and allocating resources for future activities and exacerbated the separation between top management and operating management in many companies. (Chandler, 1994, p. 20)

Porter voices essentially identical concerns. He notes that over the last two decades, US corporations have become very decentralized, involving highly autonomous business units and limited information flows both vertically and horizontally. The

> consequence is that top management has become more distanced from the details of business. Senior managers have little knowledge or experience in many of the company's businesses and often lack the technical background and experience to understand the substance of products or processes. (Porter, 1992b, p. 71)

The result for Porter is as Chandler depicted: business management and allocation of resources 'by the numbers' wherein

> unit or functional managers [must] justify investment projects quantitatively. The system rarely treats investments, such as R&D, advertising, or market entry as investments; rather they are negotiated as part of the annual budgeting process, which is primarily driven by a concern for current profitability. Intangible investments such as cross-functional training for workers may not even be tracked in the financial system – and thus may be sacrificed in the name of profitability. (Porter, 1992b, p. 72)

It is clear that both Chandler and Porter see that the emergence of a more highly diversified corporate structure makes top management decision making more reliant on quantitative data, to such an extent that important qualitative data are omitted. Lazonick, in his analysis, explains how middle management's lack of control over financial resources necessary for the management of innovation prompts them, out of self-interest, to adopt short-term, adaptive strategies which please upper management (Lazonick, 1992, pp. 466–9).[34] The concern of all three is that this phenomenon, in combination with goals seeking higher ROIs, will encourage a competitive depleting short-termism.

In conclusion it is important to note that these areas of change are interlinked and tend to reinforce one another. For example, corporations' internal capital markets mirror the equity or external capital market with which they must deal. The external capital market has become more transaction than relationship oriented. Money is now increasingly made through the frequent, speculative trading of stocks instead of through the holding of stocks for long-term appreciation. Industrial corporations, even in efforts to fend off this short-term orientation, have had to accommodate its demands to some extent and put greater focus on short-term results. This mirroring effect has also taken place among DFFs in that both securitization and extensive direct borrowing have induced them to abandon relationship banking, which is long-term oriented, in favor of transaction banking, which is short-term oriented. Yet, FFs must also respond to the same equity market pressures to which industrial corporations must respond. Thus it appears that these interconnections may make FFs more prone to short-termism than NFFs.

Increased Competition, Evaluative Pressures and Financial Fragility

Lazonick points out how increased international competitive challenges fostered short-termism among American businesses. He argues that such competition makes the success of an innovative investment strategy a much more uncertain affair. This increased uncertainty made it difficult to muster the financial commitment needed to fund innovative investment projects. 'Under these circumstances, quite apart from the transformation of U.S. financial markets, it may be rational for a company in possession of organizational and physical capital accumulated over decades to live off its past success rather than invest for the future' (Lazonick, 1992, p. 256). Such behavior results in a preference for what Lazonick calls 'adaptive investment', which is shorter term, over what he calls 'innovative investment', which is longer term. According to Goldstein, under Lazonick's adaptive investment strategies, firms strive to maintain profitability by seeking trade protection, cutting costs using current technologies, and by pursuing transactions-based gains from the reshuffling of corporate assets (Goldstein, 1995, p. 24). All these strategies are designed to improve near-term results.

Lazonick goes on to argue that changes in the market for corporate control, what Porter calls the external capital market, have weakened financial commitment by weakening corporate control over retained earnings. Managers who are interested in the innovative, long-run potential of their enterprises favor low price/earnings (p/e) ratios since they allow low dividends, and thereby high earnings retention, to fund innovative, long-term investment. Current institutional investors are interested in high p/e ratios because they favor short-term gains through generous dividends and stock-price appreciation. Therefore, corporate managers are under evaluative pressure to adopt short-term strategies which boost current earnings to mollify shareholders. Financially oriented management, because of their viewpoint, find it more reasonable to comply with these shareholder demands. This increased prominence of financially oriented management in combination with structural changes increasing shareholder pressures for high p/e ratios magnifies the use of adaptive, or short-term, investment strategies. Lazonick also discusses how the dominance of the market for corporate control and its ability to raid corporate treasuries rose through conglomeration, the merger wave of the 1980s, and the institutionalization of the savings function, giving further impetus to short-termism. Each of these factors prompted managements interested in maintaining control to adopt short-term strategies designed to comply with the demands of the market for corporate control (Lazonick, 1990, pp. 47 and 52; Lazonick, 1992, pp. 456–60, 463–4 and 466–76).

Under Goldstein's similar analysis, US corporations, in comparison to those in Japan, are not insulated from speculative financial markets, but are integrated into them, and therefore more vulnerable to their pressures fostering competitive-sapping short-termism (Goldstein, 1995, pp. 1, 8–9, 18 and 23–4). In other work, Goldstein notes how competition among institutional investors fosters greater short-termism. Goldstein argues that each institutional investor's effort to outperform his/her competitors has promoted profit-seeking innovations which increase turnover as hot stocks are acquired and cold ones are dropped more rapidly (Goldstein, 1991, pp. 88–93).

A note on financial fragility
Overlying the competitive and evaluative pressures fostering greater short-termism are the problems generated by increased financial fragility which are described in the introductory portion of Chapter 5. The problem of increased instability caused by fragile financial structures increases the level of uncertainty that must be coped with by participants. This gives corporate managers a cause, in addition to increased competition, to favor short-term investment over long-term investment.[35]

This fragility-induced short-termism is reinforced through other factors which arise simultaneously. The greater debt burden carried by corporations reduces the availability of cheaper internal funds and increases the dependence on more expensive external funds to finance investment. Lenders, because of information asymmetries, must charge a lemons premium to corporations borrowing funds. This increased cost of funds to finance investment projects will make shorter-term projects more profitable than long-term ones (Crotty and Goldstein, 1993, pp. 270–72). In addition, this greater reliance on short-term investment reduces both competitiveness and profitability. This reduces confidence which makes short-term investment projects more palatable than long-term ones (Goldstein, 1991, p. 109). Lastly, the increased debt loads carried by corporations in a financially fragile environment compel them to be more responsive to financial market signals favoring adaptive investments boosting current earnings.

Management Compensation and Evaluation

Both Chandler and Lazonick note that during the first half of the twentieth century, career corporate managers were compensated through salary. These salaries were designed to reward managers as they climbed up the corporate hierarchy. This meant that the long-run returns to top managers were directly tied to the long-term success of the corporations they operated. Therefore, individual top managers found it in their interest to maintain control over retained earnings and pursue innovative investment strategies. Top management also realized that the growth resulting from innovative investment motivated younger, lower-level managers by furnishing opportunities for their advancement. Therefore under salaried compensation, top management had strong incentives to monitor operations and allocate resources in a manner which was in the long-run interest of the firm (Chandler, 1994, pp. 15–16; Lazonick, 1992, pp. 450 and 463).

Lazonick shows that these incentives shifted as stock-based rewards came to represent a substantial portion of executive compensation. The lesson that top managers quickly learned was that the size of their compensation had become directly tied to stock market performance. According to Lazonick, top management, by keeping near-term stock price high, could exercise their options profitably, increase their base pay, and qualify for the exercise of additional options. With this 'strategic managers of industrial corporations joined the money managers of institutional portfolios in focusing on the "bottom line" of their companies' quarterly reports' (Lazonick, 1992, p. 462). '[Lazonick's] view is that the access of top management to substantial amounts of ownership income weakened the innovative response by providing them with individualistic alternatives to personal success that could best be achieved by choosing adaptive strategies' (Lazonick, 1992, p. 464). Therefore, under management compensation involving substantial ownership income, the long-term success of any corporation was often at odds with the personal success of those who managed it (Lazonick, 1992, pp. 461–6).

It was discussed earlier how extensive diversification can overload the decision-making capabilities of the corporate office, because of both the many decisions which must be made and the top management's lack of specific technological and organizational knowledge of various industries. This difficulty was resolved by basing resource allocation decisions on statistical financial reports. As was noted earlier, such an analysis by numbers results in short-term investments being more favorable than long-term ones.

Under conglomerate structures middle managers, who frequently ran their division as a separate enterprise before it was acquired, were given the responsibility to manage innovative investment, but not the resources. According to Lazonick, they quickly found that top management would not positively respond to requests for resources to fund innovative investment projects. Instead, middle management were evaluated by the corporate office on their short-term performance. This meant that advancement was best achieved by presenting top management with adaptive strategies which did not make large and sustained demands on corporate earnings (Lazonick, 1992, pp. 466–9; Lazonick, 1990, p. 52; Chandler, 1994, pp. 18–19).

Therefore, in the end, the financial orientation of senior management and their compensation with substantial ownership income combine so that middle-level management are evaluated as to how well they enhance current earnings. These incentives are reinforced by both confidence-shattering competition and market-evaluative pressures favoring short-term adaptive strategies which increase current earnings. The result is that the corporate and financial structures where managements worked, out of individual self-interest, as a team, with strategies designed to strengthen the firm's competitive position and long-term earning potential, have largely disappeared. In their place has grown a corporate and financial structure, where managers, from top to bottom, are given a strong incentive, in order to promote their own financial success, to adopt short-term strategies which bolster current corporate income.

Short-term Pressures Specific to DFFs

Wojnilower argues that financial markets are different from nonfinancial markets. He says that they are more quickly paced and are more prone to sudden, unforeseen and rapid changes. In the opening pages of his article, 'The Central Role of Credit Crunches in Recent Financial History', he makes the following comment:

> Between credit crunches the changing expectations of financial market participants play an important role in determining the rate of growth of credit and nominal GNP. These expectations, however, tend to have large and mercurial short-run swings, are often inconsistent even within particular enterprises, and appear to be influenced more by extreme and memorable events than by slow-moving processes. Thus the desired stocks of financial assets change frequently and sizably, and in directions that may make little sense to the outside (and because of random components, often the inside) observer. But because adjustment of actual to desired financial stocks can be virtually instantaneous, especially as compared with the glacial pace of the corresponding adjustments in human and physical capital mediated by changes in financial asset preference, financial behavior becomes a routinely dominant force in business fluctuations. (Wojnilower, 1980, p. 278)

In commenting on what made the stock market plunge of 19 and 20 October 1987 so violent, he says that equally or more important than better insight into economic realities 'was the souped up efficiency of the marketplace in giving full and immediate vent to the emotion of the moment' (Wojnilower, 1988, p. 1). D'Arista also notes how recent financial market evolution has resulted in increased speed and complexity (D'Arista, 1994, p. 326).

Wojnilower has also consistently warned 'about the fundamental incompatibility in speed and attitude between our genetically built-in human programing and the computer programs upon which we have structured our financial markets' (Wojnilower, 1988, p. 2). He notes that the less restrained and more free financial markets become the more unstable they will become, because of the increased incompatibility between fast paced, fast changing, computer-run financial markets and slow to change human nature (Wojnilower, 1980, p. 279).

Wojnilower frequently claims that the source of this destabilizing incompatibility is the inborn optimistic bias and proneness to gambling addiction shared to some extent by all human beings. Wojnilower notes that throughout human history people have recognized 'the narcotic attraction of borrowing and the related phenomena of gambling and asset-price speculation' (Wojnilower,

1980, p. 279). He has also argued that optimism has become so indestructible that rises in interest rates seem merely to strengthen the consensus among business debtors that rates must come down soon. Therefore, firms are inclined to hold on a little longer rather than to retrench. It appears, according to Wojnilower, that only widespread defaults effectively dampen optimism (Wojnilower, 1985b, pp. 352–3). Elsewhere, in an expansion on this point, he writes that

> the biological and historical evidence is that undue optimism – the propensity to gamble, speculate, and borrow too much and to overvalue near-term gain – are hardwired into our species. That is why most (perhaps all) societies leaving a written record were impelled to regulate their money and credit systems. (Wojnilower, 1985a, p. 2)

Wojnilower goes into some detail and describes five human biological biases which make market participants short-sighted and prone to excessive risk-taking,[36] rendering financial markets quickly paced, unstable and cyclical, subject to sudden and violent shifts. These characteristics are (1) undue optimism; (2) myopia; (3) susceptibility to addiction; (4) rote habituation; and (5) the peculiarities of group (particularly male group) behavior. These human qualities in combination with the nature of financial markets result in real-world financial market behavior much different from the atomistic markets of conventional theory. For example, past experience with financial market patterns and behavior is not a reliable guide for the future but is used because of human limitations and because of the hectic pace of markets which make only simple rules useful. These problems mean that financial market participants turn to one another, and especially those regarded as leaders, to decide which options are best. This means that 'financial market participants strongly influence one another and may be swept by highly contagious epidemics of mood and attitude' (Wojnilower, 1987, p. 10). In other words, financial markets are prone to herd-like or lemming-like behavior (Wojnilower, 1987, pp. 2 and 8– 11).[37]

Given human nature and the characteristics of financial markets, it makes good sense for DFF managers to operate with a short horizon. Goldstein notes how 'even if some traders see that speculative errors are being made, it may – given finite career horizons and sufficient costs of carrying arbitrage positions – make sense for them to ride rather than buck the bubble' (Goldstein, 1995, p. 10). Wojnilower comments that 'During the South Sea Bubble a conservative banker is said to have rationalized that "When the rest of the world are mad, we must imitate them in some measure". Market professionals and good forecasters realize that, too' (Wojnilower, 1987, p. 5).

Lastly, DFFs must not only deal with more quickly paced markets, more subject to radical shifts, than do NFFs, but they must also be more focused on maintaining adequate levels of liquidity. The DFF has to maintain much higher levels of liquidity than does the NFF so that it can honor withdrawals made by depositors. This need to remain more liquid, especially given rapidly changing financial markets, requires DFFs to focus on short-run concerns. This process is exacerbated by a deregulated environment where any core of stable deposits is depleted (D'Arista, 1994, pp. 171–5).

ASSUMPTIONS FOUR AND FIVE MULTIPLE DFF GOALS AND MANAGEMENT DISUNITY

From the earlier discussion regarding DFF entrepreneurship (assumption two) it is already clear that the DFF has multiple goals. It pursues both profit and growth goals under a security constraint composed of a balance between portfolio risk and competitive risk. For DFFs, because of the cap on financial sector growth, growth targets will focus on efforts to maintain and expand market share. These market share goals may be sought after through efforts to grow in scale and/or scope. This growth may be achieved either through expansion and diversification projects undertaken by the DFF itself, or through merger and acquisition with desired existing units. Profits are an essential part of the process. They are necessary to pay dividends, attract capital and finance expansion.

It has already been discussed, through the writings of Chandler, Lazonick, Marris, and Donaldson and Lorsch, why professionally managed firms have a strong orientation toward growth. It was also discussed how DFFs are more aggressive than NFFs in pursuing growth because, unlike NFFs, they operate in a close-to-zero-sum environment. Given the detailed discussion of all this in connection to growth resulting from the entrepreneurial nature of DFFs, there is no need to repeat that discussion here. However, it is helpful to discuss how management motivations, along with efforts to resolve conflict, result in the setting of multiple growth-oriented goals. Additionally, it is essential to discuss how short-termism affects this goal-setting process for DFFs specifically and contrast this with how the same forces affect NFFs.

Management and Goals

The importance of organizational structures

Analysis of DFF behavior requires a focus on management attitudes and motivation because DFFs more than NFFs must compete with one another with well-managed organizational structures. This is the case because DFFs lack the production units possessed by NFFs. These production units, through greater efficiencies and/or better technological and engineering capabilities, provide NFFs with a competitive weapon beyond that of a well-managed organizational structure. William J. Baumol, in *Business Behavior, Value and Growth*, illustrates a managerial attitude and approach which is especially applicable to the DFFs and the fiercely competitive conditions they face, wherein DFFs that grow at a rate faster than that at which the financial sector is capped do so at the expense of other DFFs.

> Indeed, management is not ordinarily content to play a passive role in the growth process; that is, it is not prepared to wait for fortuitous events to impose growth upon it. The businessman understands thoroughly the nature of the battle for market share. He realizes that sooner or later someone will grow and he will then be forced to fight to maintain his firm's relative position. How much more satisfactory it is to grow first, especially since it is then possible to choose one's own timing strategy. Rather than waiting passively for someone to make a first move, anticipation leads firms to undertake active programs of expansion, and the desire to maintain market share renders these programs contagious. (Baumol, 1959, p. 89)

It is apparent that DFF management will compete for market share by striving to develop more effective organizational structures. Therefore, even though DFFs will have similar resources because they compete with one another in a similar fashion, they each will have a unique pool of resources from which to draw, because of differing histories of resource use and experience. These differing abilities to exploit productive opportunities and perceive them provide each DFF with unique growth opportunities. These opportunities provide DFFs with a continuous incentive to grow because their uniqueness presents each DFF with an arena of action in which they have some degree of competitive advantage (Hay and Morris, 1979, pp. 300–301).

Keeping resources continuously employed fosters growth

Another incentive toward growth is the existence of unused or underemployed resources at any point in time. This happens because many resources, especially managerial ones, are indivisible and often are underexploited. Increased specialization exacerbates this effect. In addition, managerial resources learn through experience and acquire new skills and information over time. Therefore, even without the hiring of additional managers, managerial resources available to the DFF will grow through time. These excess resources will be used because if they are utilized in overseeing additional projects, more profits will be generated. Even without the hiring of additional resources, the new experiences gained will, through a learning process, increase the capabilities of existing management and result in yet another pool of underutilized resources. In reality, new projects almost always require the hiring of additional staff. Again, through indivisibility problems and learning, these new resources will also become underutilized, providing further profit-seeking incentives toward growth (Hay and Morris, 1979, pp. 300–301).

This management and organizational inducement toward growth is magnified by two other factors. One is managerial empire building which is done to increase a manager's earnings, status and power. The other is the organizational need to motivate lower-level managers by providing them good opportunities for advancement within the organization. These opportunities only become plentiful enough when the firm is growing (Donaldson and Lorsch, 1983, pp. 7, 40, 46–8 and 74; Marris, 1964, pp. 50–51; Chandler, 1977, p. 10; Lazonick, 1990, pp. 36–7, 39–40, 47 and 51; Letter from Albert M. Wojnilower to James S. Earley, 26 January 1986).

This growth process means that profits will always be compromised at some level below their maximum. This happens because costs are, at best, minimized under an excess capacity constraint. To fully minimize costs, only those resources necessary to run current operations should be employed. However, under the above growth process, there is always some portion of resources, above and beyond that necessary for current operations, devoted to expansion projects. In other words, to accommodate the need to grow, an excess of resources are continuously employed by the firm. Therefore, costs are not fully minimized, they include coverage of some level of excess capacity, and profits are not maximized at any point in time (Donaldson and Lorsch, 1983, pp. 7, 40, 46–8 and 74; Marris, 1964, pp. 50–51; Chandler, 1977, p. 10; Lazonick, 1990, pp. 36–7, 39–40, 47 and 51; Letter from Albert M. Wojnilower to James S. Earley, 26 January 1986).

Superior organization begets size
From any sampling of Chandler's many historical studies of the development of individual firms, it is clear that managers will frequently set ambitious expansion goals.[38] Progress toward these

goals is satisfying because it not only boosts management egos, but also lifts employee morale since rapid expansion provides a wealth of opportunities for advancement. Progress toward these goals is also contagious because rivals will eventually be forced to stress expansion in efforts to protect their market share, and keep competitive risk in check, which is essential to a firm's success. From this perspective three factors, management needs, organizational needs and competitive needs, work together to require firms to seek growth at a limited expense of profits.

Size, and what its achievement represents, is a substantial aid to any firm's success. Chandler repeatedly illustrates how excess capacity in many industries was dealt with through consolidation. Consolidation enabled firms to mop up excess capacity and stabilize markets. According to Chandler, these new, larger entities succeeded when they rationalized production. This was accomplished when firms were able to better exploit economies of speed wherein any given set of resources was able to produce more product because it was more continuously employed. Chandler argues that the primary factor for success in exploiting economies of speed (more commonly called economies of scale) is a superior organizational structure. Superior organizations did this because they were better able to coordinate the flow and processing of inputs into outputs by collecting and using information more effectively.[39]

DFFs are not in the production business, as are the manufacturing businesses that Chandler focuses on. However, they clearly are in the information business where superior organization can be very effective in speeding up the collection, transmission and processing of information. Any DFF organization which can speed up the pace at which information can be effectively used will grow to be large. As Chandler says, speed begets size, size does not necessarily beget speed (Chandler, 1988c, p. 350). In effect, we come back to the point that firms succeed and grow when their organizational structures are constantly on the watch for ways to use their unique pool of resources more effectively.

From historical observation, the excess capacity in DFF markets will drive DFFs toward the type of consolidation and rationalization process described by Chandler. In fact, the current wave of bank consolidations indicates that this process is presently under way. This consolidation process will be a hotly competitive one and will require much attention from DFF management. This will be the case because managements will quickly realize that substantial competitive advantages go to what Chandler refers to as the 'first movers', those that are first in adopting more effective organizational structures (Chandler, 1990, pp. 34–6).

Growth through resolution of management conflict

Lastly, another reason for growth-oriented goals is the natural inability of numerous and diverse managers and management teams, which exist in any large firm, to work in concert toward a single goal such as profit maximization. Each manager has an individual agenda and sees his/her career best promoted through empire building of that which he/she oversees. The same is true of each management team. Their interests are best served by promoting their branch of the business. With all parties seeking growth, an expansion of a firm's overall growth objectives makes it easier to accomplish compromise and accommodation among opposing managers and/or management teams. In other words, battles among management over resources for expansion are more easily settled when a firm, within limits, emphasizes expansion over profitability (Donaldson and Lorsch, 1983, pp. 7, 40, 46–8 and 74; Marris, 1964, pp. 50–51; Chandler, 1977, p. 10; Lazonick, 1990, pp. 36–7, 39–40, 47 and 51; Hay and Morris, 1979, pp. 231, 243–4, 248, 257–9, and 263–5; Chandler, 1988e, pp. 125–6; Moss, 1981, pp. 24–5).

The Differential Effects of Short-termism on DFFs

It was discussed earlier how Lazonick argues that American corporations as they became subject to greater international competition were prompted to favor short-term adaptive investment over longer-term innovative investment. According to Lazonick, the more intense competition increased the uncertainty and risks associated with long-term financial commitments of longer-term, innovative investment. This made it safer for managements to rest on the corporation's past accomplishments and adopt shorter-term adaptive investments. Because of the greater risks involved, American corporations, instead of developing new products, production processes and technologies, opted to modify or adapt existing ones. In essence, what happens is that near-term profitability becomes more emphasized than longer-term growth. Manufacturing firms can do this effectively because they have production units with engineering and research and development staffs where substantial cost cutting can be made. Also, the markets for manufactured goods are relatively slow when it comes to change. This enables a line of products to be quite competitive with a series of minor modifications made to them over the years.

DFFs cannot use growth-mitigating adaptive investment in this way to respond to the intense competition they face. One reason is that they do not have production units from which profit-boosting cost cutting can be obtained. Therefore, the only way to enhance profitability over the short run, given competitive limits on margins, is by expansion. Another reason is that financial markets are quickly paced; they are subject to rapid changes and shifts in outlook because participants can give rapid vent to changes in perceived need through virtually instantaneous buying and selling of financial assets. Markets for manufactured products cannot buy and sell in this manner and therefore change at a slower pace. Therefore, DFFs cannot depend on an existing line of financial products and services to keep them competitive, even with modifications, over any substantial period of time and remain viable. To remain competitive financial firms must keep pace in some way with financial market changes; they must constantly pursue growth and innovation to protect market share from encroachment by others. Remember, DFFs, unlike NFFs, play in a close-to-zero-sum game where the competition for market share is fierce, contagious and consuming.

DFFs, as competition escalates, will move from strategies which are akin to Lazonick's innovative investment strategy to Lazonick's adaptive investment strategy. When competition is less intense, DFFs will tend to expand by developing and purchasing better and more appropriate technologies and managements, and by carefully researching and investigating expansion through additional branches, through operations in related markets, or through merger. The DFF finds it advantageous to grow in this methodical way because competitive risk is quite low, making it an increased threat to security to grow with the acquisition of unnecessary portfolio risk. This process is analogous to Lazonick's long-term, innovative investment strategy.

When competition becomes more intense, the picture changes markedly. Competitive risk for DFFs rises to security-threatening levels. The only way to reduce this competitive risk is to aggressively pursue growth at a more rapid rate. The result is that to reduce competitive risk and enhance security, DFFs will accept escalations in portfolio risk to boost growth rates. The result is that the growth strategies noted above, because of time constraints, will be pursued with much less care, leading to the acceptance of greater and previously unacceptable portfolio risks or risks which were simply unforeseen. The same competitive pressures which make it worthwhile to accept greater portfolio risk to speed growth will also lead the DFF to gain business and boost returns by narrowing margins, by lowering credit standards and making riskier loans, and by making more speculative investments with a greater potential for near-term gains. All of these actions increase portfolio risk. These competitively induced, reckless growth strategies are analogous to Lazonick's short-term, adaptive investment strategy.

Therefore, the point being made here is that unlike Lazonick's NFFs, escalated competition does not lead to the adoption of shorter-term strategies by DFFs which mitigate growth. Instead, because of the different milieu in which DFFs operate, escalated competition leads DFFs to adopt more reckless, near-term result-oriented growth strategies. These strategies require the acceptance of increased portfolio risk to gain what are perceived to be more substantial reductions in competitive risk, thereby enhancing security.

ASSUMPTION SIX DFFs BOTH ALLOCATE AND CREATE CREDIT

It is clear that DFFs are in the business of allocating credit. DFFs are intermediaries. They borrow from surplus units in the form of deposits and lend these funds out to deficit units at a contracted interest rate and payment schedule. The successful DFF will allocate its available loan funds, credit, to those borrowers who are most credit worthy, who are best able and most likely to meet their contractual obligations. If DFFs only allocate credit, then the maximum amount of credit that DFFs can extend is limited by the available pool of current and prior savings. If DFFs can create credit through their own devices, then they can extend credit beyond this available pool of savings. DFF creation of credit is dependent upon an incentive to create it and upon the technical capability of creating it. Minsky's financial fragility thesis, discussed at the beginning of the next chapter, when specifically applied to both NFFs and DFFs, illustrates the incentive to create credit. A brief look at financial innovation illustrates the capability to create credit. This scenario runs counter to the Deregulationists' monetarist thinking and their contention that DFFs respond passively to market discipline, both of which render DFFs only capable of an allocative function when it comes to credit.

Financial Fragility, Credit, DFFs and NFFs

Minsky's financial fragility theory meshes precisely with the argument made in the section on DFFs' entrepreneurial behavior, where escalations in competition will prompt DFFs to pursue growth more aggressively, and reduce the greater competitive risk, by taking on more portfolio risk. All successful DFFs get caught up in this process because they must aggressively pursue growth or risk survival through the loss of market share. Over the course of an expansion, when growth rates are at their highest, competitive risk peaks and the shift toward riskier DFF portfolios will be at its highest, creating a form of financial fragility.

These riskier portfolios become acceptable for two reasons. The first was discussed earlier. Over the expansion phase, rising growth rates raise DFFs' competitive risk, threatening each DFF's security. Security is enhanced by speeding up growth through the acceptance of greater portfolio risk. The second reason, which comes from Minsky's financial fragility thesis, is that the brightening of expectations over the expansion shifts perceptions and makes what were previously unacceptable portfolio risks acceptable ones. Both of these phenomena are bolstered by the intense, close-to-zero-sum competitive game which exists among DFFs. It forces even the more cautious DFFs to protect their market share by pursuing these riskier growth opportunities and not forfeiting them to their competitors.

This process also applies to NFFs. For NFFs, however, it is the balance between competitive risk and borrowers', not portfolio, risk which shifts. During widespread expansion the security threat from competitive risk becomes prominent while that from borrowers' risk recedes into the background. Also during this phase, brightened expectations reduce the perceived risks associated with borrowing. Under these conditions, NFFs find their security enhanced by borrowing more to finance expansion projects which reduce competitive risk. Competition works in a similar fashion upon NFFs as it did upon DFFs, pressuring even more cautious firms to relax self-imposed restrictions on borrowing to pursue growth opportunities that would otherwise be lost to competitors.

In the end, competition among NFFs and competition among DFFs works hand in hand to both increase financial fragility and induce the creation of credit over the course of an expansion. NFFs increase borrowers' risk (default and interest-rate risk) to decrease competitive risk and enhance security. DFFs increase portfolio risk to decrease competitive risk and enhance security. With this, competitively induced striving after growth among NFFs generates the demand for credit, while competitively induced striving after growth among DFFs creates the supply of credit. Therefore, each sector spurs growth by providing the other sector with what it needs to grow. Each sector's growth is accomplished at the expense of greater financial fragility. This greater financial fragility is the result of credit created by increasing velocity, wherein a larger superstructure of financial assets is built on the foundation of any given monetary base. There is an incentive to create credit because both those who demand it and those who supply it are willing, out of self-interest, to accept riskier financial positions where obligations are pulled tauter, possibly to the point where there is little or no margin of safety.

Financial Innovation

The question is, where does the increased volume of credit come from? How is it created? It is created through financial innovation. Liability management, a form of financial innovation, enables DFFs to create credit by economizing on reserves. This is done by shifting liabilities out of low-cost, high-reserve demand deposits into higher-cost, low-reserve purchased funds. This releases funds previously tied up in reserves, enabling the DFF to extend more credit. Credit of this kind falls into the category of created credit because the credit arises from funds fulfilling more of a transaction than a savings function. This process, however, raises interest rates because DFFs, in order to maintain acceptable margins, must eventually pass on some portion of their higher cost of funds to borrowers.

The credit creation process does not stop here. Higher interest rates spur greater financial innovations in the form of new instruments because such innovations become more lucrative when interest rates are higher. These new instruments, which are frequently close money substitutes, escape any reserve requirements and therefore any regulatory-imposed constraints on their growth. Therefore, financial innovation of this kind allows DFFs to create additional credit without having to raise interest rates, excepting what is necessary for the attraction of funds valuing liquidity into less liquid investments (Dymski and Pollin, 1992, pp. 41–2). Under this process, DFFs essentially escape reserve requirement constraints on their growth. This breaks the linkage that credit has to savings. Therefore, DFFs will create and extend credit whenever it appears profitable to do so.

Minsky, in his book on Keynes, notes how rising interest rates alone, as a byproduct of the credit creation process, begin a process which increases financial fragility. Minsky notes that during a boom the estimation of both the borrower's and the lender's risk becomes imprudently low. Eventually, credit commitments will come to exceed income flows. The result is that loans are turned over as they come due, since they cannot be paid out of income. This refinancing, however, takes place at higher interest rates because efforts to increase the volume of credit require the tapping of funds which place a higher value on liquidity. This rise in borrowing costs turns what were once viable loans into bad loans as they come due and are refinanced at higher rates. This increases the perception of both the borrower's and the lender's risk. This causes credit costs to rise, creating more bad loans. The process then repeats itself, making finance increasingly fragile (Minsky, 1975, pp. 109–16 and 123–30, especially pp. 112–14 and 123).

The Federal Reserve has little power to stop this march toward increased financial fragility, the greater preponderance of credit in financial positions. If the Federal Reserve takes an accommodative stance, it simply makes it less difficult for DFFs to create additional credit, since interest rates are stable and DFFs are under less pressure to find ways to escape reserve requirements. If the Federal Reserve takes a restrictive stance, it increases interest rates which prompts DFFs to innovate more and create credit by escaping reserve requirements and increasing velocity. Given these problems, the Federal Reserve's primary weapon of control, open market operations, is weakened in its ability to contain the creation of credit and the associated increases in financial fragility (Dymski and Pollin, 1992, p. 42).

NOTES

1. Adolph A. Bearle and Gardiner C. Means (1932), *The Modern Corporation and Private Property*, New York: Harcourt, Brace & World; G.C. Means (1959), *Administrative Inflation and Public Policy*, Washington: Anderson Kramer Associates; G.C. Means (1962), *The Corporate Revolution in America: Economic Reality vs. Economic Theory*, New York: Crowell–Collier Publishing Company.
2. P.W.S. Andrews (1949), *Manufacturing Business*, London: Macmillan & Co. Ltd.
3. Robin Marris (1964), *The Economic Theory of 'Managerial' Capitalism*, New York: Free Press of Glencoe.
4. Edith T. Penrose (1959/1980), *The Theory of the Growth of the Firm*, White Plains: M.E. Sharpe, Inc.
5. Gordon Donaldson and Jay W. Lorsch (1983), *Decision Making at the Top: The Shaping of Strategic Direction*, New York: Basic Books, Inc.
6. William Lazonick (1990), 'Organizational Capabilities in American Industry: The Rise and Decline of Managerial Capitalism', *Business and Economic History*, 19 (Second Series), 35–54. W. Lazonick (1992), 'Controlling the Market for Corporate Control: The Historical Significance of Managerial Capitalism', *Industrial and Corporate Change*, 1 (3), 445–88.
7. G.B. Richardson (1960), *Information and Investment: A Study in the Working of the Competitive Economy*, London: Oxford University

Press; G.B. Richardson (1959), 'Equilibrium, Expectations and Information', *Economic Journal*, **69** (274), June, 223–37.

8. Charles P. Kindleberger (1989), *Manias, Panics, and Crashes: A History of Financial Crises*, Revised Edition, New York: Basic Books, Inc.

9. Hyman P. Minsky (1982), *Can 'It' Happen Again: Essays on Instability and Finance*, Armonk: M.E. Sharpe, Inc.; H.P. Minsky (1977), 'A Theory of Systemic Fragility', in Edward I. Altman and Arnold W. Sametz (eds), *Financial Crises: Institutions and Markets in a Fragile Environment*, New York: John Wiley & Sons, pp. 138–52.

10. Martin H. Wolfson (1986), *Financial Crises: Understanding the Postwar U.S. Experience*, Armonk: M.E. Sharpe, Inc.; M.H. Wolfson (1993), 'The Evolution of the Financial System and the Possibilities for Reform', in Gary A. Dymski, Gerald Epstein and Robert Pollin (eds), *Transforming the U.S. Financial System: Equity and Efficiency in the 21st Century*, Armonk: M.E. Sharpe, Inc., pp. 133–55.

11. This is a good summary of the controversy over abstract theories which are claimed to predict well and the need for theories which incorporate more realistic assumptions.

12. Most of the information in this section is gleaned from Chandler's introduction to his book *The Visible Hand*. The five propositions discussed in this section are the last five of eight generalized propositions Chandler gives regarding modern business enterprises. See: Alfred D. Chandler Jr. (1977), *The Visible Hand: The Managerial Revolution in American Business*, Cambridge, MA: Belknap, pp. 1–12. These themes run throughout Chandler's three major works, A.D. Chandler (1962), *Strategy and Structure: Chapters in the History of the Industrial Enterprise*, Cambridge, MA: MIT Press; *The Visible Hand*; and A.D. Chandler (1990), *Scale and Scope: The Dynamics of Industrial Capitalism*, Cambridge, MA: Belknap.

13. William Lazonick's arguments agree with Chandler's in this arena and bring forward Lazonick's concept of innovative investment. See: William Lazonick (1990), 'Organizational Capabilities in American Industry', *Business and Economic History*, **19** (Second Series), 35–41; W. Lazonick (1992), 'Controlling the Market for Corporate Control: The Historical Significance of Managerial Capitalism', *Industrial and Corporate Change*, **1** (3), 449–51 and 463.

14. Edith T. Penrose (1959/1980), *The Theory of the Growth of the Firm*, White Plains: M.E. Sharpe, Inc.

15. Robin Marris (1964), *The Economic Theory of 'Managerial' Capitalism*, New York: Free Press of Glencoe.

16. Gordon Donaldson and Jay W. Lorsch (1983), *Decision Making at the Top: The Shaping of Strategic Direction*, New York: Basic Books, Inc.

17. This concept of competitive risk is thoroughly described in the section discussing assumption number two – DFFs Are Actively Entrepreneurial.

18. Gordon Donaldson and Jay W. Lorsch (1983), *Decision Making at the Top: The Shaping of Strategic Direction*, New York: Basic Books, Inc.

19. Robin Marris (1964), *The Economic Theory of 'Managerial' Capitalism*, New York: Free Press of Glencoe.

20. Albert M. Wojnilower (1980), 'The Central Role of Credit Crunches in Recent Financial History', *Brookings Papers on Economic Activity*, **2**, 277–339.

21. In this article Wojnilower analyzes how well the models developed in his earlier 'Credit Crunches' article were holding up under behavior through the first half of the 1980s. In this article, he also notes how indestructible optimism and a broadening of the Federal Reserve's lender-of-last-resort function strengthens each DFF's sense of security, thereby exacerbating the atmosphere of hyper-competition.

22. For succinct statements on Chandler's notion of economies of speed, see, all in Thomas K. McCraw (ed.) (1988), *The Essential Alfred Chandler: Essays Toward a Historical Theory of Big Business*, Boston: Harvard Business School: 'Decision Making and Modern Institutional Change', pp. 349–50; 'Administrative Coordination, Allocation and Monitoring: Concepts and Comparisons', pp. 402–3; 'Scale, Scope, and Organizational Capabilities', pp. 475, 483 and 489. Otherwise refer to *The Visible Hand* or A.D. Chandler (1990), *Scale and Scope: The Dynamics of Industrial Capitalism*, Cambridge: Belknap.

23. Jane W. D'Arista (1994), *The Evolution of U.S. Finance, Volume II: Restructuring Institutions and Markets*, Armonk: M.E. Sharpe, Inc.

24. Michael E. Porter (1992), 'Capital Disadvantage: America's Failing Capital Investment System', *Harvard Business Review*, September–October, 63–82. M.E. Porter (1992), *Capital Choices: Changing the Way America Invests in Industry*, Washington, DC: Council on Competitiveness.

25. James M. Poterba and Lawrence H. Summers (1992), 'Time Horizons of American Firms: New Evidence from a Survey of CEOs', Manuscript, Department of Economics: Massachusetts Institute of Technology.

26. Donald Goldstein (1991), 'Takeovers and the Debt Assessments of Firms and the Stock Market', Dissertation: Department of Economics, University of Massachusetts; D. Goldstein (1995), 'Financial Structure and Corporate Behavior in Japan and the U.S.: Insulation vs. Integration with Speculative Pressures', Manuscript, Department of Economics: Allegheny College, July.

27. William Lazonick (1990), 'Organizational Capabilities in American Industry: The Rise and Decline of Managerial Capitalism', *Business and Economic History*, **19** (Second Series), 35–54; W. Lazonick (1992), 'Controlling the Market for Corporate Control: The Historical Significance of Managerial Capitalism', *Industrial and Corporate Change*, **1** (3), 445–88.

28.   Alexander Gerschenkron (1962), *Economic Backwardness in Historical Perspective*, Cambridge, MA: Harvard University Press.

29.   Robert Pollin (1996), 'Financial Structures and Egalitarian Economic Policy', *International Papers in Political Economy*. Also in *New Left Review*, 1995.

30.   Adolph A. Bearle and Gardiner C. Means (1932), *The Modern Corporation and Private Property*, New York: Harcourt, Brace & World.

31.   See section below – Changes in Corporate Organization.

32.   Michael T. Jacobs, Donald Goldstein, Jane D'Arista and William Lazonick wage similar arguments. See: M.T. Jacobs (1991), *Short-term America: The Causes and Cures of Our Business Myopia*, Boston: Harvard Business School, pp. 17–19, 22–3, 31–8, 41–5, 49–51, 56, 194 and 219–21; Donald Goldstein (1991), 'Takeovers and the Debt Assessments of Firms and the Stock Market', Dissertation: Department of Economics, University of Massachusetts, pp. 85–6 and 88–93; J.W. D'Arista (1994), *The Evolution of U.S. Finance, Volume I: Restructuring Institutions and Markets*, Armonk: M.E. Sharpe, Inc., pp. 223–4; William Lazonick (1992), 'Controlling the Market for Corporate Control', *Industrial and Corporate Change*, 1 (3), 458–60 and 473–6.

33.   This is primarily specific technical knowledge about an industry, that is, what technologies are promising; the tradeoffs between alternative production processes; the capabilities of the workforce; the fierceness of competition.

34.   Lazonick's concept of innovative vs. adaptive investment is described in the following section – Increased Competition, Evaluative Pressures and Financial Fragility.

35.   The introductory section referred to is Minsky on Financial Markets and Institutions: The 'Wall Street' Paradigm in Chapter 5. For descriptions of how firm behavior is influenced by fragility see: Gary Dymski and Robert Pollin (1992), 'Hyman Minsky as Hedgehog', in Steven Fazzari and Dimitri B. Papadimitriou (eds), *Financial Conditions and Economic Performance: Essays in Honor of Hyman P. Minsky*, Armonk: M.E. Sharpe, Inc., pp. 40–41 and 46–7.

36.   There is a long tradition to this thinking. Adam Smith makes a similar argument when he contends that people are prone to overvalue the chance of gain and undervalue the risk of loss. Adam Smith (1937), *The Wealth of Nations*, New York: Modern Library Edition, pp. 107–9.

37.   There is more on this from more scholarly sources in the section on assumptions nine and ten in Chapter 5 – Uncertainty, Herd Behavior and the Uninsurability of Risks.

38.   A recent *Wall Street Journal* article provides excellent journalistic anecdotal evidence of the phenomena. Robert L. Simison and Oscar Suris (1995), 'Alex Trotman's Goal: To Make Ford No. 1 In Auto Sales', *The Wall Street Journal*, Western Edition, 18 July, pp. A1 and A5. This is one of many such articles.

39. See the following Chandler articles, all in Thomas K. McCraw (ed.) (1988), *The Essential Alfred Chandler: Essays Toward a Historical Theory of Big Business*, Boston: Harvard Business School: 'The Beginnings of "Big Business" in American Industry', pp. 55–6, 66 and 71; 'Decision Making and Modern Institutional Change', pp. 349–50; 'Administrative Coordination, Allocation and Monitoring: Concepts and Comparisons', pp. 402–3; 'Scale, Scope, and Organizational Capabilities', pp. 475, 483 and 489.

5. Six Alternative Assumptions for Financial Markets

INTRODUCTION

This chapter will focus on six alternative assumptions regarding the behavior of financial markets. These assumptions regarding financial markets correspond to the Deregulationist assumptions, numbers seven through twelve, stated at the end of Chapter 3. The alternative assumptions proposed in this chapter are derived from the works of the Keynesian economist Hyman P. Minsky, similar thinking Keynesians, and those who have incorporated Minsky's theories into historical studies of financial crises.

This chapter will follow the analytical structure used in Chapter 4. First there will be a quick review of Minsky's Keynesian approach to the behavior of financial markets. Then, six assumptions regarding financial markets will be proposed. The remainder of the chapter will center around discussions of each of the proposed assumptions.

Minsky on Financial Markets and Institutions: The 'Wall Street' Paradigm

Under the alternative assumptions concerning the nature and behavior of financial markets, the barter-based, static equilibrium models used in traditional economics, which abstract from money and finance, are set aside in favor of dynamic models which bring money and finance in on the ground floor. These dynamic theories are favored because they illustrate how money and finance intimately link the past, present and future of an economy.

The perspective adopted will be that of Keynesian economist, Hyman Minsky, and his Wall Street paradigm.[1] According to Minsky, theories which abstract from finance are only applicable to simple barter economies. Such theories, by excluding finance and its influence on behavior, fail to capture the driving forces of modern capitalism (Fazzari, 1992, p. 3). Minsky describes his Wall Street paradigm in the following manner:

In our economy the behavior of 'Wall Street' is a determinant of the pace and direction of investment. A model of the economy from the perspective of 'Wall Street' differs from the standard model of economic theory in that it first sees a network of financial interrelations and cash flows and then a production and distribution mechanism. A 'Wall Street' paradigm is a better starting point for theorizing about our type of economy than the 'barter' paradigm of conventional theory. (Minsky, 1977, p. 141)

Minsky, by putting cash flows and financial networks and their interrelationships on the ground floor of his analysis comes to a strikingly different conclusion about markets. Markets are no longer filled with endogenous forces which drive them toward stability, as they are in conventional analysis. Instead, they possess endogenous forces which make them inherently unstable. This happens because the theoretical role of money and finance is no longer simply that of a lubricant which eases both the exchange of goods and services and the transference of funds from savers to borrowers. In Minsky's world, money links together past, present and future. Financial decisions made in the past shape, and may limit, options available in the present, depending on the financial commitments made. On the other hand, expectations about the future open up options for the present if they are bright, because of the ability to borrow against future earnings, and close these same options if expectations are dark (Wray, 1992, p. 164).

Under the Wall Street paradigm, money is no longer neutral. One of the reasons for this is that credit is not just something that is allocated. Rather, it is something that is created through market processes. According to the conventional economics the Deregulationists use, credit is allocated out of an existing pool of savings. Therefore savings, and the credit flowing therefrom, must precede investment. Under the alternative scenario credit is created, out of profit-seeking behavior, to finance ventures that are thought to be lucrative. Here, there is at least a portion of credit and investment which precedes and forces the savings necessary to finance it (Wray, 1992, p. 166).

It is this credit creation process fueled by profit-seeking behavior which is the source of instability in modern capitalist markets. It not only explains the instability of the US economy up through the Great Depression. It also explains the post-World War Two tendency toward both increased financial fragility and increased proneness to financial crises, the price of stability bought through big government intervention. The financial sector, as the Deregulationists claim, does not just simply reflect disruptive shocks to the real sector. Instead, the financial sector is the source of instability in the real sector or a medium through which real sector disturbances are amplified (Dymski and Pollin, 1992, pp. 28–9). The implication is that financial markets themselves are inherently unstable.

The root of this instability can be seen with Minsky's financial fragility thesis. This fragility thesis begins at the trough of an expansion when financial positions are robust. One reason for the robustness is that the debt-deflation which accompanied the previous contraction brought many of the more fragile units into bankruptcy. The other is that firms, since they were not expanding during the contraction, and therefore not investing extensively, were not taking on new financial commitments and were paying off prior financial commitments with internally generated funds. Therefore, at the beginning of an expansionary phase, debt is at manageable levels with expected earnings comfortably above payment commitments. Initially, financial arrangements remain conservative because expectations are still low due to memories of the recent downturn. However, as the expansion proceeds profits begin to exceed expectations. This shifts expectations upward and makes firms more willing to borrow to pursue profitable opportunities (Dymski and Pollin, 1992, pp. 38–41).

As the expansion continues, expectations eventually become euphoric, according to Minsky. The result is that at some point in time the growth in debt will eventually exceed the growth in profits. This happens because profit opportunities are constrained by advances in productivity while there are no such constraints on the extension of credit. This combination of constraints on profits and euphoric expectations without corresponding constraints on credit, results, at some point in time, in credit advances which exceed the profit flows from the projects the credit financed. In other words, profits eventually disappoint expectations and are insufficient to meet financial commitments. With this, the financial structure moves toward greater fragility. It becomes more fragile as NFFs borrow more to pay financial commitments they can no longer meet out of internally generated funds. Lending institutions, out of self-interest, will accommodate this demand for funds since these firms are important clients, and because they cannot afford to lose such business to competitors (Dymski and Pollin, 1992, pp. 40–41).

Minsky notes that since World War Two, the US government has successfully stabilized the economy by using expansive monetary and/or fiscal policy to prevent debt-deflations. These interventions have been highly successful but they have generated another problem. The problem is that each intervention validates each existing fragile financial structure and gives participants cause to deepen it. This happens because participants realize that the losses from fragile financial positions are socialized while the gains remain private. This is analogous to the moral hazard problem among DFFs which the Deregulationists argue is created by deposit insurance.

Therefore, government intervention to stabilize the economy makes the economy more and more unstable, requiring more frequent interventions to avoid violent contractions. With each intervention more and more fragile financial structures are validated. Thus, with each intervention smaller and smaller disruptions are able to topple the system and throw it into an interactive debt-deflation. This happens because increasingly fragile financial structures inherently involve more complex and highly layered credit networks with more intricate interlinkages. This makes trouble in one area more easily and rapidly spread to others while trouble itself becomes more likely. This process in turn further weakens the Federal Reserve's ability to contain the growth in fragility because restrictive policies are increasingly likely to trigger financial crises whose resolution will require sudden reversals in policy. In the end, government intervention to stabilize the system makes it more unstable because it makes it more fragile and more crisis prone (Dymski and Pollin, 1992, pp. 42–4; Goldstein, 1991, pp. 93–7).

The point is that with or without government intervention financial markets are unstable. Without intervention they follow a cycle. When free of government intervention, financial markets move from robust to increasingly fragile structures through an expansion phase. This eventually results in crisis, a debt-deflation and bankruptcies of more fragile units which return the financial structure to a more robust one. With this the cycle begins anew. With intervention, the structure becomes increasingly fragile and more unstable because increasingly less severe disruptions are able to trigger the crisis. It appears that the Deregulationist position that financial markets are self-regulating and self-equilibrating and therefore stable is incorrect. It is very apparent from Minsky's reasoning that some shock or disruption may trigger the crisis, but it is endogenous forces which create the conditions which spawn the crisis. Under more robust conditions the system would be resilient enough to withstand the disruption (Dymski and Pollin, 1992, p. 44).

It is clear that Minsky holds credit to be a key element of financial markets and that the behavior of credit makes free financial markets inherently subject to unstable and unpredictable cycles of boom and bust. This erratic cyclical nature is not just due to exogenous shocks, but due, primarily, to the presence of endogenous forces and behavior which fuel such cycles. Martin Wolfson[2] and Charles P. Kindleberger[3] make extensive use of Minsky's model in each of their historical studies on financial crises.

A List of the Alternative Assumptions

At this point it is helpful to provide a list of alternative assumptions which are primarily derived from Minsky's perspective on financial markets. This list corresponds directly with the last six, numbers seven though twelve, of the list of twelve Deregulationist assumptions given at the end of Chapter 3. This completes the list of twelve alternative assumptions initiated in Chapter 4.

7. Financial markets are fragile and unstable. They possess endogenous forces which produce both fragility, and unstable and unpredictable cyclical movements. This endogenously produced cycle can be triggered or magnified by exogenous forces or shocks.
8. Market signals are often inaccurate and unreliable.
9. Market participants must cope with uncertainty, the unknowable, unpredictable future. Participants' rational efforts to counter uncertainty often result in destabilizing herd behavior.
10. Market risks are uninsurable because uncertainty makes objective evaluation of them impossible.
11. A stable money supply or reserve base does not result in a stable financial system because DFFs are very capable of both circumventing constraints and creating credit. The system is inherently unstable and has little or no natural ability to recover spontaneously from disruptive shocks.
12. Federal Reserve intervention can only mitigate the cycle and has little, if any, ability to alter its instability and unpredictability. Cycle mitigation only comes at the cost of greater financial fragility which increases the system's susceptibility to crisis. The result is increasingly frequent Federal Reserve intervention to avert serious contractions.

The remainder of this chapter will center around this list of alternative assumptions regarding financial markets and their behavior. Each of them will be discussed in the order they appear in the list. The discussions, as was the case in the previous chapter, will strive to provide a rough foundation for each assumption.

ASSUMPTION SEVEN FINANCIAL MARKETS ARE FRAGILE AND UNSTABLE

At the beginning of this chapter a summary of Minsky's financial fragility thesis clearly explained why financial markets, when free of government intervention, possess endogenous forces which produce both fragility, and unstable and unpredictable cyclical movements. I shall not repeat that explanation here, but it is necessary to explain why individuals do not learn from previous crises spurred by fragile financial structures and adopt more conservative and robust financial positions. It will be shown that individuals do not learn this lesson because competitive conditions and reward structures render fragile financial structures to be in the rational best interest of all participants, be they individuals or institutions. In addition, financial market instabilities created by credit and expectations will also be illustrated. The instability caused by contagion problems will not be discussed in this section because they were already touched upon sufficiently in the discussion on DFF externalities (assumption one), in the previous chapter.

Good For Each But Not For All

During periods of relatively robust financial structures there are always firms, be they nonfinancial or financial, which will find more fragile financial postures helpful in securing better competitive positions. By assuming more relaxed financial postures, both NFFs and FFs are able to increase their rates of growth and gain market share. This threatens the competitive positions of other firms because they are losing market share. The survival of these competitors makes it necessary for them to adopt similar measures to speed up growth rates and defend market share. Thus competitive pressures bring about the initial use of fragile financial positions and then their spread, causing the financial structure to shift from robust to fragile.

This process moves forward, even though it is damaging to the system as a whole, because each individual firm finds its rewards improved by dumping cautious financial positions in favor of aggressive ones. Wojnilower notes that capital flows toward areas of anticipated growth (Wojnilower, 1990, p. 13). This is especially the case for NFF growth financed through debt and DFF growth financed through increased portfolio risk. These financially fragile positions attract capital because they provide leverage which multiplies the anticipated potential returns to capital.

The reward structure that managers face also provides incentives to pump up growth through more aggressive financial postures. During the course of an expansion or boom,

> aggressive firm managers and bank loan officers will be rewarded for pursuing profitable opportunities and gaining competitive advantages.

Cautious managers, operating with the understanding that boom conditions will end at some uncertain point, will be penalized when their more aggressive competitors surpass their short-run performance. (Dymski and Pollin, 1992, p. 45)

In addition, when the boom conditions end, the aggressive managers will fail together. The result is that aggressive managers will not be held accountable for their firm's failings. Instead, the failure will be blamed on external conditions which have also affected everyone else negatively. On the other hand, cautious managers during the boom fail in an isolated manner and cannot escape accountability. Thus, over the course of an expansion, aggressive managers will be promoted while cautious ones will find themselves demoted or dismissed. In addition, since aggressive managers are not demoted or dismissed for the widespread failings which occur at the boom's end, they have both the enhanced position and enhanced skills to aggressively pursue similar gains during the next boom period. In the end, managers come to realize that their careers are best promoted by being aggressive and adopting horizons which stop short of the expansion's end (Dymski and Pollin, 1992, p. 45).

The systemic damage done by these aggressive, financially risky firm strategies is ignored by participants simply because aggressive behavior is rewarded more and punished less than cautious behavior. Aggressive, not cautious, behavior best fulfills the interests of firms, investors and managers. These interests combine in such a powerful manner that the lessons from past cycles and crises which teach caution cannot be implemented by participants, be they firms, investors or managers, because it will lead to their decline and failure. Even when participants realize that their aggressive behavior will result in systemwide crisis at some point in time, they realize that they cannot opt out of such games because to remain in the game they must play it. The result is that behaviors which are good for each but not for all are fomented. What we have is a classic fallacy of composition problem where what is beneficial to individual units is not beneficial to the system those units compose.

Credit and Expectations

We have already established that financial intermediaries' ability to create credit contributes to the fragility and instability of financial markets. Credit itself, however, is unstable because its extension depends on subjectively formed expectations which are never deeply rooted because unavoidable uncertainty makes confidence in them easily swayed. R.G. Hawtrey's writings precede Keynes's insights, and lack much of the terminology used thereafter, but they are nevertheless valuable and provide a good foundation for reasoning because he understood the fundamentals which make credit inherently unstable. The implication is that if credit is unstable then financial markets are unstable because they mainly price and trade credit instruments.

Hawtrey finds credit to be inherently unstable because its creation or diminution automatically triggers forces which trigger its further creation or diminution. According to Hawtrey,

> credit created for the purposes of production becomes purchasing power in the hands of the people engaged in production; the greater the amount of credit created, the greater will be the amount of purchasing power and the better the market for the sale of all kinds of goods. The better the market the greater the demand for credit. Thus an increase in the supply of credit itself stimulates the demand for credit, just as a restriction in the supply of credit leads to a decline in the demand for credit. (Hawtrey, 1923, p. 13)

Another way Hawtrey expressed this is that any equilibrium in the credit markets is unstable because 'every displacement from the equilibrium position tends to magnify itself' (Hawtrey, 1923, p. 14). Hawtrey also describes in detail how the self-interest of both borrowers and lenders, in addition to price-level changes, strengthens the process whereby either the expansion or contraction of credit is continued and magnified (Hawtrey, 1923, pp. 30 and 46–7).

Hawtrey's analysis of credit describes what is today called a path-dependent process. Agents' expectations result in decisions and actions which affect economic conditions. These changed economic conditions in turn affect agents' expectations which result in decisions and actions which also affect economic conditions and so on. This process is path dependent because agents' expectations and resulting actions affect the economic outcomes upon which agents' expectations are based. Therefore, agent choices, in a cascading manner, determine the direction of the economy (Crotty, 1994, pp. 110–16). This process, when it comes to credit markets and expectations, is unstable because once any movement gets under way it feeds back on itself and becomes magnified.

Under this path-dependent process, which exists in credit markets, expectations tend to become galvanized in one direction after a change in them takes place. This source of instability is amplified under conditions of financial fragility because an increased number of disruptions are capable of generating sudden reversals in the directions of expectations. This means that episodes which result in changes in the direction of expectations will be more frequent. These changes in expectations, even though they are more frequent, will still tend to result in wide swings of movement, because of their self-reinforcing nature. This makes financial markets more volatile, more unstable, with more compressed cycles of nearly equally high amplitude.

The path-dependent expectations just described are much different from how expectations are depicted under the conventional theory used by the Deregulationists. Under conventional theory, agent choices and expectations are based on a probability calculus. Agents are deemed capable of determining all possible outcomes of a choice and calculating an accurate probability (expectation) of occurrence for each one. These are the same conditions upon which choices are made in games of dice or roulette. Under these conditions, each agent's choices, and the choices of other agents, do not affect the outcome, and outcomes do not affect agents' choices. This happens because agent choices cannot change the probabilities associated with various outcomes and because outcome patterns do not alter agents' expectations (probabilities) of possible outcomes. It is a theoretically unchanging structure, as exists in games of dice and roulette, which enables this process to unfold. Under this model instability is not an endogenously created possibility because agent choices and outcomes cannot interact in ways which tend to drive everyone's expectations in the same direction. No matter what happens, agent expectations remain unaltered (Crotty, 1994, pp. 108–10).

ASSUMPTION EIGHT MARKET SIGNALS ARE OFTEN INACCURATE AND UNRELIABLE

Market signals, the prices of financial assets, are often inaccurate and unreliable under the alternative assumptions both because of instability and because of the way in which expectations are formed. When financial markets are unstable the prices of financial assets will change erratically. Therefore, the information conveyed by a price one day will frequently be found to be invalid the next. This inability to depend on the validity of a price signal for any significant length of time renders it inaccurate and unreliable.

In addition, the prices of financial assets reflect their expected stream of future earnings. Under conventional theory, as was described in the previous section, expectations are based on an essentially constant probability calculus. This makes price signals informative. Under the alternative scenario, expectations are path dependent. Expectations are colored by economic forecasts while economic outcomes, in turn, color expectations. As described above, this process tends to galvanize expectations in one direction or the other, resulting in wide swings in economic activity. This results in traders basing their earnings on efforts to out-guess changes in the direction of the expectations driving the market. This results in financial markets being speculative where prices are no longer based on the real factors which determine earnings over the long term. This lack of attachment prices have to real factors results in them being inaccurate and unreliable as informative signals. This whole process is exacerbated by participants' efforts to cope with uncertainty. Uncertainty will be dealt with in the following section.

ASSUMPTIONS NINE AND TEN UNCERTAINTY, HERD BEHAVIOR, AND THE UNINSURABILITY OF RISKS

Uncertainty and Confidence

An absence of endogenous instability occurs under conventional theory because agents, when it comes to making choices, have nothing to learn. They have complete knowledge. The conditions in which agents operate are akin to those in a game of dice where agents can precisely calculate probabilities of all possible outcomes for each role of the dice. Agents know that six sixes rolled in a row will not change the probability of a six coming up in the next roll. Agents also know that everyone betting on a six to be rolled does not change the probability of a six being rolled. Agents' probabilities, or expectations, remain unaltered by circumstances because they have a perfect knowledge of the game and they realize its structure is unchanging; the probabilities of all possible outcomes remain constant. In other words, agents realize that their expectations and the expectations of others do not affect outcomes (Crotty, 1994, pp. 108–10).

Under the path-dependent credit movements described by Crotty, Minsky, Kindleberger, Wolfson, Goldstein and Dymski, advances or retreats of credit are magnified through an interactive process which alters expectations. This happens because agents have an incomplete knowledge of the game they are playing. Agents thus strive to learn and develop more complete knowledge by taking note of both outcomes and the choices of other agents. Through this learning process expectations are altered and tend to become aligned in one direction and become a source of destabilization (Crotty, 1994, pp. 110–16; Dymski, 1994, pp. 95–9; Goldstein, 1991, pp. 48–9 and 52–4).

Agents realize that other agents are going through a similar learning process which means that the structure of the game being played is not constant but undergoing continuous change. Therefore, agents, in unending efforts to minimize the incompleteness of their knowledge, will continuously be open to alterations in their expectations because ongoing structural change renders past decision-making guidelines obsolete. This whole process is destabilizing because agents' defensive openness to change makes outcome patterns more likely to affect expectations and makes expectations more likely to affect outcomes. Therefore, expectations, like money and finance discussed earlier, link the past, present and future of an economy through an interactive process which is frequently destabilizing.

The source of the destabilization caused by the formation of expectations is uncertainty in the form discussed by Keynes, the fact that so much of the future upon which expectations are based is unpredictable and unknowable. With this uncertainty, as opposed to the probability calculations of conventional theory, agents have no center of gravity to anchor their visions of the future upon which they develop their expectations for making decisions and taking actions. Given this uncertainty, individuals making decisions are forced to rely on the judgements of others simply because the foundations and conventions upon which they make their own judgements are so flimsy and subject to sudden and violent changes (Crotty, 1994, pp. 111–12; Crotty and Goldstein, 1993, p. 261; Goldstein, 1991, pp. 52–4).

This dependence upon the judgements of others is the explanation of the herd mentality which causes the sudden and destabilizing shifts in outlook afflicting financial markets. These shifts in outlook are destabilizing because agents in financial markets can give them almost instantaneous vent. This quickly results in outcomes which reinforce the changed outlook, magnifying the destabilizing change in direction.

In addition, this sort of market turbulence tends to diminish agents' confidence, also discussed by Keynes, in the truthfulness of their predictions. This decreased confidence results in agent opinions and evaluations which are more readily swayed, simply because they become more dependent on and influenced by other agents. This exacerbates the inherent instability of financial markets (Dymski, 1994, pp. 95–101; Crotty, 1994, p. 114; Dymski and Pollin, 1992, p. 47).

In turn, this increased market volatility prompts participants to shorten their horizons and derive earnings from speculating when and where the market will shift direction. This can be accomplished if one can outwit the market, stay ahead of the crowd, and buy before prices rise and sell before they fall. These sorts of decisions predicting market behavior are adopted by many market players because their shorter term means they can be made with less uncertainty and greater confidence than other investments. The problem is that this form of short-termism increases market turbulence through yet another interactive process which renders financial markets increasingly unstable.

Coping With Uncertainty: Firms' Organizational Structures and Management Behavior

The organizational structure

Chandler's historical analysis of business structures clearly indicates that many organizations formulated the multidivisional structure so that top-level managers could devote their energies full-time to the development and implementation of strategic plans; to have a group of managers who were focused on the needs of the firm as a whole. Conversions to the multidivisional structure took place because competitive success made extensive strategic demands which no longer allowed upper management to split their time between operational decisions and strategic planning. Instead, competitive pressures and efforts to succeed required managers who could, on a full-time basis, focus and specialize on strategic planning. The multidivisional structure accomplished this by freeing upper management from having to oversee operational functions.[4]

This change in the organizational structure of firms which swept through industry and is today almost universal, took place because success required firms to devote more management resources to strategic planning. This indicates that such plans must be quite difficult to make. The clear implication is that real-world strategic planning is probably not akin to the probabilistic risk calculation of conventional economics, but is more akin to a world rife with uncertainty as described by Keynes. In other words, the organizational development of firms indicates that firms find themselves operating in a world of uncertainty; a world where much of the future is unknowable; a world where useful strategic decisions must be based on a well-researched case-by-case basis, and not based on some formula adaptable to all decisions.

Penrose explains how firms respond to and cope with uncertainty. She writes:

> Subjective uncertainty about the future and, in particular, about the weight to be given to various outcomes, can be traced to two sources: 'temperament' (for example, self-confidence), and an awareness on the part of the entrepreneur that he possesses insufficient information about the factors which might be expected to determine the future course of events. Uncertainty resulting from the feeling that one has too little information leads to a lack of confidence in the soundness of the

judgments that lie behind any given plan of action. Hence one of the most important ways of reducing subjective uncertainty about the future course of events is surely to obtain more information about the factors that might be expected to affect it; and it is reasonable to suppose that one of the most important tasks of a firm in an uncertain world will be that of obtaining as much information as is practicable about the possible course of future events.

To obtain information requires an input of resources, and to evaluate the information requires the services of existing management. Therefore one of the important effects of subjective uncertainty is to induce a firm to devote resources to what might be termed 'managerial research'. (Penrose, 1959/1980, pp. 58–9)

Chandler's extensive historical analysis parallels Penrose's depiction of how firms cope with uncertainty. Chandler's work clearly shows that firms either developed or adopted multidivisional structures so that they could isolate and devote both managerial and staff resources to strategic planning – what Penrose calls 'managerial research'. Firms made these structural modifications because they were dealing with a world filled with uncertainty, not one filled with probabilistic risk functions.

Management behavior
The survey research of Donaldson and Lorsch also illustrates behaviors of corporate management which indicate that they see the world as an uncertain one. According to Donaldson and Lorsch, corporate executives deal with the uncertainty associated with new investment opportunities in three ways. One is that they employ staff who are capable of compiling extensive data on the feasibility of various investment projects. Second, it is the job of upper-level managers to focus on strategic concerns and make strategic decisions, to decide which investments will most likely result in success. As already noted, these efforts to focus management energies on countering uncertainty resulted in the creation of the multidivisional structure.

Third, and most important, successful managers not overcome by short-termism, when they evaluate investment opportunities, often rely little on data, but instead rely on belief systems born of experience. With experience, managers learn what leads to success and what leads to failure. From this they develop beliefs about what is appropriate and what is not. Over time, according to Donaldson and Lorsch, successful managers come to rely heavily on their belief systems for two reasons. One is that they work; they have led to corporate and personal success. The other is that they enable them to perform jobs that are demanding and complex by narrowing the focus upon which decisions are made.

These belief systems are so helpful to such managers that they can only change incrementally with additional experience.

In the Donaldson and Lorsch survey, managers express several times how data on investment opportunities are complex, how they involve intricate tradeoffs, and how, in the end, they are not reliable because the future is uncertain. To cope with these difficulties managers fall back on the belief systems which have served them well. While taking account of their beliefs about the direction of the future and the capabilities within their firm, managers tend to make important decisions on the basis of intuition, crude approximations, convention, tradition or rules of thumb.[5] In short, what has brought success in the past will be relied on to bring success in the future. As experience is accumulated, according to Donaldson and Lorsch, managers develop greater confidence in themselves than in data gathered to illuminate an uncertain future (Donaldson and Lorsch, 1983, pp. 64–6, 118–23 and 127–30).[6]

Donaldson and Lorsch conclude that managers rely heavily on their belief systems to make decisions because this provides them with a foundation upon which they can cope with uncertainty and the complexities it presents.

> Their beliefs provide a set of concepts that enable managers to make choices in areas where hard facts are often unavailing and where the tools of management science and economics are inadequate to the job. Without these belief systems, managers would be adrift in a turbulent sea with no charts. (Donaldson and Lorsch, 1983, p. 129)

It is clear that management's dependence on an experience-based belief system to make decisions is indicative of an effort to cope with uncertainty. It parallels Keynes's observation that uncertainty forces one to rely on the judgements of others when making decisions. As was noted earlier, this subjectiveness of the decision-making process regarding investment results in herd behavior which generates instability. This is far different than the approach used under conventional economics where probabilistic risk calculations essentially erase uncertainty and allow investment decisions to be made on an objective basis.

The point of this review of portions of the works of Chandler, Penrose, and Donaldson and Lorsch is that, when we take a fuller account of the real-world conditions that firms face, we find a development in both corporate organizational structures and the behavior and methods of management in the decision-making process which clearly indicates that firms are striving to better their ability to operate in an uncertain and unstable environment. Firms would not have developed and come to rely on these structures, methods and behavior if they had perceived an operational environment more akin to that presented in conventional economics.

Uncertainty and the Uninsurability of Market Risks

Under the conventional economics used by the Deregulationists, the operational environment is one of relative certitude. Expectations, and therefore market risks, are evaluated through a probability calculus. This method of evaluation is similar to the actuarial statistics which insurance companies use to calculate rates. For example, there is a huge body of statistics upon which an individual's life expectancy can be calculated. When a life insurer provides life insurance for an individual it is estimating, or placing a bet on, how long that individual will live. This bet is in essence repeatable, much like those in dice or roulette, because the insurer insures many individuals, and because overall conditions remain virtually constant. Overall conditions are virtually constant because longevity-determining elements of lifestyle change slowly and incrementally, and advances in medical technology work in the insurer's favor by extending life spans. Other forms of insurance, such as auto and homeowners', work in the same way. Under a probabilistic calculation of market risk, the assessment of risk is essentially the same as that just described taking place in the insurance industry. The bets being placed are essentially repeatable and, therefore, are insurable.

In an uncertain operational environment market risks cannot be insured simply because bets placed on them cannot be repeated. Uncertainty exists because the future is fundamentally unknowable. In addition, past events and conditions are not useful predictors of future conditions. This is the case because the structural environment in which decisions are made is constantly evolving into a new and different form as agents, because of uncertainty and confidence difficulties, are continuously learning from each other and from their pasts. A good analogy to this process is the inability to profitably set rates for earthquake insurance. Knowledge of the frequency and severity of past earthquakes will not accurately predict their future occurrence. Each earthquake alters the geologic structure, and it is this very structure which determines how and when future earthquakes will occur. This continuous evolution of the event-determining structure means that the bet placed, upon the provision of earthquake insurance, is not repeatable, as it is with life insurance. It is this lack of repeatability which makes earthquakes uninsurable. It is this same lack of repeatability which makes market risks in an uncertain world uninsurable. In other words, the fundamental lack of knowledge which exists under uncertainty makes an objective evaluation and pricing of market risks impossible.

ASSUMPTION ELEVEN FINANCIAL SYSTEM STABILITY IS NOT WROUGHT BY MONETARY STABILITY

Under the Deregulationists' model of the DFF, the DFF is only capable of performing an allocative function in matters concerning credit. This means that the supply of credit that the depository financial system can generate is closely linked to the reserve base. The consequence is that the Federal Reserve, through its control over and enforcement of reserve requirements, and its influence over total system reserves through open market operations, is able to control the supply of credit produced by DFFs. Therefore, the Deregulationists contend that as long as DFF reserves remain stable, the financial system will remain stable because the supply of credit remains stable. According to the Deregulationists, the Federal Reserve only has to intervene, to maintain stable reserves, in the rare situation when there is a run on the entire banking system. In the more typical situation where there is a run on one or a group of DFFs, reserves will automatically remain constant because of a redeposit of withdrawn funds into DFFs deemed to be safer.

Under the alternative assumptions it has already been explained, in the previous chapter, how DFFs create credit and not just allocate it. Because of this ability that DFFs have to create credit, the supply of credit is only very loosely linked to total DFF system reserves. Upon any given reserve base DFFs are able, through financial innovation, to circumvent the restrictions that reserve constraints have on the extension of credit. In other words, the ability of DFFs to extend credit is highly flexible, it is not seriously constrained by reserves, and the volume of credit will ebb and flow as market conditions and profitable opportunities for DFFs change.

The result is that if the Federal Reserve desires to stabilize the supply of credit supplied by DFFs, it will have to continuously adjust reserves in the opposite direction in which DFF behavior is driving credit supplies. This kind of Federal Reserve action may be destabilizing because efforts to curb credit by restricting reserves raise interest rates. This prompts DFFs to work harder at developing circumventing innovations because they have become more profitable. These DFF efforts increase instability because they make the financial system more fragile and more prone to crisis. When crisis does break out, the Federal Reserve will be forced to quickly reverse its restrictive policies to avert contagion and a serious contraction. In essence, the Federal Reserve, in its efforts to stabilize financial conditions, generates for itself a more fragile financial system which is more unstable and crisis prone.

In addition, this instability is not the fault of Federal Reserve action because the system itself lacks automatic stabilizers. It has been described earlier how credit interactions, competitive conditions, the formation of expectations, and efforts to cope with uncertainty and establish confidence are all factors which tend to drive the financial system from a relatively sober or stable state into unstable and unpredictable cycles of boom and bust. It has also been noted previously how these endogenous movements are either triggered or exacerbated by disruptive shocks. The end result is that the financial system is inherently unstable and, with or without Federal Reserve intervention, it has little or no natural ability to recover from disruptive shocks.

ASSUMPTION TWELVE THE FEDERAL RESERVE CAN ONLY MITIGATE THE CYCLE

The foundations of this assumption were described in detail in the opening section of this chapter summarizing Minsky's model of financial markets. Therefore, I shall only briefly outline the basics here. Under Minsky's theory of financial fragility, the financial system cyclically moves from a structural robustness to a fragile state leading to crisis and a return to relative robustness. Both shifts toward brighter expectations and rising competitive pressures move the financial system from a robust to a fragile state. The fragile conditions, by reducing margins of safety, eventually result in some crisis which reverses expectations, generating a debt-deflation. This creates a series of bankruptcies which return the system to a more robust financial state where the cycle begins anew.

In previous discussions concerning financial fragility and DFFs' ability to create credit, it has already been noted that the Federal Reserve can do little, especially in a deregulated environment, to avert the march toward increasing financial fragility over the course of an expansion.[7] Therefore, the optimal moment for the Federal Reserve to intervene effectively to stabilize the system is at a moment of crisis. By flooding the markets with liquidity, the Federal Reserve can contain the crisis and maintain the price level, thereby preventing a debt-deflation and any serious contraction. The problem is that the Federal Reserve intervention validates fragile financial structures, and increases fragility over time, by averting the debt-deflations which would normally invalidate them. The end result under continued Federal Reserve intervention is that the cycle is mitigated or flattened; its amplitude is reduced. Since debt-deflations are avoided, expansions start from a higher level of economic activity. They also come to a more rapid close, and end in crisis, because they begin with financial structures that are already relatively fragile. In addition, the recession following the crisis is made more shallow because the Federal Reserve adopts aggressively expansionary policies to contain the crisis. The Federal Reserve is also frequently assisted by expansionary fiscal policy which erects another floor under contractions. The dilemma is that this mitigation of the cycle through government intervention is bought at the price of increased susceptibility to crisis as repeated validation of fragile financial structures encourages increasing fragility. The end condition is a mitigated or flattened cycle, but also increased financial system instability, as evidenced by more frequent crises and Federal Reserve interventions to contain them.

NOTES

1. A handy collection of Minsky's work is *Can 'It' Happen Again: Essays on Instability and Finance*, and an excellent presentation of his core thesis is 'A Theory of Systemic Fragility', in Edward I. Altman and Arnold Sametz (eds) (1977), *Financial Crises: Institutions and Markets in a Fragile Environment*, New York: John Wiley & Sons, pp. 138–52. However, much of the information on Minsky's approach is taken from Steven Fazzari and Dimitri B. Papadimitriou (eds) (1992), *Financial Conditions and Macroeconomic Performance: Essays in Honor of Hyman P. Minsky*, Armonk: M.E. Sharpe, Inc. I lean heavily on the Gary Dymski and Robert Pollin article, 'Hyman Minsky as Hedgehog: The Power of the Wall Street Paradigm', contained in this worthy volume. Martin H. Wolfson, in both editions of his book, *Financial Crises: Understanding the Postwar U.S. Experience* (1986, 1994), develops an empirically based business-cycle model of financial crises which has many of the characteristics of Minsky's model. For simplicity, however, I will stick with a presentation of Minsky's model.
2. Martin H. Wolfson (1986, 1994), *Financial Crises: Understanding the Postwar U.S. Experience*, Armonk: M.E. Sharpe, Inc.
3. Charles P. Kindleberger (1989), *Manias, Panics, and Crashes: A History of Financial Crises*, Revised Edition, New York: Basic Books, Inc.

4. This is a thesis central to Chandler's three major works, *Strategy and Structure, The Visible Hand* and *Scale and Scope*.

5. This behavioral observation of Donaldson and Lorsch corresponds with Crotty's presentation of Keynesian uncertainty. See James Crotty (1994), 'Are Keynesian Uncertainty and Macrotheory Compatible?', in Gary Dymski and Robert Pollin (eds), *New Perspectives in Monetary Macroeconomics: Explorations in the Tradition of Hyman P. Minsky*, Ann Arbor: University of Michigan Press, pp. 120–21. For a similar observation see James Crotty and Don Goldstein (1993), 'Do U.S. Financial Markets Allocate Credit Efficiently?', in Gary A. Dymski, Gerald Epstein and Robert Pollin (eds), *Transforming the U.S. Financial System: Equity and Efficiency for the 21st Century*, Armonk: M.E. Sharpe, Inc., p. 271.

6. I realize that the findings of Donaldson and Lorsch (D&L) are incompatible with the numbers-driven management described in the earlier discussion on short-termism. However, the D&L survey was published in 1983 and, therefore, given research time and the fact that answers to survey questions are based on past experience, reflects management behavior of the 1970s. This was before the financial deregulation which created pressures toward shorter-term corporate planning. Shorter-term planning naturally results in more numbers-driven management because it focuses on near-term profits over longer-term growth and because it involves less uncertainty. Thus, the incompatible management behavior is the result of differing conditions in two eras. Nonetheless, the results of the D&L survey are reviewed because they show management behavior which was adopted to cope with uncertainty.

7. See section, in previous chapter, on assumption six – DFFs Both Allocate and Create Credit. In addition, under a program offering a new approach to regulation, such as that proposed in Chapter 8, the dilemma over crisis containment and increasing financial fragility should be mitigated. For example, the reimposition of deposit interest-rate ceilings and the provision of reserves being tied to the financing of productive investment gives the Federal Reserve tools with which it can slow the march toward increasing financial fragility.

6. Performance of the Deregulationist Program Under the Alternative Assumptions

INTRODUCTION

This chapter will illustrate how the Deregulationists' policies will work under the twelve alternative assumptions developed in Chapters 4 and 5 and will compare this outcome to that which the Deregulationists envision. This comparison will be accomplished by going through the Deregulationists' program point by point, as was done in Chapter 2, examining how each policy will perform under the alternative assumptions. As was done in Chapter 2, the Deregulationist policies reviewed in this chapter will be those regarding deposit insurance, capital standards, market value accounting, prompt closure, nationwide banking, allowing entrance into both investment banking and nonfinancial business, and disclosure.

DEPOSIT INSURANCE

As was discussed in detail in Chapter 2, the Deregulationists are advocates of an extensive overhaul of the deposit insurance system. Their overhaul is designed to create incentive compatibility between the insured and the insurer so that problems of moral hazard are avoided. The Deregulationists claim that limited deposit insurance, and, in earlier proposals, risk-related deposit insurance, both in conjunction with adequate DFF capital, goes far in promoting risk-averse behavior by DFFs.

According to the Deregulationists, this aversion to excessive or inappropriate portfolio risk is brought about by discipline arising from two areas. One area of discipline is the increased cost of deposit insurance, along with an increased threat of erosion to capital, incurred by the DFF when it invests in riskier assets. The other is the demand from depositors that their returns rise along with risk exposure and/or the threat that depositors will withdraw funds in response to excessive risk. Under the alternative assumptions, both of these factors promoting portfolio risk aversion are weakened.

Conditions Under the Alternative Assumptions

Under the alternative assumptions, the DFF is entrepreneurial and seeks profits and growth under a security constraint. Setting aside how management's independence may be threatened by disgruntled shareholders, the DFF's security constraint is primarily composed of a balance between portfolio risk and competitive risk, which was discussed in Chapter 4. The Deregulationists' policies, by removing regulatory impediments, intensify competition among DFFs. This goads each DFF to strive more vigorously after growth in order to survive, possibly prosper and keep competitive risk in check. As was also noted in Chapter 4, the close-to-zero-sum game in which DFFs operate, magnifies competitive risk because it makes growth campaigns to protect or promote market share both highly aggressive and highly contagious.

The problem is that DFFs face a dilemma in balancing portfolio risks against competitive risks. If the DFF chooses to avoid portfolio risk it does so at the expense of suffering greater competitive risk. This happens because aversion to portfolio risk eliminates many opportunities for growth, especially those with quicker results. Competitive risk rises as growth falters and market share is lost to those DFFs which take advantage of growth opportunities entailing additions to portfolio risk. On the other hand, the DFF can effectively reduce its competitive risk by taking aggressive advantage of available growth opportunities. This, however, usually comes at the expense of assuming greater portfolio risk. Therefore, given the heat of competition, DFFs face an unavoidable tradeoff between portfolio risk and competitive risk.

Under the Deregulationist program it is clear that the competitive risks DFFs will face will rise significantly since competition is opened as wide as possible. To reduce these risks DFFs have no choice but to accept greater portfolio risks in order to achieve adequate growth. It was argued in Chapter 4 that DFFs perceive competitive risk as an immediate threat to their survival while portfolio risk is a potentiality of the future which can be favorably modified through management skill. Given this, competitive risk is seen as far more harmful to the DFF than portfolio risk. Therefore, to enhance security, DFFs will vigorously attack increases in competitive risk brought about by deregulation by assuming greater portfolio risk.

Risk-Related Premiums, Limited Insurance and Adequate Capital

The Deregulationist program, by raising the competitive risks faced by DFFs, counteracts, possibly rendering impotent, the discipline that the Deregulationists claim is wrought by risk-related deposit insurance premiums and by limited deposit insurance. Raising deposit insurance premiums as portfolio risk rises will be seen as one additional cost of many incurred to reduce competitive risk. If DFFs are willing to incur higher costs for funds, narrower margins and reduced credit standards to speed growth and reduce competitive risk, they will very likely also be willing to incur increased deposit insurance premiums under conditions of increased competitive risk.

The risk of depositor runs from limited deposit insurance is also not likely to produce substantial aversion to portfolio risk simply because it is close to portfolio risk in character. Like portfolio risk, the risk of depositor runs is a potential occurrence in the future which is believed capable of favorable modification through management skill. Given this similarity to portfolio risks, runs are simply a part of the pool of portfolio risks DFFs are willing to incur to reduce competitive risk, the immediate threat. In addition, DFF managers realize that depositor confidence is also shaken by losses of market share which result when competitive risk is not reduced. Both of these factors render limited deposit insurance incapable of generating the sort of discipline on portfolio risks envisioned by the Deregulationists.

Lastly, the Deregulationists argue that for their modifications in deposit insurance to be effective in generating discipline against excessive portfolio risk, they must be accompanied by adequate amounts of capital being put at risk. According to the Deregulationists, when significant capital is at risk, DFFs will become averse to portfolio risks which may result in losses of capital. Under the alternative assumptions, however, capital is at risk not just from portfolio risks, but also from competitive risks. Since competitive risks present a more immediate and significant threat to the DFFs' survival, higher capital standards will probably not alter DFF behavior in the more conservative direction Deregulationists foresee. In fact, higher capital standards may induce more aggressive (reckless) pursuits of growth to satisfy a greater number of shareholders with an interest in more immediate and more lucrative returns. This can be an especially powerful force under the alternative assumptions because, as was discussed in Chapter 4, competition, evaluative pressures and market instability prompt DFFs to operate with short planning horizons. The dangers from short-termism will be magnified over the course of a lengthy expansion because competitive risks will be escalating while the downside portion of portfolio risks will be increasingly discounted.

Depositor Monitoring

The behavior of depositors is the only influence remaining which may alter DFF behavior toward an aversion to portfolio risk. The Deregulationists desire to induce depositor monitoring of DFF safety by clearly limiting deposit insurance, leaving some portion of deposits uninsured. Under the alternative assumptions this monitoring will take place, but it will likely generate episodes of instability. It will lead to sudden and violent shifting of funds as they are either moved from less safe into more safe DFFs or are moved into cash and other highly liquid assets.

To the extent that depositors have short horizons, or simply seek the highest possible returns, they will tend to deeply discount any downside risks associated with higher earnings on deposits. This tendency will be strengthened by any long-running expansion. The longer the period over which some depositors enjoy higher returns without losses from DFF failure, the less risky will such deposits appear, and even risk-averse depositors will become more willing to expose themselves to the risks associated with more lucrative deposits. This happens because the lack of losses over a period of time reduces subjective uncertainty and boosts confidence, giving all participants good reason to more deeply discount the potential costs of their risk exposure. This process will be magnified to the degree by which deposits are brokered. Competition among brokers and demands from clients for high returns will shorten horizons and induce brokers to maximize returns on deposits, giving little respect to the potential for losses. This is analogous to what has happened in the equity markets under the institutionalization of the savings function.

Depositors will remain content and will continue to deeply discount their risk exposure until some disruption occurs. (This is inevitable given increasing financial fragility over the expansion and given the inherent instability of financial markets.) This will cause depositors to suddenly reevaluate their positions and quickly shift their deposits to safer havens. These adjustments tend to be violent and herd-like because participants in making their own judgements rely on the judgements of others. This dramatic shifting of funds among DFFs will make the instability contagious, and magnify it, by disrupting the intricate and interdependent credit networks which develop among DFFs. The Deregulationists fail to see this difficulty because of their monetarist viewpoint and their use of money mechanics which neutralizes any churning of funds among DFFs, leaving reserves intact. The above scenario will be especially disruptive if few DFFs are deemed safe, with a resulting flight from DFF deposits into cash or other highly liquid assets. According to the Deregulationists, this is unlikely to happen in free financial markets because DFF trouble is an event isolated by endogenous market forces fostering stability and is an event made rare by disciplinary forces inducing conservative behavior. Under the alternative assumptions, a flight out of DFF deposits is likely to happen because competitively induced growth to reduce competitive risk will have required almost all DFFs to take on riskier portfolios. These portfolios will all tend to be loaded with loans and investments focused on those sectors having experienced the greatest growth. The result is that trouble in one DFF will often signal trouble and weakness in many other DFFs since they all come to hold similar portfolios. Therefore, under the alternative assumptions the exact opposite of what the Deregulationists foresee occurs: uninhibited competition naturally promotes the generation of an environment in which few DFFs are deemed to be safe.

CAPITAL

The Deregulationists have made several proposals regarding capital standards. They clearly favor higher capital standards and the inclusion of subordinated debt as part of capital. In their earlier proposals, as was noted in Chapter 2, the Deregulationists advocated the use of risk-related capital standards. In later proposals they have abandoned risk-based standards in favor of increasing supervisory oversight as capital falls from an ideal standard, at which the DFF is free from supervisory control. The Deregulationists claim that several factors will prompt the DFF to operate in a more cautious and conservative manner, keeping a tighter rein on portfolio risks. First, higher capital standards put more funds under risk of loss thereby inducing more cautious behavior. Second, risk-related capital standards explicitly raise the costs of holding riskier portfolios, thus giving cause to avoid them. Third, increasing supervision as capital falls provides incentives to maintain greater capital to avoid that supervision. Fourth and last, both subordinated debt and risk-related capital require meeting the test of the market to either maintain or raise more capital. Many of these incentives toward portfolio risk aversion are weakened under the alternative assumptions.

Higher Capital Standards

Higher capital standards, under the alternative assumptions, will not do much to prompt a greater aversion to portfolio risk on the part of DFFs because, as discussed regarding deposit insurance, the DFF faces a security tradeoff between portfolio risk and competitive risk. In other words, as was said earlier, DFF capital is at risk of loss not just from portfolio risk, but also from competitive risk. For the same reasons as noted earlier, any DFF with a desire to survive will very likely opt to grow, at the expense of greater portfolio risk, in an effort to reduce competitive risk to acceptable levels. It should be noted, however, that higher capital standards, by providing DFFs with a thicker capital cushion, will help to mitigate the instability which is inherent in financial markets. This happens because the thicker capital cushion reduces the incentive for depositors to run from troubled DFFs. It also gives the regulatory authorities a longer time frame over which to recognize and reorganize or shut down troubled DFFs. This extra time will make it more likely that the authorities will be able to take into account credit interlinkages and structure reorganizations or shutdowns in a manner which will minimize disruptions.

Risk-related Capital

According to the Deregulationists, risk-related capital standards, like risk-related deposit insurance, discourages undue portfolio risk by explicitly attaching a cost to it. Risk-related capital would likely be more effective than risk-related deposit insurance for discouraging portfolio risk because it would be more costly and because raising the capital requires meeting the test of the market. These disincentives toward excessive portfolio risk, however, are diluted under the alternative assumptions.

As with deposit insurance, investors, contributing capital to a DFF, who want to maximize their returns, will tend to overly discount, or even ignore, the portfolio risks to which a DFF exposes its capital. Investors looking for high returns will seek out those DFFs which are growing most rapidly. Investors, especially institutional ones, as was noted in Chapter 4, favor firms which adopt adaptive investment strategies which bolster near-term earnings. For DFFs, as was also described in Chapter 4, adaptive investment takes the form of rapid growth involving the assumption of greater portfolio risks. This reverses the market test envisioned by the Deregulationists. Under the alternative assumptions, the market test does not discourage, but encourages reckless DFF growth because capital will tend to flow in the direction of the most rapidly growing firms which are most likely to be taking undue risks (Wojnilower, 1990, p. 13).[1] This process is strengthened by long-running expansions during which almost all parties come to view downside risks (and illiquidity) as being less of a problem. This process was described in greater detail in the discussion concerning deposit insurance. This tendency to come to hold capital with higher returns, but exposed to greater risk, however, is not as destabilizing as the similar tendency to hold deposits with higher returns, but greater risks. This is the case simply because capital, unlike deposits, cannot run.

The core reason why risk-related capital standards are less effective at controlling portfolio risks under the alternative assumptions is the introduction of competitive risk into the equation. The increased capital cost of acquiring portfolio risk to accomplish growth is offset by a reduction in competitive risk which enhances security. This key benefit to security reduces the incentive that risk-related capital standards create to avoid portfolio risk.

Increasing Supervision as Capital Declines

Increasing supervision as capital declines will, under the alternative assumptions, provide strong incentives to maintain high levels of capital so that supervision is avoided. For reasons already stated, however, high capital standards themselves do not do much to encourage an aversion to portfolio risks. In fact, the need to attract more capital may encourage the assumption of undue portfolio risk to boost near-term earnings. In addition, the lack of supervision that substantial capital buys will enable such DFFs to more easily reduce competitive risk by pursuing risky growth strategies unchecked by any supervisory authority. Given the DFF's entrepreneurial drive after profitable opportunities for growth (an inherent behavioral nature magnified by competitive inducements), this is a recipe which may well result in frequent disruptions of financial markets.

Meeting a higher capital standard to avoid stricter supervision, by the greater cushion it provides, does to some degree offset the potential instability created by a laxity in supervision. The question is whether or not this offset is sufficient to generate sufficient stability. Under the alternative assumptions the offset is probably not sufficient. This is due to the aggressive nature of DFFs and due to the contagion problem generated by the entangled credit networks which will quickly evolve around DFFs free to pursue rapid growth without supervisory restrictions.

Subordinated Debt

Allowing the use of subordinated debt as capital will, as with risk-related capital, require the DFF to meet the test of the market in raising capital. The difference with subordinated debt is that the market test must be made on a continuous, contractual, regular basis and not on a sporadic basis. The problem under the alternative assumptions is that meeting the market test may encourage DFFs rather than discourage them from assuming undue portfolio risks. This situation, created by investor behavior seeking high near-term returns, was discussed with regard to risk-related capital.

The situation may be exacerbated by the use of subordinated debt and induce even greater assumption of undue portfolio risk than does the use of risk-related capital, simply because the DFF must pass the market test on a more frequent and regular basis. This gives the purchasers of subordinated debt frequent opportunities to impose upon DFFs the conditions upon which they will acquire such debts. This more frequent call to meet investor demands for high returns increases the pressure upon the DFF to adopt adaptive investment strategies which boost near-term profitability by speeding up growth through the relaxation of standards containing portfolio risks.

MARKET VALUE ACCOUNTING

The Deregulationists, as was discussed in Chapter 2, are strong advocates of market value accounting (MVA). Under MVA, DFFs are required to immediately reflect, on the books, any market change which affects the value of their assets, such as a rise in interest rates or any decline in borrowers' ability to pay. The Deregulationists claim that this will provide discipline which will induce DFFs to operate in a more conservative manner. When MVA is enforced, DFFs cannot use accounting gimmicks which enable them to appear solvent and continue operations when in reality they are not solvent and should cease operations. The cutting off of this escape, which the Deregulationists point out has commonly been used, will clearly increase the costs of downside risks, thereby creating powerful incentives to avoid portfolio risks that put capital in jeopardy. In short, MVA renders DFFs unable to avoid market judgements over valuation and how this affects its capital. To contain this danger, the Deregulationists claim that DFFs will avoid more risky and speculative holdings which are subject to more radical changes in market value. This more cautious DFF behavior will tend to help stabilize both DFFs and the financial markets in which they operate.

The Deregulationists conclude that MVA is stabilizing because they start with the premise that financial markets are stable and that the prices produced therein are trustworthy; they accurately and reliably reflect real conditions. With the alternative assumptions, we start with the premise, developed in Chapter 5, that financial markets are cyclically unstable in an unpredictable manner. This renders price signals unreliable and inaccurate. Under these conditions the use of MVA to evaluate the health of DFFs will amplify the inherent cyclical instability of financial markets.

MVA forces DFFs to dramatically decrease their size as asset values fall, and are marked to market, during a contractionary phase. This process, unlike book or historical accounting, requires DFFs to more aggressively downsize, given that it eats up capital. For example, at the cycle peak, interest rates are high and reach their maximum just as the contractionary phase begins. This means that loans made over the course of the expansion at lower interest rates will have to be marked down in value as the contraction takes hold. This will erode DFF capital and require them to rapidly decrease in size to meet capital requirements. This MVA-imposed shrinkage of DFFs is accomplished, in part, by pulling back on the extension of credit. Since traditional forms of accounting for DFFs do not impose such a shrinkage and decline in credit, the use of MVA, under the alternative assumptions, will amplify the cycle by increasing the violence of the contraction. With the alternative assumptions, the book or historical accounting typically used by DFFs is stabilizing, not destabilizing as the Deregulationists claim, because asset values are more constant due to their insulation from market valuation changes.

Unstable financial market conditions also result in MVA amplifying the cycle by helping propel expansions forward. This occurs because asset values tend to rise during expansions. If DFFs use MVA, this rise in asset values will be accounted for, increasing their capital. This bolsters their ability to expand and increases credit beyond what it would be under typical accounting regimes which do not enhance capital values through accounting methods as asset values rise. Therefore, MVA, by increasing DFFs' ability to expand credit, also gives greater momentum to expansions, thereby amplifying the cycle from both sides of the peak.[2]

Lastly, under the alternative assumptions, price changes are seen as frequently being erratic and not very informative. This means that MVA, since it requires DFFs to mark assets to market, will result in frequent and erratic changes in the values of DFF assets. This increases both the uncertainty and illiquidity risks with which DFFs must cope. This will directly increase the potential for instability. The Deregulationists come to the exact opposite conclusion because they work from the premise that financial markets are stable and sober, producing price changes which are rational and informative.

PROMPT CLOSURE

The Deregulationists, as was discussed in Chapter 2, favor the adoption of prompt closure policies to prevent the operation of DFFs with negative capital. This is accomplished by having increasing supervisory oversight of DFFs as their capital declines. This enables supervisory agencies to be prepared to reorganize or close a DFF before its capital drops below zero, if efforts to restore it to health fail. Capital is measured in terms of market value. The Deregulationists claim that the merits of prompt closure are twofold. One, it will prevent any losses to the insurance fund, inspiring depositor confidence and generating greater stability. Two, it will provide a source of discipline, akin to failure in fully unregulated markets, since it results in loss of control over the DFF for both owners and managers. These claims, in some ways, are unfounded under the alternative assumptions.

The disciplinary aspect of prompt closure is significantly moderated under the alternative scenario because of the strivings of DFFs to reduce competitive risk through growth. These strivings will be at their peak when the DFF is troubled and struggling to survive. The DFF, under these conditions, will be willing to acquire highly speculative assets, which would normally not be considered, in desperate efforts to improve or restore solvency. These acquisitions will be made with very short horizons, almost ignoring longer-term risks, because the overriding interest is in those strategies which are most likely to quickly replenish or re-establish the DFFs' capital base. In short, troubled DFFs find it in their rational interest to cope with competitive pressures by behaving in an essentially reckless manner. This sort of behavior exposes DFF capital to risks of loss which are so rapid that increased regulatory oversight may very well not be able to reorganize or shut down DFFs before capital falls below zero. This difficulty reduces the disciplinary aspects that the Deregulationists see occurring under prompt closure.

In addition, under the alternative assumptions, prompt closure, as advocated by the Deregulationists, will fail to stabilize financial markets. This happens because prompt closure of ailing DFFs takes place according to a formula based solely on solvency instead of taking place on a case-by-case basis where both solvency and contagious credit interlinkages are taken into account. The alternative DFF operates in an entrepreneurial and growth-oriented manner. This results in the creation of extensive and intricate interlocking credits being interwoven among DFFs. The existence of these complex credit relationships requires that they be disentangled before a smooth and nondisruptive closure of a DFF can take place. Failing to do this before closing a DFF will impose negative and contagious consequences upon those doing business with the DFF, thereby disrupting financial markets.[3]

Prompt closure, done on the Deregulationists' formula basis, requires that all DFFs be closed before their capital falls below zero. Closure based on this single criterion will result in the abrupt cutting off of credit linkages which will disrupt financial markets in a contagious manner. Closure, done on a case-by-case basis, will allow DFFs to operate with negative capital, for some minimized period of time, if it is necessary for the adequate unwinding of credit relationships to avert contagious disruption and provide a smooth closure. The Deregulationists fail to see this difficulty because their use of monetarist-based money mechanics blinds them to the complex credit networks which grow around DFFs.

Lastly, Deregulationist prompt closure may fail to limit deposit insurance fund losses and inspire increased depositor confidence in the safety of their funds. In fact, with the alternative assumption of inherently unstable financial markets in play, prompt closure, based on the single criterion of adequate capital, may shatter depositor confidence and further destabilize financial markets. This will tend to happen because MVA, in conjunction with the Deregulationists' prompt closure, will, during economic downturns, very likely result in so many DFF closures that the public will lose confidence in the system. As was described earlier, competitive pressures induce all DFFs to assume similar portfolio risks. Given this, under MVA, DFFs will fail in massive waves because changes in market values will degrade the asset values and capital of many DFFs in a similar manner. This process is self-reinforcing because each DFF, out of self-interest, pulls back on credit. This magnifies the decline in asset values and therefore also magnifies the decline in DFF capital, bringing about more failures. These failures of DFFs in large and sudden waves will make depositor confidence weak and will significantly increase the likelihood of systemwide runs. Such runs will tend to make losses to the deposit insurance fund high, not low.

It is clear that under the alternative assumptions, as opposed to the Deregulationist assumptions, prompt closure will only be useful when it is imposed on a case-by-case basis, not a formula basis, and when it employs more flexible accounting systems, not MVA. This difference centers around differences concerning markets and regulators. The Deregulationists see financial markets as inherently stable and regulatory interference as destabilizing. The alternative scenario sees financial markets as inherently unstable and regulatory restrictions and intervention as essential for stability. This means that the Deregulationists see a need to circumscribe regulatory discretion and systematize regulatory decision making. On the other hand, alternative theorists see a need to widen regulatory discretion and inject more imagination into regulatory decision making. This is why the Deregulationists advocate a formula-based prompt closure which emulates the behavior of free markets while the alternative assumptions point to prompt closure performed on a case-by-case basis giving regulators wide discretionary latitude.

NATIONWIDE BANKING

The Deregulationists, as was discussed in Chapter 2, support nationwide banking because they contend it will enable DFFs to diversify geographically, reducing overall portfolio risk. Under the alternative assumptions this is also the case but to a lesser degree because any reductions in portfolio risk through greater geographic diversification are offset by efforts to combat competitive risk which often entail acceptance of increased portfolio risk. The alternative assumptions, however, present additional advantages to nationwide banking. Each of them involves the generation of conditions which mitigate competition, the opposite of that which the Deregulationists think is necessary to re-establish discipline and stability.

The opportunity to expand nationwide will enable DFFs to reduce excess capacity through consolidation. Consolidation will also enable DFFs to exploit previously excluded synergies and further decrease costs by eliminating what become (after merger) duplicated services and resources. Each of these factors will reduce the intensity of the competition with which each DFF must cope after the consolidation process is complete. This will reduce each DFF's need to combat competitive risk through growth strategies which raise portfolio risk. In essence, a completed consolidation process results in an environment with reduced competitive risk which in turn reduces portfolio risk and improves stability.

The transition toward nationwide banking, however, where DFFs are rapidly merging with one another, presents some destabilizing dangers. As some mergers occur, DFFs which have not yet merged will be under significantly greater competitive risk which will pressure them to also grow through merger. As more and more DFFs are the products of mergers, the remaining, not yet merged, DFFs will come to suffer such high exposures to competitive risk that their survival will necessitate rapid merger with some other DFF. This rush to merge phase, and some settling out period afterward, will tend to be very unstable because consolidated DFFs will assume insufficiently analyzed portfolio risks and frequently be disappointed when they fall short of expected synergies and expected cost reductions. In addition, mergers of any sort, but especially rushed ones, run into many unforeseen difficulties and risks as two different corporate cultures are integrated. In short, a completed consolidation presents some stabilizing benefits, but the path toward that completed consolidation is fraught with destabilizing dangers.

A major benefit of nationwide banking, once the transition to it is complete, is that it will probably result in banking being dominated by a national, oligopolistic structure. This will probably result in a more controlled and less erratic competitive atmosphere. This calming of markets is repeatedly observed in many industries by Chandler as atomistically competitive markets suffering ruinous competition develop into oligopolistically competitive ones.[4] Fewer DFFs will allow the employment of more expert managers who will more likely have the wisdom to avoid the undue portfolio risks that less expert managers might acquire. Also, the feedback or action–reaction effects which characterize oligopolistic markets will help these more expert managers be more aware of the systemic effects of their risk exposure. This type of environment will indicate more explicitly to DFF managers how unlikely it is that they will be able to unload excessively risky assets before incurring costly damage during a disruption or downturn. Each of these factors should make national, oligopolistic banking structures more stable than the atomistically competitive banking structures which the Deregulationists see as the ideal.

The Deregulationists argue that allowing nationwide banking will not result in concentration levels sufficiently high to thwart the benefits typically attributed to perfect competition (Mengle, 1990, pp. 13–16). The Deregulationists see this much less than oligopolistic outcome to nationwide banking because they model the DFF as a passively adaptive profit maximizer. On the other hand, the alternative framework models the DFF as an active, growth-oriented entrepreneur. The Deregulationist DFF is not interested in empire building, while the alternative DFF has a direct interest in it which becomes contagious through competitive pressures. This helps explain why the alternative framework clearly leads to nationwide banking being oligopolistic while the Deregulationist framework does not.

DFF EXPANSION INTO INVESTMENT BANKING AND NONFINANCIAL BUSINESS

The Deregulationists, as was discussed in Chapter 2, desire to enable DFFs to minimize overall portfolio risk by giving them additional lines of business in which to diversify and spread risks. To accomplish this, they propose the blending of commercial and investment banking as well as a mixing of banking with commerce. Under this proposal, DFFs may underwrite and sell all forms of securities, they may operate and sell insurance, they may operate and sell mutual funds, and they may enter any commercial enterprise they find desirable. The Deregulationists emphatically claim that the conflicts of interest such diversification is typically thought to create are in reality relatively insignificant problems which do not necessitate any worry. As was noted in Chapter 3, this bold claim is based on some theoretical explanations, such as enhanced market discipline, and a reinterpretation of history. When the alternative assumptions are brought into play these Deregulationist arguments are weakened for several reasons.

The Deregulationists are incorrect to think that conflict of interest is not a problem in a deregulated banking environment. Their proposals, allowing DFFs to diversify into both investment banking and commerce, will heighten competition by expanding the number of competitors, and potential competitors, in the newly allowed lines of business. With the alternative assumptions giving DFFs an entrepreneurial and growth-driven nature, the Deregulationists' policies will worsen, and not control or contain, any problem with conflict of interest. The greater level of competition will increase the threat to security from competitive risk. This will strengthen strivings for growth to reduce competitive risk at the expense of greater, though much less immediate, portfolio risk. This increased drive for growth will be satisfied by expanding into new and previously prohibited lines of business which offer better and/or more numerous growth opportunities. The problem is that the easier and more convenient growth opportunities (those with better marketing or synergistic advantages) which DFFs are competitively driven to exploit will, when operating numerous business lines, frequently involve conflicts of interest. This conflict of interest problem is exacerbated when DFFs enter new lines of business without adequately understanding the risks associated with them because they lack the expertise to properly evaluate those risks.

Conflicts of interest frequently entail intricate interconnections among risks. When opportunities involving conflicts of interest are advantageously exploited by DFFs the risks they produce will remain unchecked. The difficulty lies with the interconnected nature of the risks, giving potential rise to contagion problems which magnify volatile and destabilizing externalities. The Deregulationists' hands-off approach gives DFFs virtually complete freedom over corporate structure, range of subsidiaries and relations among subsidiaries. These unimpeded business connections under a single corporate umbrella provide a perfect breeding ground for conflicts of interest with tightly intermeshed risks (D'Arista, 1994, pp. 187–90, 197–206, 229, 419 and 448).[5]

Lastly, all these problems associated with conflict of interest are exacerbated by the reduced regulatory discretion and oversight provided under the Deregulationist program. Without such regulatory oversight and discretion, conflicts of interest will be exploited in a dangerously uncontained manner. This happens for two basic reasons. First, taking advantage of conflicts of interest provides the DFF with relatively convenient avenues of growth which keep competitive risk in check. Second, the risks associated with conflicts of interest will not come to light through market processes because the instruments are not traded but are managed within the DFF's corporate structure. Therefore, under the alternative assumptions, regulatory oversight is essential to ferret out and contain conflicts of interest.

Another problem with allowing largely unregulated DFF expansion into investment banking and commerce is that it may result in a dangerous extension of the safety net beyond DFFs into large nonbanking segments of the economy. This would very likely result in widespread moral hazard problems akin to those the Deregulationists describe existing under flat-rate unlimited deposit insurance. This sort of difficulty arises because businesses affiliated with DFFs have an incentive to take risks they would not take without their link to the safety net. This means that business affiliates of DFFs are more likely to get into trouble than businesses lacking a DFF affiliate. A troubled affiliate is very capable of pulling a DFF into difficulties. Given management desires and competitive inducements which generate pressure to preserve corporate size and structure, rescues of the troubled affiliate will often be undertaken by tapping into the DFF's resources. This often harms the health of the affiliated DFF. In addition, the rescue of ailing DFFs by the Federal Reserve may frequently necessitate the rescue of nonbanking affiliates because of the complex interconnections which develop among corporate affiliates. Lastly, unimpeded expansion of DFFs into investment banking and commerce may lead to the problem of an unlevel playing field. This happens because businesses affiliated with DFFs have financial advantages, and therefore competitive advantages, over rival businesses lacking a DFF affiliate (Corrigan, 1987, pp. 1–8; Corrigan, 1991, pp. 1–13; D'Arista, 1994, pp. 426–33).[6]

DISCLOSURE

Traditionally, disclosure by depository firms has been limited in order to minimize the possible shattering of confidence, and resulting bank runs, which often attend unfavorable news about a bank's condition. Instead, soundness regulations were adopted to maintain the robustness of banks and, in turn, the public's confidence in them (D'Arista, 1994, pp. 16–17 and 343–4). However, the Deregulationists, as was noted in Chapter 2, claim that the disciplinary forces dispensed by the greater financial market freedoms they advocate will prompt DFFs, out of self-interest, to accurately disclose the state of their health. They claim that this will happen because there will always be healthy DFFs which will find it competitively advantageous to make such a disclosure. Competitive pressures will force other DFFs, healthy or not, to do the same. For the Deregulationists, this widely available information regarding DFF health will strengthen market discipline. This will provide additional pressure upon DFFs to behave in a manner adverse to portfolio risk. Again, under the alternative assumptions, DFFs striving after growth, to reduce the more immediate threat from competitive risk, brings into question such Deregulationist claims.

The Deregulationists view financial markets as being both stable and sober. This, for the Deregulationists, makes the market, as a whole, an effective and efficient calculating machine which, over time, relentlessly discerns the truth behind any façade. This ability of the market to reveal the truth makes inaccurate DFF statements too likely to result in the loss of their creditors' confidence. This confidence, once lost, cannot easily be regained by the DFF. This scenario is helped along by the Deregulationists' view of the DFF. They think that the DFF, when faced with full market discipline, will passively adapt by operating in a more cautious and conservative manner, more diligently avoiding inappropriate portfolio risks.

Under the alternative assumptions, the financial market is less than sober and suffers episodic instability in the form of an unpredictable cycle. In addition, the Deregulationists' model of the DFF is rejected in favor of an aggressive, entrepreneurial and growth-oriented one. As noted earlier, these conditions prompt participants to operate with short planning horizons. This may make it advantageous for DFFs not under regulatory supervision, to issue misleading disclosure statements to cover up weaknesses or exaggerate strengths of the firm for a number of reasons.

First, the need to maintain high rates of growth in the hotly competitive environment, created under Deregulationist policy, may require many DFFs to issue misleading disclosure statements in order to maintain and/or attract capital. In addition, untruthful positive disclosures will enable the DFF to better preserve and/or attract deposits than when a more honest and negative disclosure is issued.

Second, the falsely positive disclosures will assist the DFF in its effort to succeed and grow rapidly. To the extent that it does grow, the growth will enable the DFF to overcome, or make good on, any misrepresentations it may have made to foster growth.

Third, the DFF has the greatest control among market participants over what kind of information concerning it becomes public. This gives the DFF an advantage over other participants in shaping the public perception regarding troubling revelations about misrepresentations not overcome through growth. This advantage provides the DFF with a lever by which it can control and limit, to some significant degree, the damages which arise when misrepresentations come to light.

Fourth, any negative consequences from misrepresentations are not immediate, while those from insufficient growth are immediate. Misrepresentations are capable of being covered up and, if they are ever revealed, they will only be revealed over the course of time. Insufficient growth, however, inflicts almost instantaneous competitive disadvantage upon the DFF. This situation is analogous to that involving the balance between portfolio risk and competitive risk taking place under the DFFs' security constraint.

Fifth, financial markets, under the alternative assumptions, have erratic evaluative powers. This frequently produces contradictory information which leads to wide-ranging opinion on the solidity and wisdom of various financial positions. This helps to blur just how extensive disclosure misrepresentations might be, thereby softening the negative impact of their revelation.

Therefore, in conclusion, under the alternative assumptions, disclosure results in behavior in direct opposition to the behavior the Deregulationists foresee under their assumptions. With the alternative assumptions, accurate disclosure requires supervisory oversight, not free financial markets, to weed out and prevent misrepresentation prompted by the DFF's competitive striving after growth. Without such supervision, disclosure will fail to produce information which is truthful and helpful to participants in making rational decisions.

CONCLUDING SUMMATION

In essence, the alternative assumptions, in combination with the Deregulationists' policy recommendations, result in both financial markets and DFFs becoming more unstable, contrary to what the Deregulationists claim. In closing this chapter, the reasons for this increase in instability will briefly be recounted to show more clearly their reinforcing, interconnected nature. The following chapter offers two case studies and an analysis of the empirical evidence which substantiates the arguments made in this and the two preceding chapters.

1. The entrepreneurial nature of the DFF, in combination with the more competitive markets of Deregulationist policy, will increase competitive risk and, therefore, DFFs' pursuit of growth to reduce it. This strong need to grow will require each DFF to accept a riskier portfolio. This greater portfolio risk will make DFFs and their markets more unstable, not more stable.
2. This entrepreneurial, growth-oriented behavior of DFFs will amplify the cycle of expansion and contraction as DFFs act in their own self-interest. This amplification occurs because aggressive behavior on the part of DFFs results in a volatility in credit which propels and strengthens both expansions and contractions. In addition, both the contractionary and expansionary phases of the cycle, as explained above, are further amplified by the use of MVA (which the Deregulationists advocate), thus contributing to greater instability. MVA, because of the erratic nature of markets under the alternative assumptions, also raises the potential for instability by increasing DFF uncertainty and by increasing DFF exposure to illiquidity risk.
3. The opening up of financial markets, under the Deregulationist program, will result in more extensive and intricate interlocking credit relationships among DFFs and their business associates. This will make financial markets more conducive to contagion, rendering them less, not more, stable.
4. The prompt DFF closure policies that the Deregulationists recommend will also increase financial market instability because their imposition may abruptly cut complex and intertwined credit relationships, creating extensive and possibly far-reaching ripple effects. DFF closure must be done on a discretionary case-by-case basis, and not on a rigid formula basis, to sufficiently unwind credit relationships and avoid destabilizing ripple effects. As noted previously, this tendency is counteracted to some extent by

heightened capital standards which are urged by the Deregulationists.
5. Lastly, the increased instability and unpredictability of financial markets will encourage, if not make necessary, the use of shortened planning horizons by DFFs and other market participants. This will result in longer-run risks being more deeply discounted or even ignored by each individual DFF or other participant. This kind of behavior will further increase financial market instability. The result, as noted before, is macroeconomic instability creating microeconomic behavior which further increases the macroeconomic instability.

NOTES

1. This observation of Wojnilower regarding DFF capital markets is in agreement with the observations made by Porter, Lazonick and Jacobs, presented in Chapter 5, regarding the capital markets of nonfinancial firms.
2. The Japanese have recently experienced such an exacerbation of the cycle similar to that described here. This has occurred because Japanese banks are allowed to include equity as capital. This has effectively marked-to-market the value of their banks' capital.
3. This problem is clearly seen in the next chapter in an analysis of the shutdown of Penn Square National Bank, wherein the regulatory authorities allowed uninsured creditors to suffer substantial losses.
4. See any of Chandler's major works cited in Chapter 4.
5. On the pages cited, D'Arista offers several examples of conflicts of interest which illustrate the problems enumerated above.
6. The similar problems noted by D'Arista arise in the context of the parallel banking system.

7. Two Case Studies

INTRODUCTION

Chapter 6 considered how DFFs would probably behave when the alternative assumptions are in play under the program advocated by the Deregulationists. The essence of the argument in Chapter 6 was that the entrepreneurial drive and growth orientation of DFFs lead, under deregulation, to a highly charged competitive atmosphere. Under this sort of environment, DFFs find it in their self-interest to opt for strategies fostering growth and the risky portfolio holdings those options entail. The use of more conservative tactics, which is what the Deregulationists claim their program would promote, may build a more robust portfolio but leads to competitively induced failure through the loss of market share. This chapter will attempt to provide an empirical foundation for this argument by examining two case studies.

One is the failure of the Penn Square National Bank of Oklahoma City and the other is the failure of the Financial Corporation of America (FCA), or American Savings and Loan, of California. Penn Square has been chosen as one example because its behavior was so unusual that it ended up essentially operating in its own pocket of deregulation, and because its closure mirrored the kind of closure advocated by the Deregulationists. The losses imposed by this closure led directly to massive losses, liquidity problems and near failures at two much larger banks. Seattle First National Bank (Seafirst) avoided failure through an emergency merger with Bank of America. Continental Illinois National Bank and Trust Company averted failure through an unprecedented government bailout that could reasonably be called a nationalization of the bank.

The FCA has been selected as the other example because for several reasons it operated in a genuinely deregulated environment. At the Federal level the passage of the Depository Institutions Deregulation and Monetary Control Act in 1980 and the passage of the Garn–St Germain Act in 1982 gave Savings and Loans substantial freedoms so that they could grow out of portfolios that had become troublesome as interest rates rose. In addition, the Reagan appointees heading regulatory agencies were free market proponents who were lax in evaluating the character of Savings and Loan owners and were generous in granting charters (Mayer, 1984, p. 198). Lastly, the California Savings and Loan Commissioner, under the leadership of Larry Taggart, paralleled the climate at the Federal level by generously issuing new Savings and Loan charters and by strongly favoring the allowance of new investment powers for them. Taggart's approach was backed up by changes in California law at the beginning of 1983 which allowed state chartered Savings and Loan to use deposited funds in almost any manner they thought best (Mayer, 1990, pp. 5, 66 and 108–11).

The two case studies examined in this chapter are divided into two parts. The first part of the chapter will provide fairly detailed historical narratives describing both the Penn Square and FCA failures. The second part of the chapter will provide an analysis of how well the empirical evidence from each of these two financial institution failures meshes with the earlier arguments made in support of the alternative framework.

THE PENN SQUARE FAILURE AND ITS REPERCUSSIONS

Beginnings

Bill Jennings began his career as an executive vice-president at Penn Square Bank, a small retail bank located in a shopping mall. In his four years there he became president of the bank and developed a solid reputation. To advance his career, Jennings accepted an executive vice-presidency offered by Grady Harris, president of Fidelity Bank, a larger bank in Oklahoma City. Through his alliance with Harris, Jennings hoped to succeed Harris as president of Fidelity and fulfill his dream to become chief executive officer of a major bank. Under Harris, Jennings learned aggressive lending practices but also acquired sloppy management practices. Jennings, following Harris, became popular in the Oklahoma business community for making loans that other banks would not make. In his early years at Fidelity, Jennings had full lending authority and the responsibility and prominence that came with it. However, as the years passed Jennings's authority waned as Fidelity grew and established a loan committee system, which took Jennings out of the loan approval process. In addition, Jennings's involvement in a conflict of interest situation, which required Fidelity to hire legal counsel to extract itself from the fray, brought Jennings's judgement into question. Upon Harris's death in August of 1974, Jennings was never considered as his replacement. With this, Jennings realized that he had no chance of moving up into the position he had long sought (Zweig, 1985, pp. 22–7).

To fulfill his dream Jennings decided to return home by purchasing, with a few wealthy partners, Penn Square Bank, under the agreement that he would run it. Jennings established First Penn Corporation, a bank holding company, to purchase Penn Square stock. In December of 1975 Jennings's takeover of Penn Square Bank was approved, permitting First Penn to be a one-bank holding company. (Jennings had been in charge of operations for a period of time before this date.) This bank holding structure would allow Penn Square to engage in activities that stand-alone banks were forbidden to engage in. Unlike banks, one-bank holding companies can establish real estate and venture capital subsidiaries and tap needed funds through the commercial paper market. It was Jennings's intention to transform Penn Square from a small retail bank into a prominent oil and gas bank. Jennings also intended to prove to his superiors at Fidelity that he was the better banker (Zweig, 1985, pp. 27–9).

Growth

Jennings quickly moved to achieve his growth goals. Jennings proudly announced at the January 1976 stockholders' meeting that Penn Square had grown by 40 percent over the course of 1975. The typical growth rate of other Oklahoma City banks was about 4 percent. In a rather casual way Penn Square established an oil and gas department in early 1976. To get Penn Square growing, Jennings would book oil and gas loans at the legal limit with only potential oil and gas production as the collateral, in spite of warnings from Bill Lakey, the head of the oil and gas department, that this was a risky thing to do. Essentially, loans were being rapidly extended based solely on the estimated value of reserves. The borrowers' income stream, or cash flow, was usually insufficient to even meet interest payments (Zweig, 1985, pp. 30–35).

Jennings was not pleased with growth at this rate. He wanted Penn Square to grow faster so that it could become the biggest bank in Oklahoma City. To do this Jennings needed to get around two growth-limiting factors. One was the legal limit on loan size, the other was Oklahoma's unit banking laws. Penn Square got around these limitations by doing two things. One, it began to market and sell large oil and gas participation loans to the large money center banks. Second, to meet the liquidity demands of such an activity it began to depend heavily on purchased funds. It bid for funds from deposit brokers who represented large institutional investors. These actions helped put Penn Square on a path of incredibly rapid growth (Zweig,

1985, pp. 38–9, 71, 368 and 379). Between 1977 and 1982 Penn Square grew from a $30 million bank into a $500 million one (Mayer, 1984, p. 198). Eventually, Penn Square sold more participation loans than it had loans on its books, which was a rarity in the business (Zweig, 1985, p. 39). By July of 1982, Penn Square had sold a total of approximately $2 billion in participation loans to its top five correspondent banks (Wolfson, 1994, p. 87).

In the later half of 1977, with the resignation of Lakey and the hiring of Bill Patterson as head of the oil and gas department, Penn Square lost any serious internal constraints on the risks it would accept to maintain rapid rates of growth. Patterson and Jennings were kindred spirits in that they both were willing to extend loans based solely on optimistic appraisals of collateral value, without adequate documentation. In short, Penn Square grew rapidly because it dropped any loan quality standards (Zweig, 1985, pp. 60–61).

From late 1977 through 5 July 1982, when Penn Square was shut down, Penn Square's growth and prominence were based on a sophisticated pyramid or Ponzi scheme concentrated in oil and gas loans. When loans went sour they were simply renewed so that they could look good on paper. This was easily done because the oil and gas boom allowed the appraisal of reserves or drilling equipment serving as collateral to be inflated over time with some justification. Once this had been done a few times, and the loan would obviously be bad to examiners, it was made good again, on paper, by extending loans to other apparently more credit worthy borrowers so that they could take over the bad loans. In short, more and bigger loans were continuously being made to cover earlier loans that had gone bad. Money was made through loan origination fees, the payment of up-front interest, and through joint ventures and partnerships with borrowers. This shell game became so complex that Penn Square was able to successfully use the same collateral to cover more than one loan, a further boon to growth (Zweig, 1985, pp. 40, 61, 109, 118–19, 144, 160–61, 202, 247 and 270).

With all these bad loans on its books one wonders how Penn Square satisfied the big money center banks to which it had sold loan participations. They convinced these big banks that the loans they purchased were good in one of two ways. One method was that they always bought back loans that any of these banks became dissatisfied with. They would then repackage it and resell the loan to some other big bank. Penn Square was successful at this because of the ignorance of correspondent banks about energy loans and because of the widespread expectation at the time that oil and gas prices were going to continue to rise for many years. The other method was simply to cover up the fact that the loan had gone bad. This was done by Penn Square up-streaming interest to its correspondent banks even when interest was going unpaid by the borrower, which was often the case. These ploys made the Penn Square slogan that 'no one has ever lost a nickel on a Penn Square loan' believable to the big banks who had bought loan participations from Penn Square (Zweig, 1985, pp. 206–7, 237–8 and 246–8).

The Façade of Success

The oil and gas boom
There are a number of reasons as to why Penn Square was able to successfully maintain a façade of success for several years. One was the oil and gas boom. From the time Jennings bought Penn Square up through April of 1981, oil and gas prices were on a continuous rise, helped along by price decontrol in the United States. Even at the tail end of the boom, energy industry experts were forecasting continued price increases for the foreseeable future. With this there was a willingness to accept energy loans only backed by collateral simply because the reserves in the ground were going to continuously escalate in value. In fact, it was believed that energy loans when unpaid could profitably be rolled over because the collateral behind the original loan could be reevaluated upward because of energy price increases (Zweig, 1985, pp. 73–4, 93, 109, 174–5, 191–2 and 209–14).

Ignorance about energy loans
Another reason for Penn Square's success was the ignorance of both examiners and correspondent banks in evaluating the quality of energy loans. The examiners who came to inspect Penn Square were not trained in evaluating energy loans. There is a mystique and flexibility to energy loans that examiners do not understand because they are used to loans that are less speculative and are more concrete and ordinary in how they are evaluated. Thus examiners can be fairly easily persuaded, by those being examined, that an energy loan is good, especially during an oil and gas boom. This is the case because escalating energy prices make it relatively easy to make risky or even bad loans appear to be good. Until the last examination which shut Penn Square down, examiners focused on poor loan documentation, operational shortcomings and lack of liquidity. They failed to focus on the real problem, which was poor loan quality. The officials overseeing energy loans at both Continental Illinois and Seafirst, the two upstream banks that purchased the most participations from Penn Square, had the same shortcomings as did the examiners. Neither Lytle at Continental

Illinois nor Boyd at Seafirst, who headed each bank's energy division, had the background necessary to evaluate properly the quality of an energy loan. They both insisted, along with their superiors, almost right up to the time of Penn Square's failure, that the trouble they had with their Penn Square participations was due to poor documentation and due to operational procedures unable to cope with the massive volume of Penn Square loans. They maintained this viewpoint in spite of warnings from lower-level officials that there were serious loan quality problems. Lastly, Penn Square continued to succeed because concerns expressed in examination and audit reports were never made public while Penn Square reported respectable profits. The end result was that for five years Penn Square was able to operate in a reckless manner because it was never seriously challenged by regulatory or market discipline (Zweig, 1985, pp. 53–4, 57–8, 121–2, 174, 219–22, 228–34, 237–8, 242–6, 253–4, 257, 261–2, 264, 276, 283–4, 286, 297 and 299).

Growth focus of Continental Illinois

Probably the biggest factor which contributed to Penn Square's appearance of success was the very strong growth orientation of both Continental Illinois and Seafirst. The quest for heightened growth rates at each institution resulted in them either skirting, or ignoring, appropriate loan quality standards. In 1976, Continental Illinois, under its chairman Roger Anderson, embarked on a radical new business strategy by making a conscious decision to be more aggressive in putting new business on the books. Anderson announced his intention to take Continental from being the eighth largest bank in the United States to among the top three in commercial and industrial loans by 1981. Both the recession, which was just ending, and competition lent justification to a more aggressive stance. During the recession loans had fallen off and needed to be replenished to maintain profitability. Competition from commercial paper, foreign banks and nonbanks also pointed to the ability of greater aggression to win back business lost to these sectors (Zweig, 1985, pp. 68–70).

This sort of strategy made additional sense for Continental because of the state of Illinois unit banking laws. Continental could not grow through branching and therefore could not use such a mechanism to secure a stable core of retail deposits. In addition, focusing on business loans would enhance profitability simply because they were not subject to the usury ceilings imposed on consumer loans. Therefore, if Continental wanted to grow in a state like Illinois it would focus on business loans and obtain deposits by purchasing them through the money market. Continental became heavily dependent upon short-term purchased funds. Continental would eventually reach the point where it rolled over more than eight billion dollars in purchased funds every night. It would be this dependence on purchased funds that would eventually lead to crisis at Continental and a full-scale bailout by the federal government (Zweig, 1985, pp. 71–2).

Under its aggressive growth campaign, Continental was scouring the entire country for new business. This included participation loans. During this period, one of the most rapidly growing industries was domestic oil and gas exploration. Therefore, when Continental and Penn Square connected they made a perfect match. Penn Square needed the money it received from the sale of participations to Continental and Continental needed the extra business it could book from Penn Square. The expectation that the boom in oil and gas would be long term, because of the worldwide shortage in known energy reserves, made the relationship appear even more beneficial to Continental's growth goals. Lastly, Continental was pleased with the Penn Square participation loans because it saved itself overhead costs and because it earned fatter margins than it could in the more hotly competitive markets in which it made direct loans (Zweig, 1985, pp. 72 and 82).

There are several reasons as to why Continental so eagerly purchased shoddy loan participations from Penn Square. Almost all of them are related to the growth culture that came to dominate life at Continental. To obtain additional oil and gas business Continental needed to attract borrowers away from the institutions with which they traditionally did business. Continental did this by lowering credit standards, by giving customers more of what they asked for. In addition, John Lytle, who eventually headed the oil and gas division at Continental, and was always closest to the purchase of Penn Square participations, did not have the background necessary for judging the quality of an energy loan. This culture of reduced credit standards to meet growth goals and Lytle's ignorance made it easy for Penn Square to convince Continental its loans were solid through gimmicks such as repurchase agreements and the up-streaming of interest (Zweig, 1985, pp. 72–4, 82 and 156).

There are other factors which led to the acceptance of Penn Square loans at Continental. One was the prestige of the energy division at Continental. The division was established in 1954 and quickly gained status as one of the premier lenders to energy industries. By 1973 Continental's energy division was bringing in one-quarter of the bank's earnings. With such a glowing track record the methods that the energy division used to promote growth failed to be questioned in detail by upper-level officials. Another factor which contributed to this laxity of oversight was the adoption of a reorganization promoted and popularized by McKinsey and Company which stressed decentralization to foster growth. The central theme of this restructuring was to decentralize into specialized units, giving each unit the authority it needed to keep its customers happy. At Continental, this significantly increased the lending authority of junior officials and reduced loan reviews by more seasoned senior officials. With this decentralization, Continental's loans were reviewed by an upper-level committee only after a commitment had been made, thereby weakening the enforcement of any loan quality standards. The last and probably overriding factor which led to the booking of overly risky loans such as those from Penn Square was the superheated growth culture that developed under the leadership of Robert Anderson. In this environment, senior officers at Continental felt that their career would be irreparably damaged if they allowed their division's growth to be impeded by difficulties such as personnel shortages or a lack of qualified borrowers (Zweig, 1985, pp. 73–5 and 220).

Growth at Seafirst
An emphasis on growth at Seafirst led it into willingly purchasing loans from Penn Square in much the same way as it did at Continental. Seafirst became acquainted with the oil industry when it extended lines of credit to the major oil companies during the construction of the Alaskan oil pipeline. This experience, even though it was relatively risk free, gave Seafirst the feeling that it was relatively accomplished when it came to oil finance. In addition, Seafirst had for years extended loans based on equipment as collateral with the aviation, fishing and logging industries located in its home territory, the Pacific Northwest. Seafirst's link to the oil industry, along with its experience in collateral lending, made it easy for John Boyd in Seafirst's fledgling energy division to become heavily involved in the collateral-based energy loans championed by Penn Square. Besides, the expectations of seemingly everyone were that the oil industry had nowhere to go but up (Zweig, 1985, pp. 96–7).

Seafirst's William Jenkins, like Continental's Roger Anderson, set highly ambitious growth goals. Jenkins's goal was a growth rate of 15 percent per year. To accomplish this level of growth, Jenkins had Seafirst reorganized along the same decentralization model sponsored by McKinsey and Company as was done at Continental and other large banks. As at Continental, this resulted in substantial lending authority being pushed down to junior officials. Jenkins pushed the McKinsey decentralization so far at Seafirst that he abandoned the bank's well-respected loan review committee. This sort of structure and climate signaled divisional leaders that their rewards would be based on the contribution that their division's expansion made to overall growth at

Seafirst. This made the temptation to grow by reducing credit standards irresistible, especially given Jenkins's acknowledgement that to achieve the kind of growth he wanted he would have to take on more difficult business (Zweig, 1985, pp. 96–9).

Jenkins set such ambitious goals at Seafirst because he was looking forward to the probable emergence of nationwide banking. He wanted Seafirst to have sufficient clout to have a chance at being a player in this new market. This meant that Seafirst had to become big enough to become an absorber of smaller institutions rather than being one that was absorbed during the construction of nationwide banking networks. In addition, Seafirst's growth ambitions became extraterritorial; they looked beyond the Pacific Northwest region, because the lumber and aviation industries dominant in the area were severely slowed by Federal Reserve chairman Paul Volker's tight monetary policies begun in 1979. In spite of Seafirst's core of retail deposits supplied by its extensive branch network, it found it necessary to turn heavily toward short-term purchased funds to finance the needed growth opportunities which it most readily found outside its traditional business territory. It was these highly volatile purchased funds, the availability of which was dependent upon sellers' confidence in Seafirst, which brought on the initial trouble that led to Seafirst's emergency merger with Bank of America. This corresponds with the initial cause of crisis at Continental (Zweig, 1985, pp. 100–101, 106–7 and 142).

Because of the potential for growth in a booming energy industry, Boyd was able to campaign successfully to get the energy loan ceiling bumped up from 1 percent of total loans to 15 percent of total loans at Seafirst. To fill the growth potential this higher ceiling provided Boyd, he reduced loan standards by enthusiastically accepting lease line and rig loans. Lease line loans are loans based on the value of an oil lease. An oil lease simply provides the right to drill in a specified site and its value is based on the likelihood of finding oil or gas. Lease line loans are very risky because lease values are volatile and change wildly with the success or failure of finding oil in neighboring lease sites. Rig loans are loans where the oil drilling rig serves as collateral, typically the rig's scrap value or the cash flow it will generate. Seafirst made the mistake of lending on the scarcity value of oil rigs which appear safe during a boom because rigs are difficult to obtain and their value is rising. However, such loans are risky because scarcity can be rapidly relieved from either the supply or demand side. On the supply side new domestic or foreign rig producers may enter the market, while on the demand side the buoyant expectations driving demand may suddenly become dark. The sudden end to the oil boom was what eventually soured Seafirst's rig loans. Because of Seafirst's growth ambitions it allowed itself over the course of two years to become the world's biggest rig lender (Zweig, 1985, pp. 156, 161–2, and 192–4).

Boyd was praised by Jenkins and other superiors for the growth he oversaw at the energy division. There seemed to be no concern about the risks to which the loans in the energy division were exposing Seafirst. In fact, internal audits of the energy department had given it a clean bill of health and the conclusions were backed up by the views of expert oil industry analysts. Given the growth goals at Seafirst, and the praise and rewards they received in helping meet them, it is no wonder that Boyd, who regularly made direct loans as bad as or worse than those at Penn Square, gladly purchased packages of questionable loans from Penn Square that were so large that they overwhelmed his operations department. Seafirst, like Continental, was assured, in its ignorance, by Penn Square's offer to repurchase loans and by Penn Square's covering of bad loans through the up-streaming of unpaid interest (Zweig, 1985, pp. 254, 260–64, 280 and 283).

The role of faulty market evaluations
Faulty market evaluations also had a role in assisting Penn Square to maintain an appearance of success. Both Continental Illinois and Seafirst were darlings of both bank analysts and the financial press who praised both institutions for their high rates of profitable growth. This growth was fueled in part by Penn Square participation loans. In 1978 *Barron's* praised Continental for its success and traced it to its penetration of, and solid record in, energy lending. In the same year *Dun's Review* named Continental as one of the five best-managed companies in the United States. In late 1981 the financial press continued to praise Continental for its remarkable growth and profitability and lauded its conservative management and style. Up through the first quarter of 1982, Continental remained a favorite of the financial press due to its aggressive lending and its consistency in reporting ever-increasing profits. Also, as late as 1982, Continental's local competition assumed that there was some grand plan, involving a major move into interstate banking, behind Continental's relationship with Penn Square (Zweig, 1985, pp. 79–80, 232, 298 and 310).

Seafirst received similar accolades. In 1978 the San Francisco securities firm of Robertson, Colman called Seafirst one of the highest quality bank stocks available, months before Seafirst accepted a ten million dollar deal with Penn Square. In 1980, Seafirst confounded its competition by coming off its twentieth straight year of increased earnings. Given the dismal state of the Pacific Northwest economy both Jenkins and his energy division head John Boyd looked like miracle workers. In early 1982 the local financial press and the business community continued to be impressed with Seafirst's growth and profitability given the weak Pacific Northwest economy. They attributed Seafirst's long-term success to conservative practices and an enormous emphasis on loan quality control (Zweig, 1985, pp. 102, 194 and 285–6).

All these market evaluations of Continental and Seafirst, given the above analysis, were wrong. However, the confidence they delivered to the two banks enabled them to buy up shoddy Penn Square loans without being questioned. The success of these two banks was not based on masterful leadership that had insights that others lacked. It was not based on conservative management practice and considered containment of risk. It was, instead, based on an aggressive pursuit of growth which fostered inappropriate risk-taking, the kind of risk-taking that led to the purchase of loans of the ilk sold by Penn Square. Market evaluations covered up, instead of revealed, as they are supposed to do, what was really going on. This failure helped enable Penn Square to sell almost worthless loans with abandon.

Another market evaluative failure which allowed Penn Square to function successfully was the ease with which Penn Square was able to attract brokered deposits. In its last days of operation, when Penn Square officials were frantically trying to rescue the bank from regulatory action and when the bank's troubles were publicly known, Penn Square was still able to bid successfully for brokered deposits (Zweig, 1985, p. 379). This ability must also have given Penn Square hope that it could raise the capital it needed to satisfy the regulatory agencies and remain in business. Penn Square was unable to attract such capital.

Why the difference? Why did brokered deposits not impose the same sort of discipline that capital did at Penn Square? The volume of typically brokered deposits meant that a large portion of them were uninsured and subject to loss. One difference is that deposits are short term while capital is long term. Therefore, deposit brokers, because of an ability to withdraw funds quickly, may find it worthwhile to place uninsured deposits with a troubled institution to get the higher returns such institutions offer. In short, deposit brokers think that through quick and astute moves they can manage away the risk of obtaining higher returns.

Another factor is that uninsured depositors may have assumed that even if Penn Square failed, then they would be made whole. This would be a fair assumption because under the last major bank failure, that of Franklin National Bank in 1974, the regulatory agencies shut it down in a manner where uninsured depositors suffered no losses (Wolfson, 1994, pp. 56–9). The fact of the matter is that uninsured brokered deposits had so little fear of loss at Penn Square that they did not act as a disciplinary brake on Penn Square's reckless operations. In fact, the desire of deposit brokers to obtain the highest possible returns encouraged Penn Square's reckless operations by funding them (Wolfson, 1994, p. 88).

The Shutdown of Penn Square

In May of 1982 the Comptroller's Office began the examination that would result in the sudden shutdown of Penn Square Bank. This examination was preceded by negative publicity in the financial press concerning Penn Square and its two biggest correspondent banks, Continental Illinois and Seafirst. The examination revealed concerns immediately due to Penn Square's concentration in energy loans and its heavy reliance on purchased funds. However, the examiner's job went very slowly because of poor records and an initial lack of cooperation on the part of an upper-level Penn Square official. During June the examination was broadened and the Federal Reserve Bank of Kansas City was informed of the mounting problems at Penn Square. When only the portion of the portfolio containing loans greater than a million dollars had been examined, the identified losses were already approaching $20 million. During the entire examination, Penn Square, in an effort to rescue itself from failure, continued to play its shell games, purchased brokered funds, sold Certificates of Deposit (CDs), and tried to raise capital (Zweig, 1985, pp. 321–5, 332 and 346).

In late June, the Comptroller's staff of examiners was strengthened and on 25 June 1982 the Comptroller's Washington headquarters was informed of the shocking dimension of the problems at Penn Square. At this point both the Federal Reserve and the FDIC were brought in. At the same time things began to unravel at Penn Square, with checks bouncing and big depositors pulling out their funds (Zweig, 1985, pp. 344–54).

At the outset the three regulatory agencies could not agree on what needed to be done. The FDIC was focused on a least-cost solution, ranging from the traditional purchase and assumption (P&A), wherein all depositors are made whole, to a payoff involving losses. The FDIC would only do a P&A if it could obtain an agreement from Penn Square's correspondent banks that would limit its exposure to losses. This agreement, however, would never be obtained, on account of the inability of any party to reliably calculate the potential losses on the Penn Square loans they held. Therefore, in the end, the FDIC favored a payoff involving uninsured depositor losses, a position strongly breaking with tradition at the FDIC. The Federal Reserve favored any solution that would minimize destabilizing repercussions by avoiding uninsured depositor losses. Thus, the Federal Reserve both negotiated with Penn Square's correspondent banks and pushed for a P&A. The Comptroller's Office was of two minds. Conover, the head of the Comptroller's Office, and some of his deputies favored a payoff, while others held in high regard favored a P&A (Zweig, 1985, pp. 353–4, 356, 370–73, 382–5, 389–92 and 394–403). The speed and pressure of events forced a solution upon the three bickering regulatory agencies. On Thursday 1 July rumors began to fly about the shaky condition of Penn Square and the *American Banker* published an article detailing the troubles at Penn Square and how they seriously spilled over into its correspondent banks. On the same day Seafirst issued a release admitting to its difficulties which gave substance to both the articles and the rumors. On Friday 2 July the problems at Penn Square were reported throughout the financial press. On Saturday 3 July Penn Square experienced a run in which it could not pay out withdrawn deposits in cash. That day Penn Square issued $1.8 million in cashier's checks (Zweig, 1985, pp. 367–8, 376 and 388–9).

The three regulatory agencies realized that Penn Square would not survive the weekend and that they would have to have a solution in place before the bank opened on Tuesday 6 July. The regulatory agencies had only a few days to do what they usually did in a few weeks or months. Penn Square's five biggest correspondent banks refused to assist in a bailout of Penn Square both because of unknown loss exposure and because of fear of litigation by shareholders. The regulatory agencies found that a P&A was out of the question for a few reasons. One, there was not time to arrange one. Second, it was doubtful that any healthy institution would agree to one, because of all the unknown possible losses. Third, the FDIC no longer saw any way in which a P&A could prove to be a least-cost solution. The only solution the crisis and its time constraints allowed was a payoff. This, however, was held up because the Comptroller's examiners were finding it difficult, with sufficient certitude, to declare Penn Square insolvent. The FDIC nonetheless geared up for a payoff (Zweig, 1985, pp. 373–4, 382–3 and 396–7).

The holdup came to an end on the afternoon of Monday 5 July when the Comptroller's examiners were finally able to report to Washington with sufficient certainty that Penn Square was indeed insolvent. That evening Penn Square was shut down and was reopened the next day by the FDIC as a Deposit Insurance National Bank. Insured depositors would be able to access their accounts as if nothing had happened. Uninsured depositors would suffer losses. They would be given receivers' certificates and would be partially compensated upon liquidation of Penn Square's assets. This was a break with tradition wherein the regulatory agencies had kept losses contained to shareholders (Zweig, 1985, pp. 404–5 and 409).

The repercussions of the shutdown

That break with tradition led to far-ranging repercussions, the fear of which had maintained the tradition of no depositor losses for so long. A number of credit unions and S&Ls had uninsured deposits totaling $119.7 million at Penn Square. Seventeen of the credit unions had deposits in excess of their capital. In addition, many local, Oklahoma City businesses and financial institutions were also hurt by the payoff at Penn Square. The biggest repercussion of the Penn Square payoff was the developing funding crises at both Continental Illinois and Seafirst which brought both institutions to the verge of failure (Zweig, 1985, pp. 410–11).

Both Continental Illinois and Seafirst were highly dependent on purchased funds. The heightened fear of loss among uninsured depositors created by the Penn Square payoff not only increased the cost of such funds but also made them much more likely to bolt if any bad news arose. The Penn Square loans at both Continental and Seafirst raised depositors' security concerns at both banks. As information leaked out about additional bad loans at both banks it became increasingly difficult for each of them to raise sufficient funds. When both banks eventually began to report losses resulting from the bad loans they both immediately suffered massive depositor runs which threw them into crisis. Depositors had good reason to run because they feared what was done at Penn Square would also be done at their banks.

Seafirst was the first to succumb. In January 1983, Seafirst's serious problems began when it reported losses for the fourth quarter of $90.2 million. At the same time it announced that it had assembled, with 13 of the nation's largest banks, a $1.5 billion safety net. Seafirst also announced that all parts of it were up for sale. This safety net, however, did not do enough to bolster confidence in Seafirst and losses continued to mount. As April approached and Seafirst was preparing to announce even bigger losses, it knew it was near failure and needed to find a way to bail itself out. This came about with a complex emergency merger with Bank of America which required legal permission from the Washington state legislature. This merger only came about because Bank of America had, for a number of years, been toying with a scheme to acquire a large Washington state bank as part of an interstate banking strategy, but had repeatedly been disappointed. The growing disaster at Seafirst provided Bank of America with the opportunity it had long sought, and the merger averted a major banking crisis (Zweig, 1985, pp. 436–8).

Over the first quarter of 1983, Continental reported that its problem loans had risen from $400 million to $2.3 billion, an amount exceeding the bank's capital base. During the week of 8 May, as a result of rumors spawned by the announcement, Continental suffered a major global electronic run which forced Continental on 10 May to go to the Federal Reserve for $4 billion to replace lost funds. On 14 May, Continental announced that with the help of Morgan Guaranty it had assembled 16 banks agreeing to supply a $4.5 billion line of credit. This, however, was not enough to stem the run. At this point bank regulatory agencies intervened in a big way to contain the crisis. By assembling a consortium of 28 banks they increased Continental's line of credit to $5.5 billion. In addition, the FDIC infused $2 billion and guaranteed all, even uninsured, deposits. In the meantime, Continental failed to attract any merger partner because suitors quickly discovered that the bad loans were not limited to the energy portfolio. With this, the crisis continued and on 26 July 1983 the three bank regulatory agencies announced a $4.5 billion rescue package. It called for 80 percent ownership of Continental by the FDIC, reducing shareholder ownership to 20 percent. In turn, the FDIC pumped in $1 billion in new capital to compensate for Continental's second quarter loss of $1.1 billion. In short, the containment of the crisis at Continental, and the maintenance of both domestic and foreign confidence in the US banking system, required a virtual nationalization of the bank (Zweig, 1985, pp. 438–40).

FORBEARANCE AT FCA

Deregulation of the Thrift Industry

At the time of the Federal Home Loan Bank Board's intervention in the management of the FCA, it was the largest thrift in the United States. FCA had adopted a growth strategy in an effort to battle the income problem created by a low fixed interest income from mortgage assets combined with more expensive deposit liabilities. The idea of rapid growth was to dilute the influence of low-interest mortgage loans by aggressively adding to the portfolio new higher-interest fixed rate mortgages. The problem with this strategy is that it depended on a downturn or at least a stabilization in interest rates. If interest rates continued to rise then the loss problem would simply be compounded.

In the early 1980s both legislation and regulatory policy regarding thrifts tried to alleviate their structurally induced losses through deregulation. In 1980 the 5 percent limit on brokered deposits was eliminated (Pizzo et al., 1989, p. 19). Also in 1980 the Depository Institutions Deregulation and Monetary Control Act phased out interest-rate ceilings on deposits and increased deposit insurance coverage from $40,000 to $100,000. These changes were designed to enable thrifts to bid effectively for the deposits they needed. In 1981 all federally chartered financial institutions were allowed to issue adjustable rate mortgages. In spite of these changes thrifts were in a bind by 1982 because their deposits were more expensive than what they earned on the long-term fixed rate mortgages they held as assets. This resulted in passage of the Garn–St Germain Act which took deregulation of the thrift industry much further.   The provisions of this complex legislation of interest here are that it allowed thrifts to offer money market funds and it significantly liberalized their investment powers by allowing much riskier nonresidential real estate and commercial lending.

Lax Regulators and a Broke FSLIC

Regulators also got into the game of easing the rules. In order to attract more innovative and entrepreneurial thrift operators they eased the ownership and chartering rules. They now allowed a single shareholder to own a thrift and allowed the issuance of charters without the establishment of a clear community need. Also, to encourage more business, they did away with down payment requirements and allowed provision of 100 percent financing. They also permitted thrifts to make real estate loans anywhere, not just in their own market area.   The regulatory agencies also allowed and encouraged the use of liberal accounting rules to squeeze thrifts' balance sheets into compliance. For instance 'goodwill' defined as customer loyalty, market share and other intangibles could be counted toward net worth. By 1986, 40 percent of the industry's net worth was in the form of goodwill (Pizzo et al., 1989, pp. 12–13). Other accounting gimmicks were the issuance of net worth certificates, which essentially created thrift capital out of thin air; the use of a five-year averaging method to calculate required capital; and the creation of artificial profits by allowing the sale of securities that rose in value while burying those that had fallen in value at historic cost in the portfolio (Mayer, 1990, pp. 102 and 153).

The Federal Savings and Loan Insurance Corporation (FSLIC) encouraged the full exploitation of both the new deregulatory laws and liberalized accounting rules because it did not have the funds to properly shut down S&Ls, especially large ones such as FCA. In fact, FCA's

$32 million portfolio was so large that efforts to cover losses under a proper shutdown would have fully depleted the FSLIC. Given the lack of funds, the FSLIC adopted a policy of forbearance (a policy later written into the 1987 FSLIC recapitalization bill) where it kept insolvent thrifts running with minimal losses. This meant that such thrifts had to write new business so that growth to some extent could offset losses. Typically, the business these failed thrifts attracted was of lower quality and this sort of competition put undue pressure on both the earnings and credit standards of healthy thrifts. The point is that with an impotent FSLIC, troubled thrifts, especially larger ones such as FCA, were operating in an almost completely deregulated atmosphere. They were allowed to do almost anything, from accounting gimmickry to the writing of unduly risky new business, to keep themselves afloat.[1] They did this with the FSLIC's blessing because the agency did not have the funds to properly shut them down and because the losses from full-scale free market-like failures would be dangerously destabilizing. The FSLIC was trapped; its only option was to keep ailing S&Ls up and running (Mayer, 1990, p. 235; Pizzo et al., 1989, p. 178).

State Savings and Loan

The story of FCA and its incredible growth is really the story of Charles Knapp, its owner. FCA starts as the owner of State Savings in Stockton California, a relatively small S&L. Under Knapp's management, State grew very quickly through extensive use of purchased funds and aggressive lending, with poor documentation, to low-quality borrowers, at very narrow profit margins. Most of the loans were in the form of fixed rate mortgages which indicates that FCA/State was betting on a decline in interest rates, a risky prospect. In 1980 State grew by 60 percent and in 1981 by 111 percent. In short, State grew at such high rates because it made bad loans, which other institutions avoided, and financed those loans with purchased funds (Mayer, 1990, pp. 105–6).

State developed a rather typical strategy to cover its bad loans. It simply made more and larger loans to cover old loans that had gone bad. To cover property it had repossessed it simply extended loans to new borrowers who would purchase it. The key to success for such a strategy was continued rapid growth. That growth drew the attention of regulators (Mayer, 1990, pp. 107–8).

Merger with American Savings and Loan

Examiners were moving in on State in late 1982 when several things happened that got State and Knapp off the hook. One factor was the passage of Garn–St Germain at the federal level and the Nolan Act in California. Both acts, especially the one in California, extensively deregulated S&Ls, giving them wide-ranging, new opportunities for growth. Also, Larry Taggart became the state commissioner over S&Ls and he had an admiration for maverick operators such as Knapp. With this change in atmosphere came the opportunity for Knapp to buy First Charter, the holding company for American Savings and Loan. If Knapp could swing such a merger he would become the largest S&L operator in the country (Mayer, 1990, pp. 107–8).

Knapp accomplished the merger by promising regulators that with American he would be large enough to become a more docile, less aggressive S&L operator. The regulatory authorities thought that this argument made sense and allowed the merger to go through. They thought that with American's extensive branch network and large core of stable retail deposits, Knapp would have little reason to fund excessive growth through the use of expensive and fickle purchased funds. FCA started operating under the American Savings name and Knapp did not reform. While operating as American Savings and Loan, Knapp opened his own money desk through which he purchased brokered deposits and sold jumbo CDs to ease the financing of more rapid growth (Mayer, 1990, pp. 108–9; Pizzo et al., 1989, p. 178).

Continued Reckless Growth, then Crisis

FCA continued to invest billions in fixed rate mortgages and also got involved with commercial development projects in California and Texas. However, in addition, FCA got involved in sophisticated hedging instruments, which both S&L regulators and the Securities and Exchange Commission (SEC) had a very difficult time understanding and evaluating. Over the year 1983–84, FCA grew from $22 billion in assets to $32 billion in assets, a phenomenal rate of growth. Growth of this kind is so enormous that it is very difficult if not impossible to maintain organizational control (Pizzo et al., 1989, p. 178; Mayer, 1990, p. 109).

FCA drew the attention of both S&L regulators and the SEC because it was reporting profits when they both knew that the institution was heavily burdened with both bad loans and repossessed real estate. The use of complex and difficult to understand financial arrangements involving hedging instruments also raised suspicions.

Upon inspection, the SEC discovered that FCA was using deceptive practices involving securities to report profits. The SEC forced FCA to reverse a reported profit of $75.3 million in the second quarter of 1984 into a loss of $79.9 million. With this information and the concerns following the depositor losses at Penn Square, $6 billion in purchased funds bolted FCA. In spite of American's extensive branch network, half of FCA's funds came from volatile market sources. FCA was in trouble and the FSLIC needed a quick resolution. FCA could not fail. It was absolutely necessary that it be kept afloat (Pizzo et al., 1989, p. 178; Mayer, 1990, pp. 109–10).

Regulatory Efforts at Resolution

First, Knapp was ousted and William Popejoy, a trusted and experienced thrift operator, was installed as Knapp's replacement. Second, the FSLIC in conjunction with the Federal Reserve scraped together, out of the FCA portfolio, $4 billion in collateral worthy of the Federal Reserve loaning on to pay off big depositors. Third, and last, Popejoy thought that the solution was to shrink the company by selling off branches to build net worth and to switch to adjustable rate mortgages. But Popejoy found that he could not do this. Upon the merger, a billion dollars of goodwill had been assessed to the branches. This meant that any funds generated from the sale of branches would not add to net worth because it would be offset by required write-offs against goodwill. Popejoy also discovered that the cost of liquidation would be $5.5 billion, something the FSLIC could not afford. The only solution was that which Knapp had long used: growth to carry the bad assets (Mayer, 1990, pp. 111–13; Pizzo et al., 1989, p. 352).

Popejoy did use Knapp's basic growth strategy to keep FCA afloat but he did make some significant changes and also had some significant advantages. Popejoy tightened credit standards to avoid the problem of additional bad loans. He continued the use of all available accounting gimmicks to maintain the appearance of positive net worth with the approval of Washington. In fact, all of Popejoy's strategies were approved or mandated by Washington. At first, Popejoy, with Washington's blessing, tried to avoid the use of brokered deposits. This came to an end on 14 September 1984, the day after Treasury Secretary Don Regan emphatically answered 'no' to a query about FCA being bailed out in the same manner as Continental Illinois. The panic generated by Regan's comment resulted in a run that day at FCA amounting to $400 million. It was the largest single day run in thrift history. This derailed the rehabilitation efforts at FCA and required the extensive use of brokered deposits to counter the massive outflow resulting from Regan's remarks. Over time, the FSLIC helped Popejoy minimize this use of brokered deposits by writing comfort letters to Wall St houses that had lent FCA needed funds through repurchase agreements. The letters assured these various Wall St houses that the FSLIC stood behind all of FCA's borrowings (Mayer, 1990, pp. 112–14; Pizzo et al., 1989, p. 181).

The problem with this growth strategy was that Popejoy was taking a gamble that interest rates would fall, a gamble that he never won. Over the next couple of years FCA remained a troubled institution. FCA essentially became a semi-autonomous unit of the federal government. By the middle of October in 1987 the condition of FCA was becoming an unacceptable burden, in spite of a decision earlier that year to sell FCA. The Bank Board had hired Saloman Brothers to find a purchaser. After frantic negotiations over the weekend of 17–18 October, the Federal Home Loan Bank Board was prepared to announce on the following Monday that FCA had failed and that the FSLIC would be unable of pay off depositors at American Savings. This unprecedented move was stopped by the crash of the stock market on 19 October 1987. With the flight to quality caused by the crash, FCA's losses receded because of price increases in government and government-insured paper, some of which was held by FCA. In addition, the Wall St houses became more willing to continue to lend through repurchases to FCA because of a self-interested desire of not adding any more negatives to a market in crisis. Even with these helpful events, FCA entered 1988 more than $3 billion in the red. The FCA problem was resolved later in 1988 when FCA was sold to Robert M. Bass in a heavily subsidized deal designed to shield Bass from losses. In the end, FCA cost the FSLIC more than $2 billion. It is interesting to note that in January of 1984, long after the recklessness at FCA had begun, the Big Eight accounting firm of Arthur Anderson and Company had given FCA a clean bill of health in accordance with consistently applied and generally accepted accounting principles (Mayer, 1990, pp. 114–15 and 254–5; Pizzo et al., 1989, p. 329).

LIMITED HISTORICAL EVIDENCE AND THE ALTERNATIVE FRAMEWORK

Introduction

Chapter 6 looked at how the Deregulationist program would operate under the alternative assumptions. That chapter ended in a summation of five points which demonstrated why the Deregulationist program would result in both unstable DFFs and unstable financial markets. This section will use two approaches to show how the above historical examples indicate that the alternative assumptions better mirror reality than the more traditional, marginalist ones used by the Deregulationists. Both approaches will be related to the five points of summation. One approach will point out how the two historical examples described above indicate how DFFs and their financial markets operate in accordance with the alternative assumptions. The other approach will look at the destabilizing nature of DFF behavior in the two historical examples.

DFFs and Growth

All four of the DFFs discussed above placed a strong emphasis on growth. Jennings wanted to make Penn Square the largest bank in Oklahoma City, and prove to his former employer that he was the better banker. Anderson wanted to make Continental one of the three largest business and commercial lenders in the United States. Jenkins wanted Seafirst to maintain a 15 percent annual growth rate to ensure that the bank would become a player in nationwide banking. Lastly, Knapp, at FCA, was apparently addicted to growth and its rate increased even after he had constructed, through merger, the largest S&L in the country.

Deregulation, FCA and Penn Square

At two of these DFFs, FCA and Penn Square, growth became reinforced internally. Both of these DFFs had reduced credit standards so much to maintain high rates of growth that they had to continue to grow at high rates to remain viable. Both firms had to continuously make more and larger loans, be it through rollovers or new business, to carry, or cover, the loans in the portfolio that had gone bad. This need for an increasing volume of loans encouraged a continuous erosion in credit standards. This in turn increased the number of bad loans which further increased the required rate of growth for viability, and so on.

Both FCA and Penn Square operated in almost fully deregulated environments. FCA as an S&L was operating in an environment that had been legally deregulated at both the federal and state level. As a California chartered S&L, FCA had virtually unlimited investment powers due to legal changes that went into effect at the beginning of 1983. In addition, regulatory agencies at both levels had loosened their policies in a major way as they tried to deal with an industry in a serious net worth crisis. Lastly, the FSLIC did not have the funds to close ailing S&Ls. Its only viable option was forbearance, where

S&Ls were essentially assisted and encouraged in their schemes to appear solvent.

Penn Square, as a bank, did not operate like an S&L in an industry that had been deregulated. Instead, Penn Square operated in what I would call a pocket of deregulation. Penn Square's unique methods were so reckless that it took time for examiners to grasp the dimensions of what was taking place. First, Penn Square was deeply into collateral-based oil and gas loans, a type of loan that is speculative and difficult for knowledgeable people to evaluate. Penn Square's examiners were not trained in evaluating such loans and were easily duped for a period of time. This was especially the case because the oil and gas boom kept collateral values rising which helped loans appear to be good when they were not. Second, the loan documentation and operations procedures were so poor at Penn Square that examiners naturally focused on them as the core problems at the bank, not poor loan quality. Third, Penn Square's heavy dependence on purchased funds, and the liquidity concerns this created for the examiners, drew attention away from the quality of the loans that Penn Square was making. Lastly, the fact that most of the loans that Penn Square had made were not on the books, but were sold as participations, gave additional cover to Penn Square's reckless lending. With this, Penn Square essentially operated in an environment that was akin to the one in which S&Ls were operating.

Growth of this type was not uncommon. Much of the S&L *débâcle* in the United States was due to this sort of growth. Its grandest example is what took place in Texas where the industry, as in California, was also deregulated in an extensive way at the state in addition to the federal level. The vast majority of Texas S&Ls grew at phenomenal rates and those that did so failed (Pizzo et al., 1989, pp. 20 and 183–4). This sort of behavior in a deregulated environment points out two things. The rapid rates of growth that were so quickly achieved indicates that a pursuit of growth is an inherent characteristic of DFFs. The reasons for its inherent nature were cited in the earlier presentation of the alternative assumptions. Some of the reasons for growth are competitive pressures, an organizational need to provide motivation, managerial infighting and resolution, the need to sop up excess capacity, the rewards it provides management, and the force of management personality in driving it. The behavior also clearly indicates the use of short-term planning horizons. The growth at both FCA and Penn Square was based on a pyramid or Ponzi scheme which can show impressive growth and profits only for a short period of time. The problem is that such schemes can work quite impressively for a time. The higher than normal profits and growth they appear to generate successfully attract the funding they need to keep going.

Weaknesses in the deregulationist argument
The Deregulationists argue that this sort of behavior is due to deposit insurance and the method by which DFFs are closed. They claim that the unlimited nature of deposit insurance, wherein all depositors are made whole upon DFF failure, eliminates any depositor discipline that would enforce more conservative DFF behavior. In addition, they say that DFFs are encouraged to take risks because they enjoy all the profits while the taxpayer bears the burden. They have proposed two solutions. One is to clearly subject uninsured depositors to losses. The other is to prevent expenses to taxpayers by closing down DFFs before net worth becomes negative. It appears, given the above historical evidence, that neither of these proposals is as viable as claimed.

Penn Square Bank was shut down in such a manner that both depositors and correspondent banks were subject to losses. Uninsured depositors at Penn Square were given receivers' certificates and they would get back whatever could be had after Penn Square's assets had been liquidated. The losses would be significant because so many of Penn Square's assets were worthless. Penn Square's correspondent banks, such as Continental and Seafirst, were put on a par with other creditors. In addition, the FDIC disavowed any letters of credit issued by Penn Square as collateral for loans made to oil companies by Penn Square. Many of these loans were held by both Continental and Seafirst (Zweig, 1985, pp. 435–6).

These losses led to high levels of instability in the financial markets until the crises at both Continental and Seafirst were resolved. After the closure of Penn Square, large uninsured depositors became incredibly skittish. They abandoned Seafirst *en masse* when losses were reported, even though Seafirst had assembled an impressive safety net. Typically such a safety net would mitigate a run to a manageable size. It did not work this time because depositors feared losses like those imposed at Penn Square. Depositor nervousness was more clear at Continental. Depositors were not comforted by an impressive line of credit assembled by Morgan Guaranty. They were not comforted by government assistance which expanded the line of credit, infused billions of dollars and guaranteed *all* deposits. They only became comfortable, and stopped withdrawing funds at unmanageable levels, when Continental was, in actuality, nationalized. Again, depositors behaved in this destabilizing manner because they feared the sort of losses that came out of the Penn Square closure. Stability returned to the markets only when the regulatory agencies clearly returned to convention and kept uninsured depositors whole.

From this scenario it does appear that subjecting depositors to losses does impose discipline upon DFFs. The problem is that the discipline is so swift, volatile and severe that it sends the system into bouts of dangerous instability that can only be contained and kept at bay by a fully-fledged return to a policy of keeping depositors whole. Fears of loss were so intense that depositor runs did not stop until extraordinary measures were taken. At Seafirst it required merger with a much larger bank. At Continental it required a nationalization. Here, depositor discipline was inducing instability, not the stability claimed by the Deregulationists.

It also appears that these sudden and massive flows of uninsured deposits out of DFFs is due to the disposition of depositors. They appear to seek out the highest returns with little regard for safety. They seem to think that any risk of loss can be managed away by immediately withdrawing funds upon the first sign of trouble. An example of this was Penn Square's ability to attract uninsured brokered deposits, until just before it was shut down, by offering high returns. Part of the sense of security may have been the belief that all depositors would be made whole upon failure, as was the tradition (note Franklin National). But the inconvenience of failure and the possibility of loss it presents also indicates that part of the sense of security comes from the belief that high returns can be had and losses avoided through quick, strategic withdrawals of funds.

The other Deregulationist solution is to shut down DFFs before they become insolvent. The stories of FCA and Penn Square make this policy questionable. At FCA the use of securities in sophisticated hedging operations made it difficult for inspectors to understand and evaluate just what was going on at FCA. By the time they did figure things out FCA was insolvent. FCA's behavior had long drawn extra attention from regulatory agencies. The same sort of thing happened at Penn Square. Its operations had long drawn special attention from examiners, but because of poor documentation and poor operations it took examiners between six and eight weeks to fully determine that Penn Square was insolvent.

Given these occurrences it appears that the Deregulationists' prompt closure policy, wherein a DFF is subjected to increased supervision as its net worth declines, is not as simple and straightforward as they claim. Both FCA and Penn Square had received a lot of examiner attention but it was still difficult and time consuming to determine solvency. There are at least three major reasons for this. One is that a DFF, to cover its tracks, may adopt complex and sophisticated financial arrangements which are difficult and time consuming to evaluate. Another is that both documentation and operational procedures are so sloppy that it is difficult and time consuming to understand what has happened. The third is that the assets in the portfolio are not commonly marketed, they are unique and specific to the institution, making it difficult and time consuming to determine a fair market value. All three of these factors applied to the situation at Penn Square.

Growth at Continental Illinois and Seafirst

Growth at Continental and at Seafirst clearly centers around both personality and competitive risk. Both Continental and Seafirst were headed by leaders with forceful and ambitious personalities. They both had a strong desire to be business leaders of distinction and prominence. The best way to obtain this is to be head of an enterprise that is big and growing, especially if that head is perceived as having built the enterprise from a relatively small and obscure one. Roger Anderson of Continental and William Jenkins of Seafirst set the goals of their banks; they were not set for them by market pressures and shareholder interests which some argue enforce a goal of profit maximization.

Both Anderson and Jenkins were able to create very heated growth cultures at their firms by motivating their management teams to enthusiastically support growth. This was done in a couple of ways. One is the traditional pep talk. The other is to create reward structures which benefit those who help foster growth. This can be done by rewarding better performing divisions with greater resources, greater freedoms and greater responsibilities. This is also done at the individual level by compensating and promoting those individuals who successfully work at generating growth. The result, over time, is a management team that sees growth as being not only in their firm's interest, but also in their own interest. Growth alone motivates employees to work toward company goals because it clearly opens up opportunities for advancement. This process is reinforced by glowing reviews by both analysts and the financial press, and probably in a bigger way by competitors or similar enterprises who adopt the praised growth strategy. Management in these rapidly growing firms, such as Continental and Seafirst, tend to become cocky and disrespectful of risk. They come to believe they can do no wrong. This is certainly not a wholly rational way to run a firm.

A sign of this cockiness at both Continental and Seafirst was how senior management ignored both changing market conditions and the warnings of lower-level officials that trouble either lay ahead or was being generated by actions undertaken by a division or the firm. For example, at both banks, managers severely discounted the danger of lowering credit standards to win additional business. Their success over a short period gave them such a high level of confidence in their abilities that they thought that they would never have to confront the seeds of potential disaster that they were sowing. In addition, they refused to admit that the oil boom, which gave them comfort over low credit standards, was winding down until it was too late to escape the fallout. This is certainly not long-term forward-looking behavior focused on long-term profitability and risk avoidance. It is, instead, short-term behavior focused on immediate rewards without serious regard for the level of risk exposure.

Some other factors supporting the alternative firm model
There are other factors in these examples which indicate that banks, and firms in general, do not operate in the manner depicted in marginalist models of the firm. It has already been noted that goals are not necessarily rational, that goal setting is more internally determined than imposed by external forces, that goals are determined by managers' personal agendas, not firm-wide or market-driven agendas, and that short-termism is prevalent.

One of these other factors is that the firm is not unified. In a heated growth environment various divisions are going to be driven to compete for the resources they need to grow. One of the best ways to obtain such resources is to be growing in the first place. Division managers may very well find it worthwhile to do this by growing in risky and irresponsible ways to attract resources. Managers in a growth culture realize that rewards will probably come to them over the short term, and that their careers are harmed by allowing impediments to growth to get in the way. This encourages managers to actually remove them or, given the short-term reward structure, to use undue risks or deceit to make it appear that they have been removed. Thus in the end, growth-oriented firms are not only not unified, but the information which flows through them, because of various incentives, is not necessarily accurate or objective.

Another factor is that growth-oriented firms have multiple and at times conflicting goals; they do not have a clearly defined single goal that all elements find in their best interest to pursue. First, because of the disunity that exists in a growth-oriented firm, there are conflicting goal agendas at various levels in the firm, be it overall firm, divisional or individual. In addition, growth requires profits to fund it. The neverending issue becomes how to balance the two and how to time changes in that balance. Growth can be increased immediately by sacrificing current profitability, but this hinders future growth by depleting the funding which fuels it. On the other hand, more rapid growth in the future can be obtained by slowing current growth to increase the profits which will be available to fund that future growth. The question becomes, when is it most advantageous to grow? This is an especially difficult question because growth itself can promote additional growth because of the strategic advantage or market presence gained thereby.

The important role played by profits leads to complementary goals regarding cost containment, and when, and at what rate and expense, to develop and/or adopt new technologies or innovations. The goal-making process again becomes complex because a firm with the latest in technology or innovation may either attract or drive away customers, depending on how it is received. Thus, in the end, goal setting is not a simple clear-cut process predetermined by outside forces. Instead, it is affected by the personalities of prominent managers, by interactions within the firm, and by interactions with other firms.

Competitive risk and the logic of growth

Growth at both Continental Illinois and Seafirst was logically spurred on by real issues of competitive risk, a concept introduced earlier in Chapter 4. Continental had understandable concerns about competition from several sources eroding its market share. They were concerned about competition from foreign banks, from nonbank financial institutions and from the commercial paper market. Continental decided to counter this loss of business by aggressively pursuing the making of loans to those who had, or might, turn to such sources for funds. Seafirst saw its competitive risk coming from developments leading toward nationwide banking. Seafirst realized that its survival in such a banking market would require it to become a much larger institution. This competitive need for increased size is what caused Seafirst to aggressively pursue business outside of its traditional territory. The leadership at both banks realized that they would have to reduce credit standards to a level below those of their competition to win the additional business necessary for growth (Zweig, 1985, pp. 96–7). In other words, they clearly saw a tradeoff between competitive risk and portfolio risk. It is obvious from their decisions that they saw the threat from competitive risk to be greater than that from portfolio risk. Both banks adopted growth campaigns because they saw lack of sufficient market share, competitive risk, as being a greater threat to their bank's survival and prosperity than those posed by any additions to portfolio risk.

A problem with growth based on the logic of competitive risk, is that it spreads to other institutions and fosters instability. Continental and Seafirst grew by attracting business away from competitors, by bringing new lower-quality borrowers into the market, and by heavy dependence on purchased funds. This puts a great deal of pressure on competitors to adopt similar growth strategies simply because competitive risk has increased for them and has become a much more immediate threat to survival than portfolio risk. First, competitors have to deal with an increased cost of purchased funds squeezing margins. This encourages a fattening of margins by making more risky loans bearing higher returns. Second, to keep current customers from defecting to the likes of a Continental or a Seafirst, competitors have to ease any burdens they place on borrowers and this usually entails lowering credit standards. Third, any business lost must be replaced by doing business with the lower-quality borrowers who have been pulled into the market.

Thus there are three circuits through which competitive risk is heightened and spread through depository financial markets after some institutions adopt aggressive growth strategies. This fosters instability for two reasons. One is that increased portfolio risks spread among competing institutions. For instance, local Oklahoma City banks had to reduce credit standards to prevent a wholesale loss of business to Penn Square. The other is that the portfolios among such competitors become similar as they all loan to the more vibrant sectors of the economy to protect market share. This makes trouble in one or a group of institutions indicative of similar trouble in other institutions. Trouble at Penn Square indicated trouble at Continental, Seafirst and other correspondent banks which had also grown by emphasizing energy loans. Aggressive S&Ls such as FCA also spread increased instability in their industry through the same three circuits. In the case of the S&Ls, the focus was usually on highly speculative real estate loans centered around construction and development (Pizzo, 1989, pp. 20 and 183–4).

Lastly, growth campaigns based on the need to reduce or contain competitive risk have a planning horizon dissonance which contributes to the logic behind them but also contains the seeds of self-destruction. When these growth strategies are initially planned out, they appear solid and conservative because they are focused on improving competitive position over the long term. At Continental, they developed a five-year plan to move Continental from being the eighth largest bank in the United States to being one of the top three in business and commercial loans. Continental managed to meet its goal (Zweig, 1985, p. 310). Seafirst was basing its 15 percent annual growth goal on the desire to be a player in nationwide banking which was years away. Seafirst, not long before its demise, celebrated twenty straight years of growth and increased earnings. The problem is that both banks met their long-term growth goals by adopting short-term growth tactics that either overly discounted, or disregarded, the acquisition of unduly high portfolio risks. What both banks did was to allow the ends, the long-term growth strategy, to justify the means, the use of short-term growth strategies which brought rapid growth at the expense of increased down-the-road risk. At both banks the striving after long-term growth resulted in a growth culture in which short-termism came to prevail, even though the initial growth strategy had a solid and logical long-term orientation. It is this dissonance, displayed in the use of risky short-term tactics to meet long-term goals, that frequently steals away both the logic and rationality of growth strategies designed to reduce competitive risk. The tragedy of this is that the use of short-term growth tactics increases the level of competition and therefore the competitive risk faced by others. This also induces them to adopt short-term growth tactics, which spreads again through the same mechanism. This all leads to heightened instability as down-the-road risks are given little respect throughout DFF markets.

DFFs and the Problem of Instability

In the preceding section on DFF growth, three sources of instability have already been discussed in sufficient detail, and will not be gone over again here. These three sources are instability produced by skittish depositors fearing losses, instability produced by the competitively induced spread of lower credit standards and instability produced by the competitive spread of a risk disregarding short-termism. There are, however, a few other sources of instability that should be mentioned before closing this chapter. There are three main ones that will be reviewed. One is how excessive lending by DFFs feeds the boom and thereby the ultimate crash. The second is how abrupt or prompt closure of DFFs results in destabilization by suddenly cutting off credit sources and by suddenly disrupting financial interlinkages. The third is how the use of MVA would have led to massive instability in both the S&L and banking industries.

Credit and the cycle of boom and bust

Penn Square's extensive lending fed the boom in the Oklahoma oil patch and made it bigger than it otherwise would have been. The competitive challenge that Penn Square presented to other Oklahoma institutions also induced them to increase their lending, adding additional fuel to the boom. Lending at such high levels tends to boost collateral values which helps to brighten expectations and spur additional lending. The result is a situation where the boom becomes self-perpetuating for a time.

The boom process unfortunately plants the seeds of its own destruction. Over the course of the expansion or boom, financial fragility rises as loans become increasingly speculative and increasingly dependent upon price increases for their viability. The crash unavoidably arrives because the increasingly fragile financial arrangements that become acceptable through competition inevitably lead to some participant being unable to meet its financial obligations. Because of the prevalence of fragile financial arrangements this leads, through a chain reaction, to the failure of many other participants. This chain reaction occurs and is far ranging because each participant has become increasingly dependent upon others meeting their obligations to it to be able to meet its obligations to others.

Therefore, the tightly interlinked credit networks which develop around and among DFFs as they compete with one another in a growth-oriented atmosphere result in bigger, more buoyant and euphoric booms which lead to bigger and more violent busts. This can be seen in the conditions in Oklahoma City before and after the collapse of Penn Square. Before the collapse, economic conditions throughout the city were vibrant and expectations were bright because of the positive ripple effects of lending. Soon after the collapse economic conditions became lethargic and expectations were darkened because of the breaking-up of complex, interwoven credit flows (Zweig, 1985, pp. 419 and 425; Pizzo et al., 1989, p. 210).

Prompt closure and instability
It has already been discussed how the sudden closure of Penn Square induced significant instability by imposing losses on both uninsured depositors and correspondent banks. In addition to this form of instability, another was caused by the sudden cutting off of dependable credit sources and/or sudden disruption of the typical flow of funds that had grown up around Penn Square's operations before it was shut down. Many of the leading oil enterprises in Oklahoma City depended upon Penn Square's largesse for their funding. Businesses that contracted with these enterprises would only be paid if Penn Square's funding were to continue. The funding and payment obligation difficulties spread as the incomes of many entities dried up as past services went unpaid and future services became unaffordable by former customers. This domino-like reaction clearly happened after the closure of Penn Square because all of Oklahoma City went into a depressed economic state, not just the oil and gas sector or those directly linked to Penn Square.

This disruption took place and was so massive because of the manner in which Penn Square was closed. The regulatory agencies that dealt with Penn Square had to move unusually quickly because of the publicity that surrounded Penn Square and the destabilizing panic generated thereby. This need for speed induced a decision to essentially liquidate Penn Square, because the complex and incalculable web of liabilities that surrounded it made other traditional options unattainable. The result was Penn Square's sudden disappearance from the banking scene.

The prompt closure schemes advocated by the Deregulationists also involve such a liquidation. Liquidations are disruptive and destabilizing because they suddenly remove from a banking market or credit network a set of financial relationships. Other forms of intervention ranging from rescue and installation of new management to a P&A avoid liquidation and the instability it induces because financial relationships are allowed to remain intact. If some form of liquidation is chosen it appears that some period of forbearance must be allowed to enable financial relationships to be unwound to prevent destabilizing disruptions. This leads into the next section.

MVA, forbearance and stability

The Deregulationists are strong advocates of MVA. They argue that at any point in time, the best way to evaluate the health and solvency of a DFF is according to what its assets and liabilities can fetch in the market at that time. Their prompt closure policy is clearly based on the use of MVA. They want DFFs closed before a market-determined insolvency occurs so that upon liquidation, disposal of assets by market sale, no creditor will be subject to losses. From the above historical examples, we observe that there are serious problems with such a policy.

It has already been discussed how difficult it may be to determine the solvency of an institution. At both FCA and Penn Square financial arrangements became highly complex and yet poorly documented so that it was doubly difficult for examiners to both understand and evaluate them. Another difficulty is that some assets which DFFs hold are unique, that is, they are not traded in the marketplace. This makes it difficult to attach a reliable market value to them. In the above examples, this was true for any institution which held an energy loan originated at Penn Square.

However, there is another problem with MVA that centers around competition and how entire groups of institutions come to hold similar portfolios as they all strive to combat competitive risk through growth. An example of how many institutions come to hold similar portfolios is the S&L industry. Many of them combated earnings problems in similar fashion with growth campaigns emphasizing residential and/or commercial real estate construction and development loans. This clearly happened in Texas. This also happened during the 1980s with banks that fought competitive risk in similar ways by either focusing on energy and/or foreign loans (Wolfson, 1994, pp. 117–19). This process of coming to hold similar portfolios is quite normal. When competition induces many DFFs to strive after growth, all of them will naturally gravitate to those sectors to which large volumes of loans can be made.

The problem is that this tendency makes the use of MVA and prompt closure highly destabilizing, not stabilizing as the Deregulationists claim. The strict use of MVA during the 1980s would have been destabilizing to both the S&L and banking industries. As already noted, many S&Ls came to hold similar portfolios as they tried to grow out of earnings difficulties. They all came to hold similar troubled assets. If MVA had been used to evaluate the solvency of S&Ls many of them over a very short period of time would have been found insolvent and would have closed under Deregulationist guidelines. As the assets of failed S&Ls were liquidated this would have driven down the asset values of other S&Ls, throwing them into a market insolvency and failure. Through this process S&Ls would have gone down like a row of falling dominoes, shattering confidence in the industry. The use of MVA in this case is clearly destabilizing because it at least quickly maims, if it does not destroy, an entire industry.

It appears that the use of forbearance by S&L regulators was correct in that it maintained confidence and prevented massive destabilization caused by an enormous number of failures. What forbearance did was to keep S&Ls up and running by creating an artificial appearance of solvency. This was done through net worth certificates, the use of goodwill as capital, and other accounting gimmicks. Forbearance here is clearly stabilizing because it keeps large numbers of firms in business rather than forcing them into closure as would be the case with the strict use of MVA. The problem with forbearance in the S&L industry is that it was used for too long, allowing massive losses to mount. This happened because political games prevented the regulatory agencies from getting the funding they needed to shut down ailing S&Ls. Even if the regulatory agencies had always had sufficient funding to close ailing S&Ls, the judicious use of forbearance would have led to stability while the use of MVA through the massive number of shutdowns it would have caused would have led to serious instability.

The use of MVA to evaluate banks in the 1980s would have led to instability in a similar way. Because of energy and foreign loans that had gone bad, many banks had become troubled at the same time. The strict use of MVA would have brought many banks, including a number of very large ones, to the brink of failure. Instead, stabilizing measures were taken so that the banks could keep operating while they worked out the problem loans. For instance, troubled international loans were given renewed viability through international negotiations and agreements along with assistance from the International Monetary Fund (Wolfson, 1994, pp. 89–91 and 118–19). Here it is clear that the strict avoidance of an attachment of market values to troubled assets, a form of forbearance, averted a financial disruption with international implications. Thus it appears from both the S&L and banking industries that the judicious use of various forms of forbearance tends to nurture both confidence and stability while the use of MVA tends to seriously erode both.

CLOSING COMMENTS

It is clear from the analysis of the historical examples given above that the alternative assumptions presented in Chapters 4 and 5 mirror reality more fully than those of the Deregulationists evaluated in Chapter 3. The behavior of the DFFs and the interactions among them closely parallel the twelve alternative assumptions while in many ways they clearly deviate from the twelve Deregulationist assumptions. In addition, the implications of Deregulationist policies such as prompt closure and MVA displayed in the examples closely correspond to the abstract analysis of the implications of such policies given in Chapter 6. In conclusion, the historical examples selected for analysis in this chapter lend extensive support to the alternative framework regarding both the behavior of DFFs and their markets, and the destabilizing implications of the Deregulationists' program. With this historical perspective lending support to the validity of the alternative framework, the following, concluding, chapter will offer an outline of a new approach to regulation suggested by the alternative assumptions.

NOTE

1. This situation lines up precisely with the Deregulationists' criticism of forbearance and how it magnified, over time, the losses in the S&L

industry. As was noted earlier, the Deregulationists propose that such losses can be avoided with the prompt closure of ailing institutions.

8. A New Approach to Regulation Suggested by the Alternative Assumptions

INTRODUCTION

The study, in Chapter 6, of how the Deregulationists' policies would work under the alternative assumptions makes it clear that the two sets of assumptions lead to largely opposing programs. Both programs are intended to strengthen the stability of both financial markets and DFFs. The Deregulationists' assumptions lead to policies which remove regulatory restrictions from DFF operations, open up financial markets and intensify competition. On the other hand, the alternative assumptions lead to policies which establish and enforce DFF soundness guidelines and limit competition. This chapter will give a brief summary of the policies suggested by the alternative assumptions for enhancing stability. It will then analyze an apparent overlap which exists between the two opposing policy programs, and conclude with an argument as to which program is preferable.

AN ALTERNATIVE POLICY PROPOSAL

The following is a rough sketch of policies suggested by the unstable financial market conditions and risk-prone DFF behavior illustrated under the alternative assumptions. The policies outlined below counter these problems by limiting competition and restricting DFF behavior to make both DFFs and the markets they operate in more robust and stable. Of note is the fact that some of these policies resurrect or maintain, in altered form, policies developed in response to the banking crisis of the early 1930s.

Level the Playing Field Upward, Not Downward

The Deregulationists correctly contend that many DFF troubles are due to their inability to effectively compete with less-regulated nonbank competitors. These nonbank competitors escape the regulatory costs imposed upon DFFs and are therefore able to offer clients duplicate services at lower costs. DFFs, in efforts to compete, either cut margins to dangerously low levels or maintain sufficient margins by accepting and pursuing riskier business. As has been explained previously, the Deregulationists' solution to this problem is to deregulate DFFs and level the playing field by eliminating the costs of regulatory compliance. The Deregulationists claim that the greater competition fostered by deregulation will impose a high level of market discipline upon DFFs. This discipline, according to the Deregulationists, will produce a level of soundness which will more than substitute for the regulatory standards which previously imposed soundness.

This downward leveling of the playing field through deregulation will not work under the alternative assumptions. Under the alternative assumptions, heightened competition will make DFF behavior more, not less, risky. This means that any leveling of the playing field is going to have to be done in an upward, not downward, direction to maintain regulatory constraints on competition. This can be accomplished by imposing uniform soundness standards upon all financial entities performing bank-like functions. Under such a regulatory umbrella, both banks and their currently unregulated competitors, D'Arista's parallel banking system,[1] compete on an equal footing because they must all operate under similar regulatory guidelines. In essence, the destabilizing competitive inequities between DFFs and their unregulated rivals are overcome by broadening the application of regulatory standards rather than by removing them.

The erection of a regulatory umbrella covering all financial entities performing intermediation functions is a logical overall policy approach to adopt under the alternative assumptions. When operating under these assumptions, it has been shown that a stable financial system requires that DFFs must comply with soundness regulations to check their entrepreneurial and growth-oriented nature. The fact that the parallel banking system has been a formidable competitor of DFFs indicates that the financial entities comprising the parallel system must also be highly entrepreneurial and growth oriented. This competitive success also indicates that an absence of regulations in the parallel banking system has allowed the firms therein to be more imaginative entrepreneurially, and more aggressive as to growth, than have DFFs. This strongly suggests that all financial units performing bank-like functions need to meet strict soundness standards to have stable financial markets.

A broadening of regulatory oversight to include all forms of financial intermediation helps to enhance financial system stability in three ways. First, it brings under regulatory purview the previously unchecked and frequently inappropriately risky behavior occurring in the parallel banking system. Second, bringing the parallel banking system under the same soundness standards imposed upon DFFs will reduce both DFFs' competitive pressures and their need for risky undertakings to survive. Third, the Federal Reserve's influence over money, credit and economic activity is enhanced through the expansion of the reserve base under central bank control into all bank-like financial entities. In effect, leveling the playing field upward contains risk-taking and instability by equalizing and limiting competition, by imposing uniform soundness standards, and by strengthening the central bank's control over financial activity through expansion of the reserve base.

The Financial Industry Licensing Act proposed by Jane D'Arista and Tom Schlesinger is a good example of how this upward leveling of the playing field can be accomplished. The essential characteristic of this proposal is that it requires all financial firms to be licensed and comply with the same regulations with respect to soundness. This licensing basically applies to any entity whose regular operations result in even relatively limited forms of financial intermediation.

In very cursory form, some operational aspects of the D'Arista/Schlesinger proposal are that after licenses are first issued, wherein adequate managerial and financial resources have been demonstrated, they are to be renewed on a regular, periodic basis. Renewal is only to be granted when the entity demonstrates that it can fully comply with soundness guidelines. The core of these guidelines is comparable reserve, capital and liquidity requirements. Capital requirements are uniformly set by a risk-weighting of the assets and off-balance-sheet items held by each entity. Extensive portfolio risk diversification standards, including asset quality and sectoral concentration, are also to be uniformly imposed. For transparency, licensed entities are to comply with a regular and uniform disclosure of their performance. Adequate competition is ensured by consistently complying with applicable anti-trust law. Lastly, to promote sufficient monitoring of entities, the development of institutional structures promoting self-regulation is to be encouraged (D'Arista and Schlesinger, 1993, pp. 191–4; also in D'Arista, 1994, pp. 449–53).

Insure Individuals, Not Institutions

The S&L crisis and the taxpayer bailout of its insurance fund, along with weaknesses in other depository financial sectors, has made concern over deposit insurance almost universal. It was noted earlier, in Chapter 2, that the Deregulationists' solution to the problem is to remove the moral hazard problem presented by deposit insurance by clearly limiting its coverage. The Deregulationists argue that under the current deposit insurance system, where virtually all deposits are covered in a *de facto* sense, financial intermediaries are encouraged to behave recklessly in their pursuit of profits because their ability to attract funds is not impaired, because of the security generated by insurance coverage. Clearly limiting coverage exposes depositors to a definite risk of loss. This will prompt depositors to discipline financial intermediary behavior, toward greater conservatism and caution, by monitoring them for safety and by withdrawing funds from those financial intermediaries they deem not to be sufficiently safe.

It was argued in Chapter 6 that under the alternative assumptions, both depositor and financial intermediary behavior would be destabilizing under a program limiting deposit insurance coverage. The question therefore becomes, if we cannot limit deposit insurance coverage because of destabilization problems, then how can we contain deposit insurance losses within limits that can easily be covered by the insurance fund? One method of protecting the insurance fund is by enforcing strict soundness standards. This was a central part of bank regulations from the 1930s until the wave of bank deregulations beginning in the late 1970s and early 1980s. The already proposed broadening of soundness regulations, operating in conjunction with a shifting of deposit insurance coverage from institutions to individuals, holds good promise of limiting fund losses to manageable levels without risking instability. Instability does not become a problem because insurance coverage is not limited in ways which give depositors cause to panic in the form of bank runs. Yet, fund losses are sufficiently limited because the shifting of coverage will eliminate the need for bailing out or rescuing troubled institutions to contain negative repercussions, an expensive process.

A deposit insurance scheme proposed by D'Arista provides an example of how deposit insurance losses can be contained without creating undue instability. A rough sketch of her proposal is that all individuals and households are required to purchase financial guarantee insurance to cover savings up to a given amount. This insurance premium on savings deposits would be paid by accepting a lower return than that on uninsured assets. Insured savings would be held in a variety of accounts in federally regulated institutions. Deposited savings beyond the given amount may be held by uninsured accounts offering higher returns. In addition, transaction accounts of individuals, especially those of businesses, would be fully insured with unlimited coverage.

D'Arista argues correctly that transaction deposits must have unlimited coverage because failure to access them has extensive negative repercussions. The too-big-to-fail doctrine has been adopted because it recognizes the massive negative contagion effects created by a disruption in transaction flows. Protecting transaction accounts in this manner is costly because it fails to separate out the differential protection needed for savings and transaction balances. The criterion for protection becomes the size of institution, not the size or function of the account. Under a deposit insurance program which shifts coverage to individuals and their needs, insurance costs are reduced because the extent of coverage on a deposit is determined by function, not by size.

D'Arista proposes that in exchange for unlimited insurance coverage, transaction accounts will earn no interest. To control and limit their risk of loss, funds deposited in them are only to be invested in assets approved under regulatory oversight. In addition, the insurance premiums on transaction accounts are to be paid out of the residual remaining after financial intermediaries deduct an established fair profit and costs.

The zero interest on transaction accounts is beneficial for two reasons. First, it will give financial intermediaries a cheap and stable source of loanable funds which will not only enhance stability but also pass on lower costs to borrowers. This lower cost of borrowing ought to lengthen horizons and encourage productive over speculative investment. Second, it will give individuals and businesses incentive to limit the amount of funds held in transaction accounts to minimize losses of interest income, thereby limiting the overall exposure of the insurance fund. These are substantial benefits given the current financial system's problems with both instability and the insolvency of insurance funds (D'Arista, 1993, pp. 210–17; also in D'Arista, 1994, pp. 402–10).

The key advantage of shifting deposit insurance coverage from institutions to individuals is that it clearly segregates insured funds from those that are uninsured. By removing insurance coverage from institutions, it will no longer be necessary to cover uninsured funds in order to recover insured ones as efforts are undertaken to preserve institutions. D'Arista's scheme makes this segregation clear, and removes many current obligations toward financial institutions, because the insurance premiums are no longer paid by the institutions, but are instead paid by individuals and businesses. This ability to keep insured funds intact, and contain negative contagion without bailing out or subsidizing the buyout of intermediaries, significantly reduces the cost of deposit insurance and decreases the likelihood of a taxpayer bailout of the insurance fund. This, in turn, will give financial intermediaries good cause to more strictly limit their risk exposure because the regulatory authorities are in a better position to let them fail.

Dymski, Epstein and Pollin point out two potential problems with D'Arista's deposit insurance scheme which need to be addressed. One is, what prevents financial institutions from paying a premium on insured savings accounts and then using those funds to make especially risky loans? The other is, what prevents the automatic transfer of funds from uninsured accounts into fully insured transaction accounts? The first activity allows intermediaries to make risky investments, because of the protection of deposit insurance. The second activity enables institutions to circumvent investment restrictions on transaction accounts while offering clients interest income and unlimited insurance coverage at the same time. In addition, when firms are threatened with failure, individuals could use automatic transfers to gain insurance benefits (Dymski, Epstein and Pollin, 1993a, pp. 14–15).

The payment of premiums to attract insured savings accounts and using those funds to make inappropriately risky loans can be controlled in two ways, one of them already proposed by D'Arista. The aggressive regulatory enforcement of soundness standards advocated by D'Arista ought to prevent, to a substantial extent, the use of insured savings accounts to fund risky loans. A second device of control, a three-tiered system of floating interest-rate ceilings on deposits, is proposed in the next section. This would prevent the payment of premiums to attract deposits.

D'Arista's deposit insurance plan is vulnerable to the difficulties Dymski, Epstein and Pollin demonstrate are created by the automatic transfer of funds, on an as needed basis, into transaction accounts. Automatic transfer also threatens any advantage banks may gain with transaction accounts providing a cheap and stable source of funds. This advantage is only in place for financial intermediaries, and will only offer the stabilizing benefits of lengthened horizons and increased productive investment as lower costs are passed on to borrowers, if transaction balances are actually held in transaction accounts. Transaction balances are unlikely to be held in transaction accounts when they can earn interest income under a system of automatic transfer based on need. Therefore, transaction balances will only be held in transaction accounts if automatic transfers are prohibited, with all transfers into transaction accounts channeled through a deliberately slow and cumbersome process. The costs of enforcing this prohibition on automatic transfers are acceptable because they are very likely outweighed by the gain in stabilizing benefits.

In addition, transfers of funds into transaction accounts when a financial institution is troubled also ought to be prohibited because the insurance coverage gained goes beyond the purpose of insuring funds earmarked for transaction purposes. The purpose of such a transfer in time of institutional trouble is to secure nontransaction funds against loss. This extension of coverage beyond what is truly needed to cover transaction needs threatens the solvency of the insurance fund. The precedent for this sort of prohibition is the analogous suspension of withdrawals, but maintenance of check-writing privileges, private clearinghouses invoked in times of stress before the formation of the Federal Reserve. These actions enabled necessary transactions to continue while giving the troubled institutions the space they needed to manage their affairs and restore confidence. The suspension of the transferring of funds into transaction accounts in times of trouble works in a similar manner. The existing transaction accounts remain fully covered, thereby preventing any disruption in business transactions. At the same time, abuses of the system are prevented, thereby avoiding a depletion of the insurance fund, and its potential insolvency, for unintended purposes.

Limit Competition Through Interest-Rate Ceilings

The development of a set of twelve alternative assumptions in Chapters 4 and 5 and the analysis of how the Deregulationists' program would function under them in Chapter 6 illustrated a need to limit competition in some way. Limits on competition are necessary to keep the competitive risk with which financial intermediaries cope sufficiently low so that they do not make common a practice of accepting destabilizing levels of portfolio risk to keep competitive risk at bay. One method of limiting competition, which was a successful part of the 1930s banking legislation, is to impose ceilings on the interest rates that intermediaries may offer on their deposits. This limits competition by containing the extent to which financial intermediaries can competitively bid with one another to attract funds. Troubled intermediaries, those at greatest competitive risk, will, if allowed, outbid competitors to attract additional funds and, they hope, grow out of their difficulties. This bids up the cost of funds for all intermediaries, requiring them to invest in more lucrative, and therefore more risky, assets to maintain margins. This, for reasons already explained, increases instability.

With the deposit insurance program proposed in the previous section in force, interest-rate ceilings on deposits will have to be reimposed in a three-tiered manner. Transaction deposits would have an interest-rate ceiling of zero percent. Time deposits, which are insured as savings deposits, would have interest-rate ceilings above zero but less than the percentage allowed for uninsured time deposits. Uninsured time deposits would be awarded the highest interest-rate ceilings. This three-tiered system of interest-rate ceilings fits with D'Arista's three tiers of insurance coverage on deposits. The ceilings will limit total insurance coverage and liability by allowing higher returns on deposits as their liquidity and insurance coverage falls. In addition, it will prevent abuses of the insurance fund by disallowing the payment of premiums, under the protection of deposit insurance, to fund inappropriately risky endeavors.

However, to avoid the problems with disintermediation which ceilings presented in the past, the interest-rate ceiling on the three forms of deposit ought to be set by the Federal Reserve. The ceilings should be set in such a fashion that they move in concert with the interest-rate changes allowed or imposed by the Federal Reserve. The ceilings must float in this manner so that as market interest rates change they remain high enough for episodes of disintermediation to be avoided. In short, Federal Reserve interest-rate policy and interest-rate ceilings on deposits become tied together. These floating ceilings allow financial intermediaries to adjust deposit interest rates as market rates change, but prevent them from entering into competitive bidding wars which raise competitive risk to destabilizing levels.

A regulatory umbrella covering all financial intermediaries, which was adopted as part of the alternative policy package earlier, limits the outlets for disintermediation by imposing upon all intermediaries a uniform standard of regulation. However, disintermediation is still possible through direct markets, foreign markets and as yet unknown innovations. Disintermediation of domestic origin can be countered to a substantial degree through continuous and vigilant regulatory innovation which either shuts off the path of disintermediation or incorporates it into the system of uniform regulation. However, foreign disintermediation remains the problem it is today. Foreign disintermediation will only be resolved through a uniformity in, and coordination of, the many national financial regulatory structures.

These floating ceilings should help limit competition and dangerous strivings after growth by denying financial intermediaries the free use of interest-rate premiums to attract deposits. However, this need to contain competitive risk cannot be overzealous because it must be balanced against an equally important need that financial firms have sufficient ability to innovate. If innovation is overly impeded, then financial firms will not have the flexibility and capacity to create the volumes of credit necessary to finance the potentially lucrative investments which drive market systems and maintain their vitality. Therefore, the interest rate allowed on a deposit should rise, and the reserve requirement should fall, as the liquidity of the deposit declines. (The presented proposal on deposit-rate ceilings incorporates this requirement.) This fuels and encourages intermediary growth through liability management and other forms of innovation, thereby supplying ample flexibility in the creation of credit. Lastly, it may be discovered that the maintenance of sufficient innovation will require that financial intermediaries, on a case-by-case basis, be allowed exemptions to the ceilings under Federal Reserve approval and supervision.

Allow Nationwide Banking

The impediments to nationwide banking should be removed. This will allow for the development of an oligopolistic market structure at the national level. This will provide an institutional structure which, in addition to regulatory imposed interest-rate ceilings on deposits, helps to limit competitive rivalry. Oligopolistic financial intermediaries will be more aware of the systematic repercussions of their risk-taking in efforts to grow. This occurs because of the feedback or action–reaction effect which occurs under oligopolistic market structures. With a small number of rivals, each intermediary will be aware of how others counter their competitive strategies, especially those entailing greater portfolio risk, and how this will increase systemic financial fragility, creating potentially negative consequences for all. This interaction, which limits growth efforts based on increased portfolio risk, is akin to how oligopolists avoid competing for market share on the basis of price because it can lead to succeeding rounds of price cuts which destroy profitability for all. This feedback effect will tend to moderate the behavior of oligopolist intermediaries, thereby reducing competitive risk and, therefore, the drive to take on excessive portfolio risk in an effort to grow.

Under more atomistic competition, the sheer number of rivals keeps competitive risk very high, encouraging the acquisition of portfolio risk for growth. In addition, the lack of any feedback effect, and the information on systemic conditions it can provide, results in each intermediary thinking that it can escape any negative consequences which may arise from the acquisition of a risky portfolio in efforts to grow. In other words, the behavior of atomistically competitive intermediaries remains unchecked and becomes aggressive, out of self-interest, because there is no feedback which informs the intermediary of the negative repercussions of its actions. On the other hand, oligopolistically competitive intermediaries moderate their behavior, out of self-interest, because they get feedback which informs them of the negative repercussions of their actions. In short, the microeconomic interest of the oligopolistic financial intermediary is more in line with what is needed for macroeconomic stability than is that of the more atomistically competitive intermediary.[2]

This process is analogous to the ruinous competition caused by herd-like behavior in atomistically competitive markets, noted by Chandler and others in nonfinancial markets. Chandler describes this process in detail in his book on the rise of the Du Pont Corporation (Chandler and Salsbury, 1971; Galambos, 1966; Fickle, 1980). The basic problem under atomistic competition is that under boom conditions, when profits are high, many new firms enter the business, thereby increasing capacity. The result is that when demand declines many firms at once strive to dump their goods on the market either to get rid of unsold inventory or to prevent heavy capital investments from becoming idle at great expense. These actions would result in price declines steep enough to eliminate profits and create losses. With the failure of trade agreements designed to constrain output to keep prices at profitable levels, the problems of overcapacity and unpredictable cycles of profit and loss were overcome through consolidation and the emergence of oligopolistic market structures. In short, oligopoly brings stability because it removes causes of the herd-like behavior and instability observed in atomistically competitive markets. As already described, this is seen in atomistically competitive financial markets, through the reckless expansion and contraction of credit as participants act in their own microeconomic self-interest. As has happened historically in nonfinancial markets, oligopolistic structures ought to bring greater stability to financial markets by moderating the causes of herd-like behavior, such as excessive competition and growth needs so great that they encourage recklessness.

In addition, the small number of financial intermediaries under national oligopoly will allow the typical manager to be more expert, given that fewer of them will be needed. They will continue to be highly entrepreneurial, but their greater expertise, in conjunction with feedback effects, should result in management decisions which more frequently strike a better balance in risk-taking with less likelihood of destabilizing intermediary behavior or failure. Lastly, these large nationwide banks would naturally develop into full-service banks, capable of meeting the credit needs of any, even very large, customers. This provides intermediaries with the synergies and broad-ranging, highly interconnected interests which lengthen horizons. In other words, an oligopolistic national banking structure results in the development of characteristics which will shift the US banking system from a capital market-based system, what Michael Porter calls fluid capital, into a bank-based system, what Porter calls dedicated capital.[3]

This change will allow for the development of institutions which will enable the greater use of voice-led or administrative-type decisions, as opposed to exit-led or market/transaction-based decisions. The banks in this new oligopolistic financial structure are unlike the banks in operation in the United States today. These new, larger banks are more akin to the universal banks dominant in both Germany and Japan. Current US banks provide fluid capital and generate returns by rigidly enforcing loan contracts, by making frequent market transactions, and by speculating. These banks do not own equity interests in their customers and will rapidly exit loan markets which become troubled. Their decisions are market based. They also tend to enforce their claims on the revenues of firms in a manner which erodes both their organizational and their competitive capabilities. Bank behavior of this sort tends to be destabilizing.

The envisioned universal bank would provide dedicated capital and generate returns by being flexible in the enforcement of loan contracts and by holding equity interests in its customers in perpetuity. Such banks become partners of their customers. Within this partnership, banks work for, and share in, the success of their customers. In this atmosphere, decisions are of the voice-led or administrative type. This means that when trouble arises, banks have a self-interest in providing troubled clients with advice, counsel and financial assistance. Banks operating in this manner find it detrimental to enforce their claims on the revenues of firms in a manner which would erode their organizational and competitive capabilities. This kind of banking behavior tends to be stabilizing.

Porter and Michael T. Jacobs both offer specific reasons as to why the envisioned banks just described would help stabilize the financial system. Both argue that allowing financial intermediaries joint ownership of both debt and equity interests increases financial intermediaries' long-term orientation simply because they have a greater stake in their clients and therefore have a strong incentive to monitor them and promote their success. In addition, equity ownership under more perpetual conditions will also provide financial intermediaries with inside information on firms. This will help alleviate information asymmetries and enable intermediaries, out of self-interest, to commit to financing the long-term investment projects of firms (Porter, 1992a, pp. 16, 34–5, 40, 42–3, 46, 48 and 82–3; Jacobs, 1991, pp. 157, 160–61 and 238–9). This sort of financial intermediary behavior enhances stability because productive and innovative investment is favored over speculative and adaptive investment. Productive investment is stabilizing because it produces income with which to pay off any debts incurred while speculative investment, outside of possibly generating positive synergies, essentially redistributes income. Innovative investment is stabilizing because it increases competitive capabilities, while adaptive investment allows competitive capabilities to erode (Pollin, 1993, pp. 321–54; Lazonick, 1990, pp. 35–54; Lazonick, 1992, pp. 445–88).

Before closing this section it should be noted that Minsky favors a banking structure which is the exact opposite of that being advocated here. Minsky favors a banking system composed of many small, independent banks. One benefit of such a structure is that it enables the Federal Reserve to allow some financial intermediaries to fail, and generate some degree of discipline, before it must intervene as a lender of last resort and contain the negative contagion of a crisis (Minsky, 1986, pp. 313–32, especially pp. 319, 322 and 327; Minsky, 1982, pp. 152–3; Minsky, 1988, p. 28; Wray, 1992, p. 176). However, this potentially major benefit is countered, and probably outweighed, by two factors, both discussed in Chapter 5, which promote instability under atomistically competitive conditions. One is micro-level rationality which encourages participants, out of self-interest, to take on destabilizing risk (Fazzari, 1992, p. 8). The other is the fallacy of composition wherein the rationally calculating firm's behavior does not take into account, and is not inhibited by, rising aggregate fragility (Dymski and Pollin, 1992, pp. 44–5). Additionally, shifting insurance coverage, as proposed, from institutions to individuals, ought to help contain the repercussions of financial intermediary failure. Also, the formation of large, full-service, voice-oriented banks will encourage financing of productive over speculative investment. This produces more robust financial structures and greater stability, reducing both the likelihood and the repercussions of any financial intermediary failure. In addition, independent capitalization and administration of each subsidiary of financial conglomerates or holding companies (as proposed in the next section) will help isolate failures to subsidiaries, limiting contagion by leaving the remainder of the firm intact.

Lastly, a banking system dominated by many small banks creates an outsider information problem, encouraging exit-led over voice-led behavior. Small financial institutions would not be large enough to provide continuous financial services for large corporations. Instead, they would provide finance sporadically, focused on specific projects. Under such conditions financial institutions would have little reason to hold equities in perpetuity. Without such holdings, smaller institutions would not be privy to inside information. Instead, they would be dependent on sketchy outside information. This leads to uncertainty and a dependency upon the judgements and actions of others. This dependence on the judgements of others for uncertainty-reducing and confidence-building information results in herd-like behavior as each participant watches and responds to the decisions and actions of others. These information, uncertainty and confidence problems are overcome by large full-service financial institutions which have insider information through perpetual equity ownership. This argument also applies to the democratization of the investment process, wherein individuals make investment decisions instead of leaving such decisions in the hands of money managers heading up entities such as mutual and pension funds. Individuals would have the same outsider information problems just described for small financial institutions which would result in the same destabilizing herd-like behavior. Managed funds are more likely to avoid such behavior, because their size and clout gives them an incentive to hold equities long term. This gives managed funds access to inside information and its stabilizing tendencies. This is more likely to be the case under the proposed regulatory package in this chapter because it is designed to foster long-term over short-term behavior. This will especially be the case if managed funds become subsidiaries of large full-service financial institutions.

Full-service Banking and Conflicts of Interest

Given that financial intermediaries are strongly growth oriented, they will, in the normal course of business, acquire portfolio risks in their strivings for growth. One group of portfolio risks are conflicts of interest. Conflicts of interest present intermediaries with attractive growth opportunities involving interconnections among risks, wherein trouble in one activity negatively affects an apparently separate activity. The depth and reach of these interconnected risks are difficult to calculate and therein lies the danger from portfolio risks entailing conflicts of interest. Therefore, the tendency of intermediaries to exploit conflicts of interest, and the potentially widespread danger they create, requires that these sorts of portfolio risks be contained to maintain the stability and soundness of both intermediaries and financial markets. This, however, can no longer be done in the old way by separating commercial and investment banking. This separation, along with changes in technology and financial structure, has spurred an exacerbation of the US capital market-based financial system by commoditizing debt and by promoting the use of exit over voice, both of which have fueled a destabilizing short-termism.

The attributes and differences between the current US capital market-based financial system and an envisioned bank-based financial system, characterized by dedicated capital and dominated by administrative or voice as opposed to market- or exit-type decisions, was described in the previous section. It was argued that such a bank-based system is more stable than the capital market-based system operating in the United States today. It was also pointed out that the desired greater levels of dedicated capital and increased prominence of administrative-type decisions are encouraged under the formation and operation of full-service banks. Full-service banks, it was noted, have a strong incentive to develop relationships with their customers and take a long-term interest in their prosperity. The formation of these relationship-oriented, full-service banks will be made fully possible by expanding bank powers and allowing a full blending of commercial and investment banking. This involves allowing financial intermediaries to hold limited equity interests in their customers. As noted earlier, equity ownership increases a financial intermediary's commitment to the financing of a customer's long-term investment projects by providing the intermediary with an interest in the customer's long-term prosperity.

The allowance of full-service banking of this sort requires that conflicts of interest be contained through a holding company structure wherein different banking functions are housed and operated in subsidiaries separated by firewall restrictions. This does allow more opportunities for conflict of interest than does a full separation of commercial and investment banking, but this danger is outweighed by other considerations. These are:

- Since the 1920s the pressure from financial markets has inexorably pushed toward full-service banking. Financial institutions have been persistent in their efforts to circumvent restrictions designed to separate commercial and investment banking. Technological advances, the globalization of banking and the rise of the parallel banking system indicate that any regulatory system, if it is to remain effective for any length of time, will have to embrace full-service banking.
- US financial institutions, to compete with their foreign counterparts under a global financial market, must be able to offer their customers similar services. This requires the allowance of full-service banking.
- The United States currently suffers difficulties with the interconnected problems of instability and a decline in competitiveness. These problems can be countered by fostering the emergence of a more bank-based financial system, where capital is more dedicated and less fluid, and where all forms of financial intermediation operate under the same soundness principles and voice-led relationships. Under such a system, financial

intermediaries have incentives to become partners with their customers wherein they have substantial concern about customers' long-term prosperity. This is important to customers because it makes credit, when difficulties arise, more flexible since their financial institution is willing, out of self-interest, to renegotiate payment schedules. This greater flexibility of intermediated credit reduces its risk and therefore, in essence, its cost. This makes the firms which borrow better able to develop long-term investment and planning horizons and gives them a compelling reason to use intermediated over direct sources of credit, thereby enhancing the central bank's stabilizing control over the amount and type of credit extended. However, financial intermediaries will only have an interest in developing these close ties to the success of their customers if they can become more intimately involved with them. In today's environment, this requires not just allowing financial intermediaries an equity interest in their customers. It also requires the lifting of excessive restrictions, designed to prevent conflicts of interest, which prohibit the formation of full-service banks, those with the synergies and wide-ranging, interconnected interests which make it profitable to monitor the activities of customers. In essence, changes in financial markets make it beneficial to accept greater potential for conflicts of interest to promote a shift from the current capital market-based finance to a more bank-based and voice-led system of finance. The benefit of such a shift is that it will increase overall competitiveness, stabilizing both the economy and banking, by giving financial intermediaries an incentive to favor the making of longer-term, productive loans over shorter-term, speculative ones.

D'Arista proposes the formation of full-service banks through a conglomerate or holding company structure. She couples this proposal with reforms in deposit insurance wherein the accounts of individuals are insured instead of institutions. The main thrust of her proposal is to make sure that financial conglomerates do not escape the soundness regulations imposed upon their more specialized rivals and that adequate firewalls be erected between affiliates. Escape from soundness guidelines is prevented by requiring both a parent and its affiliates to meet the same licensing requirements as do other financial institutions. Firewall protection is obtained by requiring each affiliate to be separately capitalized, incorporated and managed, and by imposing antitying and other restrictions designed to promote more arm's-length transactions among affiliates (D'Arista and Schlesinger, 1993, pp. 192–

3; also in D'Arista, 1994, pp. 450–51; Jacobs, 1991, pp. 146–61, 169 and 238–9).

What is wanted is a structure where separate functions (each housed in its own affiliate or subsidiary) within the holding company compete with one another, yet are able to coordinate the services of affiliates or subsidiaries sufficiently to function as a full-service financial institution for their customers. This is very much like the highly successful General Motors divisional structure developed by Alfred P. Sloan, Jr. and adopted by others.[4] Under this structure, separate automotive divisions operated in distinct markets pyramided according to price. The object was to retain customers over their lifetimes as they moved from economy models to more luxurious ones. At the same time, each division, even though it served a different market, competed with one another in terms of performance, such as profitability, relative size and technological advancements, to gain, through merit, resources from the central office. In turn, the central office and its staff, in addition to providing the divisions with expert technical and financial advice, coordinated the internal competition among divisions and melded these drives into strategic plans which would best enable the entire corporation to maintain or gain market share.

In essence, the various affiliates or subsidiaries operate as a unified whole when it comes to both strategic planning, largely involving the allocation of resources, and the coordination of efforts designed to retain or gain customers. Yet, affiliates function with a great deal of independence when it comes to operational concerns and the development and introduction of new products or services. Under this structure, a large business enterprise has highly coordinated efforts but avoids many bureaucratic inefficiencies by instituting competition among divisions which both promotes efficiency and drives forward the innovation necessary to sustain growth. This development among nonfinancial firms is reviewed because it clearly indicates that institutional structures have already been developed where separateness and cohesiveness can effectively coexist. The success of these structures indicates that it is possible to develop institutional and regulatory structures in the financial world which would contain conflicts of interest while at the same time allowing exploitation of the benefits of full-service banking.

To summarize, the following regulatory efforts are used to contain conflicts of interest under the condition of full-service banking:

1. Multiservice financial firms are organized as a holding company composed of functional subsidiaries, separately managed and capitalized, and subject to firewall restrictions.

2. All financial entities performing intermediary functions are brought under a single regulatory umbrella requiring compliance with similar soundness guidelines.
3. Competition is bridled by interest-rate ceilings and by limits on entry (see next section).

Limits on Entry

The new powers granted financial intermediaries under the above proposals may make it necessary, for purposes of stabilization, to further limit competition by limiting entry into the banking industry. This would be especially helpful during the period of extensive consolidation which will occur during the transition to full-service, nationwide financial intermediaries operating under an oligopolistic structure. Many risks from merger are unforeseen and can only be limited if mergers are well thought out. Well-planned consolidation will more likely take place if the intensity of competition is limited by reducing entry during the transition phase. After the transition is complete, limits on entry, if they prove necessary, would be less strict. Potential, if not actual entry, must be kept at that level where competitive pressure is sufficient to spur adequate financial innovation. As noted earlier, some minimum level of innovation is necessary for the creation of sufficient volumes of credit to maintain the health and vitality of a market system.

Capital Standards, Subordinated Debt and Closure

Higher capital standards would also be helpful in enhancing stability. This would provide a thicker cushion which would help maintain depositor confidence during periods of trouble, reducing the likelihood of any runs. The thicker capital cushion will also give regulators a longer time frame over which they can identify ailing financial intermediaries and either take action to rehabilitate them, or, if rehabilitation efforts fail, reorganize them or shut them down on a case-by-case basis, a necessary process discussed in Chapter 6. The additional time increased capital provides makes it more likely, if reorganization or closure of an institution proves to be necessary, that credit relationships can be unwound before capital falls below zero.

In addition, the shifting of deposit insurance coverage from institutions to individuals will keep depositors more fully intact, thereby limiting the negative contagion of failed credit relationships. This will help contain the repercussions from the reorganization or closure of any financial institution offering insured deposits. In fact, the proposed firewall restrictions for financial conglomerates, along with ample provisions promoting each division's independence, will frequently limit reorganization or closure to divisions within a financial firm. This will further limit the disruption caused by reorganization or closure. These three factors will help minimize regulators' use of forbearance, wherein financial intermediaries are allowed to operate with negative capital in order to avoid destabilizing disruptions. This will increase the disciplinary effects of reorganization or closure in two ways. First, it increases the likelihood that it will occur. This promotes discipline by clearly increasing the threat to management's control. Second, the regulatory authorities are freed to more aggressively pursue reorganization or closure because its potentially destabilizing ramifications are effectively limited.

Lastly, it is questionable whether or not subordinated debt provides a uniquely effective form of discipline. To the extent that it serves the same function as capital, it will contribute to stability by thickening the capital cushion. (One advantage of subordinated debt is that it may be a form of capital more easily raised by financial institutions, especially smaller ones.) The Deregulationists claim the use of subordinated debt as capital is an effective disciplinary device because it must pass a continuous market test, while its creditors, unlike depositors, cannot run. However, as was discussed in Chapter 6, the behavior which is invoked by this test depends on the nature of the market. If the market has a speculative, instead of a more long-term outlook, the market test may foster greater, not less risk-taking by financial institutions holding subordinated debt. A speculative market helps increase the risk exposure of banks using subordinated debt because attracting creditors requires giving them lucrative returns comparable to available speculative investments.

The policy reforms which have been proposed should shift the financial structure to a more voice-led system characterized by dedicated capital. This will generate financial markets which are less speculative and more interested in longer-term productive investment. To the extent that this does occur, the continuous market test induced by the use of subordinated debt will help make it an effective disciplinary device. However, to the extent that financial markets remain speculative, market tests will counter, possibly even erase or reverse, any disciplinary effects wrought by subordinated debt. Therefore, the extent to which subordinated debt can function as a disciplinary device is directly related to the degree to which voice-led financial structures become dominant.

Limit Speculation and Encourage Productive Investment

The proposals above, which pave the way for formation of an oligopolistic network of nationwide, full-service banks, are adopted in the hope that productive investment will be encouraged over speculative investment through the development of a more voice-led financial structure. Pollin effectively illustrates how a favoring of productive over speculative investment can be accomplished in a more direct manner. He describes how this can be done by having the Federal Reserve put a heavier emphasis on use of the discount window, as opposed to open market operations, as a way of providing bank reserves. An adjunct to this change in emphasis is the adoption of asset reserve requirements. The balance of this section summarizes, in very brief form, Pollin's policy proposal.[5]

A central bank providing reserves through the discount window instead of through open market operations can more closely monitor financial intermediaries' balance sheets because it can make the provision of reserves conditional upon bank lending favoring productive investment over speculation. This sort of monitoring cannot be done when the central bank influences bank system reserves through the purchase or sale of government securities, as is currently done. Lending for productive investment is stabilizing because it creates an income stream in both the micro and macro sense; it increases both output and income. Lending for speculation is destabilizing because, outside of any positive synergies it may create, it will only generate income (loosely defined) in the micro sense; output remains constant while income is redistributed. The Federal Reserve can have an influence over the forms of lending only if intermediaries regularly use the discount window. This can be accomplished through encouragement by keeping the federal funds rates a percentage point or two higher than the discount rate.

If so substantial an emphasis on the discount window is too heavy an administrative burden on the central bank, reformed open market operations can be used toward the same goal. This would be done by shifting open market purchases from government securities to the commercial bills market. Bank bills eligible for purchase would be those that met the same standards necessary for acceptance at the discount window.

Lastly, asset reserve requirements serve as an additional incentive for financial intermediaries to lend in the desired areas. This incentive is created simply by setting lower reserves for productive assets and higher reserves for speculative assets. The international risk-based capital adequacy standards formulated at Basel in 1988 are based on this idea.

Direct Credit Controls

In spite of efforts to limit speculation, it may prove necessary that the Federal Reserve, especially during periods of rapid economic expansion, closely monitor the flow of credit from financial intermediaries and move to limit its expansion if it becomes excessive. Credit extension becomes excessive when it is used to support a rise in asset values which is unrealistic and unsustainable. The prices of assets become unrealistic and unsustainable when euphoric expectations about an asset's future earnings exceed technically possible earnings which are constrained by productivity gains. This, as noted earlier, is an argument Minsky makes, concerning credit and expectations, in developing his financial fragility hypothesis. The Federal Reserve can probably contain excessive credit extension by deploying its current arsenal of credit controls. It will likely be necessary to periodically limit the expansion of intermediated credit in this manner because of: the entrepreneurial and growth-oriented nature of financial intermediaries; competitively induced short-termism; and the ability of financial intermediaries, especially when under competitive pressure, to circumvent restrictions designed to limit their expansion. As noted previously, all these characteristics are amplified by the conditions which arise during expansionary phases.

A Single Regulatory Agency

The comprehensive regulatory oversight required for the successful implementation of the above policy proposals, would best be done by a single, integrated regulatory agency housed in the Federal Reserve. This would enable a full and effective coordination of the various strands of regulation. This single agency would license all financial intermediaries, control their entry, examine and monitor them, minimize conflicts of interest, insure individual savings and transactions accounts, and shut down troubled firms. Additionally, the agency, as part of the Federal Reserve, would be able to correlate interest-rate ceilings on deposits with interest-rate policy, thereby avoiding problems with domestic disintermediation.

With a single regulatory agency in operation, all financial intermediaries are licensed by it and come under its purview. This means that the dual banking system would be dropped and all licensed entities would have national licenses/charters, whether or not they operate across state lines. This is a logical direction in which to move given how the above proposals encourage the formation of an oligopolistic network of full-service, nationwide banks. A single regulatory agency of this sort is preferable to multiple agencies, based on functional considerations or customs of duality, not only because it avoids a competition in laxity, but also because it enjoys the synergistic benefits of a natural monopoly.

Lastly, a single regulatory agency would be more effective than multiple agencies because of the absence of both turf fights among agencies and/or the ducking of responsibility to another agency. Without these problems it is much more likely that an account will be taken of how regulations in one area affect others, thus enabling regulatory action to be more effectively coordinated. The Deregulationists favor the exact opposite because they think that multiple regulators will compete with one another in a fashion which will minimize regulation and foster innovation. From the alternative viewpoint, this creates an additional level of competition which generates additional destabilizing conditions.[6]

FIVE AREAS OF POLICY OVERLAP

Given the policy proposals just made and the Deregulationists' program reviewed in Chapter 2, it is clear that the two different sets of assumptions concerning both intermediaries and financial markets lead to starkly different conclusions. The general thrust resulting under the Deregulationists' assumptions is an opening up of competition. The general thrust resulting under the alternative assumptions is a limiting of competition. In spite of these clearly opposing thrusts there is a surprising area of overlap between the two opposing sets of policies, that is, there are five policy areas where there is at least agreement that there are problems which make change necessary. These areas are nationwide banking, full-service banking, higher capital standards, prompt closure and insurance reform.

Nationwide Banking

Both sets of assumptions lead to a recommendation that nationwide banking be implemented. The reasons for its implementation are different, but the result of increased stability is the same. The Deregulationists argue that it will increase stability by allowing intermediaries geographic diversification which will help reduce portfolio risk. This is helpful, but under the alternative assumptions it was argued that nationwide banking will also enhance stability through the formation of oligopolistic market structures which will reduce competition risk, thereby limiting both the drive toward growth and the need to acquire portfolio risk to grow. This happens because of both the existence of fewer rivals and the presence of feedback (action–reaction) effects. It was also noted that: (1) fewer firms decrease the demand for top-level managers, allowing greater expertise, which decreases the likelihood of destabilizing events; and (2) larger firms have greater incentives to cultivate close relationships with their customers, which lengthens horizons and promotes stability.

It is true that either set of assumptions finds nationwide banking to be stabilizing. However, a major difference is that the Deregulationists see it occurring in an environment lacking soundness guidelines where the discipline of competitive pressure will induce firms to diversify geographically, thereby enhancing stability. In contrast, the alternative approach sees nationwide banking fostering greater stability with oligopolistic structures and full-service, voice-oriented intermediaries operating under strict and broadly inclusive soundness standards. Therefore, even though both sides favor nationwide banking, they strongly disagree over the regulatory structure under which it should be implemented. In fact, each side's theoretical approach leads to the conclusion that the structure under which the other side would promote nationwide banking would be destabilizing, not stabilizing.

Full-service Banking

Both sides favor the formation of full-service banks but for different reasons and under different conditions. The Deregulationists do not see conflict of interest as a problem. This arises out of their theoretical view that the intermediary is basically a passively adaptive profit maximizer. As noted earlier, the Deregulationists also develop historical evidence indicating that intermediaries have never been extensively involved in conflicts of interest as is commonly believed. This historical analysis is buttressed not only by their theoretical view of the intermediary, but also by their theoretical view of markets that competition is a dispenser of discipline which automatically limits risky behavior, including conflicts of interest. Given this, the Deregulationists have no problem with commercial intermediaries entering both investment banking and nonfinancial business in a highly deregulated environment. In fact, they claim that full-service banking will enhance stability by generating more robust financial intermediaries. The greater robustness is generated because with full-service banking, more broad-ranging financial intermediaries can reduce risk exposure by becoming more diversified and because such intermediaries are enabled to exploit once unattainable synergies which will increase profitability.

Under the alternative assumptions, any financial intermediary is entrepreneurial and highly growth oriented. This means that, under competitive pressures, financial intermediaries will find some conflicts of interest attractive because they so often present lucrative opportunities for growth. Therefore, financial intermediaries, under the alternative assumptions, as they expand into full-service financial institutions, should only be allowed to do so under clear restrictions designed to prevent and/or limit conflicts of interest. The reasons, under the alternative assumptions, for allowing full-service banking and how to structure restrictions were discussed earlier in this chapter. Basically, potential conflicts of interest are accepted, but limited by regulation, to gain a more bank-based and voice-led financial structure and its stabilizing benefits.

In this sector of overlap, agreement is limited to the allowance of full-service banking. The conditions under which each side finds full-service banking to be advantageous are in full opposition. In the end, the opposition over favored conditions for full-service banking is so great that each side finds the other side's conditional ideal destabilizing. The Deregulationists find the conflict of interest limiting regulations of the alternative approach to be destabilizing because they will prevent the full exploitation of both risk-reducing diversification and profit-enhancing synergies. On the other hand, the alternative approach finds the minimal regulations favored by the Deregulationists to be destabilizing because they fail to limit exploitation of conflicts of interest and the risks they entail. As was the case with nationwide banking, agreement on full-service banking is limited to the direction of policy, over whether or not to allow a certain activity, while there is major disagreement over the conditions under which that policy should be implemented.

Higher Capital Standards

Both sets of assumptions generate arguments favoring the enforcement of higher capital standards, but for different foundational reasons. The Deregulationists see a high capital standard putting greater capital at risk. They think that this will modify financial intermediary behavior, especially under conditions of enhanced discipline fostered by deregulation, toward a greater aversion to portfolio risk to protect the greater capital from loss. In essence, greater capital is stabilizing because it magnifies the conservative behavior induced by the discipline of a competitive market. In addition, the Deregulationists find greater capital stabilizing because it enables increasing regulatory supervision as capital erodes, thereby making closure before losses occur more certain.

Under the alternative assumptions, as was noted earlier, capital is at risk not only from portfolio holdings, but also from competitive risk. The financial intermediary's dilemma is that growth, in order to reduce competitive risk, frequently requires the acquisition of a riskier portfolio. The result, under the alternative assumptions, is that having greater capital at risk will not alter financial intermediary behavior in a more conservative direction as the Deregulationists claim. What greater capital does provide is a thicker cushion with which to calm depositors during periods of trouble. As well, it gives regulators a longer time frame over which to rehabilitate, reorganize or close distressed financial intermediaries. This gives regulators additional time over which they can more fully unwind intricate credit relationships and avoid destabilizing situations or actions.

In this area of overlap we are dealing with the adoption of a regulatory standard, instead of the allowance of a new activity. Both sides agree that there is a need for regulators to enforce higher capital standards, and it appears that both sides can agree to a large extent on the general regulatory methods to enforce those standards. However, as already noted, the reasons for favoring greater capital are quite different. These different reasons are due to opposing views as to how financial markets behave. The Deregulationists see financial markets dominated by thermostatic-like mechanisms which maintain stability. The alternative approach, however, sees financial markets under the influence of endogenous forces which generate unpredictable waves of instability.

Prompt Closure

Both sides support some form of prompt closure, because of the discipline it creates through its threat of certain loss of control for both owners and managers. The Deregulationists advocate closure under a formula basis whereby financial intermediaries are definitely closed before capital falls below zero. Under the alternative approach, this is seen as potentially destabilizing because it may result in the abrupt cutting off of credit interlinkages. Therefore, the alternative approach favors prompt closure on a case-by-case basis. Under this closure process, financial intermediaries may be allowed to operate for minimal periods of time with negative capital to allow credit interlinkages to be adequately unwound before closure.

In short, the difference over prompt closure centers around foundational theoretical differences. The Deregulationists adopt a monetarist viewpoint wherein stability is ensured, short of an unexpected external shock, as long as the money supply remains stable or intact. This makes the immediate closing of an intermediary, before capital falls below zero, stabilizing because it prevents the destruction of a portion of the money supply. The alternative approach adopts a creditist viewpoint wherein maintenance of the flow of credit is essential for stability because it is a primary determinate of economic activity. This renders immediate closure before capital falls below zero likely to be destabilizing because it results in the breakup of credit relationships, and therefore credit flows, before they can be replaced. Instead, prompt closure only becomes stabilizing when it is done as soon as possible after credit relationships are unwound. This requires allowing regulators limited use of forbearance, wherein intermediaries may operate for a short period with negative capital. To the Deregulationists, forbearance is dangerous because it erodes the money supply. Under the alternative approach, however, it is a necessary though precarious action because it keeps credit flows intact. In this arena, as with nationwide and full-service banking, each side finds the other side's recommended policy destabilizing, instead of stabilizing.

Insurance Reform

Both sides see the need for deposit insurance reform. Both sides, in their reforms, recognize the need to limit the costs of the insurance fund devoted to rescuing distressed or failing financial intermediaries. The Deregulationists do this by limiting deposit insurance coverage to increase the market discipline intermediaries face from depositors, who become more concerned about safety. Under the alternative assumptions, insurance costs are limited by shifting deposit insurance coverage from the institution to the individual, while coverage is expanded both for deposits themselves and across institutions. In essence, the Deregulationists are limiting insurance losses by limiting *de jure* coverage to generate behavior which will minimize *de facto* losses and thereby enhance stability. Meanwhile, the alternative approach fosters stability by expanding *de jure* coverage and limits *de facto* losses by shifting coverage to depositors themselves, thus avoiding costly bailouts of institutions.

This stark difference over how a policy should be implemented, as opposed to the commonality over a need for change, again centers around foundational theoretical disagreements. The Deregulationists are not alarmed by limited *de jure* coverage and the bank runs it may generate. This is because of their monetarist approach. They do not see negative contagion from depository institution distress or failure to be a problem because withdrawn funds will be redeposited in healthy depository institutions. This keeps the money supply intact. In addition, the Deregulationists oppose generous deposit insurance coverage because it creates incentive incompatibility between the insured and the insurer which both enables and encourages depository institutions to pursue inordinately risky endeavors.

On the other hand, the alternative framework, because of its creditist approach, sees depository institution distress or failure causing much negative contagion because it disrupts credit flows. This disruption threatens the failure of a number of depository institutions in a domino-like manner, further depleting the flow of credit. This is why the alternative approach favors making depositors secure, to limit destabilizing runs, through ample *de jure* coverage, while limiting *de facto* losses through changes in institutional structure.

Once again we find agreement limited to the need for reform. With deposit insurance, both sides find reform necessary to limit losses. Beyond this, however, the gulf between the proposed recommendations is so vast that each camp finds the other's policy recommendations to be destabilizing and not stabilizing as claimed.

POLICIES, EVEN IN AREAS OF OVERLAP, ARE STRONGLY OPPOSED

The analysis of the five areas of overlap existing between the two approaches shows that the possible areas for agreement are only apparent and not real. Both approaches do have a common goal of increasing financial system robustness and stability. But disagreement is so profound that even in four of the five areas of apparent policy overlap (nationwide banking, full-service banking, prompt closure and insurance reform) each approach advocates a policy formulation which the other approach thinks will detract from the common goal of increased financial system robustness and stability. Beyond the area of overlap, the differences between the two approaches become even more drastic with the alternative approach advocating regulations which the Deregulationists find to be destabilizing.

To state the core difference one last time, the Deregulationists think that increased soundness and stability is achieved with minimally regulated financial markets because the increased competition will dispense doses of discipline. This will force intermediaries to operate in a more cautious and conservative manner. Under the alternative scenario, desired soundness and stability are accomplished through extensive regulation aimed at limiting the competition which prompts financial intermediaries to assume excessive portfolio risks in their strivings for growth. This is why the alternative assumptions lead to behavior-limiting policies such as single regulators and licensing requirements, interest-rate ceilings, limited entry, extensive oversight of full-service banking, supervision through the discount window, asset reserve requirements and credit controls. All these are regulations which the Deregulationists argue are the source of our current financial system difficulties in the United States. These severe differences, given the preceding analysis, are the direct result of a reliance on different, even opposing, theoretical frameworks.

CONCLUDING ARGUMENT

The absence of any agreement between the two theoretical frameworks as to how both financial intermediaries and markets operate, leads to continuous disagreement as to whether or not they require regulatory constraints to function in a desirable manner. This fundamental opposition means that a decision as to which framework offers the better approach will center around which framework better anticipates the results of a proposed policy recommendation. All economic theories must abstract from reality to be both understandable and useful because reality is so complex and full of opposing forces that any effort at a full accounting results in confusion. The abstractions used in economic theories become enlightening, and are useful in developing policy, when they select those motives and behavior which are elemental in determining the direction of actual economic activity. Therefore, a decision about which approach is more likely to be correct, centers around which theoretical framework better anticipates results. This is accomplished by discerning which one, through its abstractions, better selects and incorporates those motives and behavior which are most fundamental in determining the course of actual economic activity.

The conventional, marginalist economics employed by the Deregulationists has earned a reputation for frequently anticipating in an accurate manner the behavior of both markets and the participants therein. However, when it comes to financial markets, and the firms in those markets, I think that the alternative approach provides a better understanding of what takes place in reality. This better understanding provided by the alternative approach can most easily be illustrated by first looking at how the two approaches model markets.

The Two Market Models

It was noted earlier, in Chapter 3, that conventional, marginalist theory bases its approach to markets on a barter-based system. In this structure, money is essentially another commodity with some unique characteristics. These characteristics are that it eases transactions that would otherwise be cumbersome and it enables and encourages saving and, therefore, borrowing of that saving. In short, money is grafted on to the theoretical model and its basic effect is that it lubricates the economic machine, enabling it to run smoother and more efficiently. The presence of money does not alter the essential behavior depicted in barter-based markets. At the end of each market cycle, markets clear and it is only the distribution of endowments inherited from the previous cycle which affect the succeeding one. This meshes well with the monetarist theory also employed by the Deregulationists, which describes money as being a veil which has no long-term effect on real activity. With money playing this kind of role, markets are perceived as being both self-equilibrating and stable, providing best possible outcomes.

Under the alternative approach, money is incorporated into the model of markets at the outset. It is noted that with money comes financial systems composed of profit-seeking entities which generate all sorts of instruments, but especially credit, which link together past, present and future. Another characteristic of such a system is that the extension of credit, the ability to borrow, becomes detached from any pool of prior and current savings. As was noted earlier, in Chapters 4 and 5, these attributes of finance result in markets which are unstable and subject to violent and unpredictable cycles of boom and bust. For example, payment commitments of past debts influence present behavior, as do expectations which determine one's present ability to borrow. Additionally, expectations and the ability to create, not just allocate, credit interact in a manner which drives the boom, setting the stage for crisis and bust. Lastly, markets which behave in this erratic manner bring in concerns about uncertainty and confidence, and how respective efforts to cope with or develop them regularly result in herd-like behavior which exacerbates instability. Thus, under the alternative approach, markets are perceived to be inherently unstable and less than optimal. The cause of this instability is money and the financial system it generates.

Why the Alternative Model is Preferable

The model of markets presented by the alternative approach is preferable because it better anticipates actual behavior by incorporating two interconnected characteristics which are commonly observed in modern capitalist economies. These two common characteristics are the pervasive presence of both cyclical instability and oligopolistic markets.

The Deregulationists, in their approach to markets, claim that market instability is an abnormality caused by either unexpected external shocks or monetary mismanagement. They argue, often with historical examples, that markets left to their own devices will develop mechanisms which provide rapid recovery, and tight containment of negative consequences, from any disruption. Therefore, continuing instability and market calamities are due to government interference thwarting development of the natural self-equilibrating capabilities of markets. The central weakness of this reasoning is twofold. One is that only government agents commit mistakes which disrupt markets while private agents do not. The other is that common phenomena, such as episodes of instability, are explained by appealing to forces outside the theory.

An example which touches on this second point of weakness is how the Deregulationists deal with oligopoly. The arguments they develop depend on the existence of a competitive atmosphere which closely emulates that found in theories of perfect competition. This causes them to produce arguments explaining why the oligopolistic structures common in real-world financial markets produce a competitive environment which is similar to that in models of perfect competition, but not like those in models of oligopoly from the same theoretical framework. The result is that both reality and theory are either adjusted or denied in ways designed to maintain the persuasive power of their argument. These shortcomings do not bode well for the predictive capabilities of the market theory employed by the Deregulationists.

The alternative approach escapes these theoretical deficiencies. It sees instability as being a normal phenomenon in capitalist markets. This instability is largely the result of endogenous forces and behavior. In addition, episodes of instability can be either triggered or exacerbated by external shocks or central bank mismanagement. The approach also realizes that oligopolistic structures are the natural result of business efforts to overcome atomistically competitive markets which are too unstable for effective business operations. By directly bringing instability and oligopoly into the theoretical model, as opposed to being exceptions to it, the alternative approach better reflects actual conditions and behavior. This makes the alternative approach capable of explaining behavior more fully and, therefore, more likely than the Deregulationists' more conventional approach to accurately anticipate responses to policy.

The Same Argument Extends to Firms

The superiority of the alternative theoretical framework also extends to firms. A common observation is that firms are in a continuous pursuit of growth. Under the conventional theoretical approach used by the Deregulationists, growth is the result of adaptation. The firm either grows to meet increased demand or it grows to exploit economies of scale or scope to reduce costs and remain competitive. Under this adaptive explanation of growth, a firm's size is dictated by the extent of the market and/or by technologically determined optimal firm size. This modeling of growth fails to explain why firms frequently grow into large oligopolists whose rates of growth exceeded that suggested by increased demand and/or economies of size.

The alternative theoretical approach explains this strong growth orientation by incorporating factors which cause it. Some of these factors are: the separation of ownership and management and how this generates differing interests which foster growth; how empire building and resolution of management disunity generate growth; how integration into capital markets promotes short-termism which pushes financial firms into reckless pursuits of growth; and how competitive pressures and organizational need and motivation produce continuous efforts to grow. When this growth drive is taken into consideration, the financial firm is modeled as actively entrepreneurial, not passively adaptive. This model of the firm better reflects reality because it explains, rather than obfuscates, why and how oligopolistic structures have come to dominate market economies. The alternative approach does with firms what it does with markets. It more clearly reflects reality. This makes it better able to anticipate the actual outcomes of policy.

Conclusion

From the above arguments concerning both markets and firms there is good reason to conclude that the alternative theoretical framework provides a better understanding of the real world. The benefit of this is that its use will provide more accurate predictions of outcomes than will the conventional approach employed by the Deregulationists. This is the case because the alternative approach, in its abstraction from reality, selects out a broader range of motives and behavior, which are fundamental to the direction of economic activity, than does the conventional approach of the Deregulationists. By embodying this greater number of direction-determining factors, the alternative theoretical framework clearly shows that the Deregulationist program would result in unacceptable financial system fragility and instability. This better understanding of reality also explains why the regulatory program of the alternative approach is necessary for the establishment of a robust and stable financial system. In the end, it is the enhanced understanding produced by the greater complexity of the alternative theoretical framework which gives merit to the claim that the alternative regulatory approach ought to be adopted over that advocated by the Deregulationists.

NOTES

1. I will frequently use D'Arista's apt phrase, 'parallel banking system', to refer to DFFs' unregulated rivals.

2. There is a great deal of historical evidence indicating that oligopolistic markets are more stable than atomistically competitive ones. Chandler chronicles in many different industries how atomistically competitive markets developed into oligopolistic ones. This happens because with the passage of time in which profitability is highly uncertain, market leaders eventually emerge which strive to make profits more predictable and continuous by stabilizing and rationalizing the market. This is done by internalizing, and making administrative transactions, out of what were previously market, or externally, coordinated transactions. The efficiencies wrought by this internalization result in the development of large firms and an oligopolistic market structure which is relatively stable, with firms earning relatively predictable and continuous profits. See, for example, Alfred D. Chandler, Jr. (1977), *The Visible Hand: The Managerial Revolution in American Business*, Cambridge, MA: Belknap.

3. These points were discussed earlier. For bank-based vs. capital market-based systems see Robert Pollin (1996), 'Financial Structure and Egalitarian Economic Policy', *International Papers in Political Economy*, also in (1995) *New Left Review*. For dedicated vs. fluid capital see Michael E. Porter (1992b), 'Capital Disadvantage: America's Failing Capital Investment System', *Harvard Business Review*, September–October, 63–82.

4. Alfred D. Chandler, Jr. documents the development of the divisional structure at General Motors under Sloan in his lengthy chapter on General Motors in (1962), *Strategy and Structure: Chapters in the History of the Industrial Enterprise*, Cambridge, MA: MIT Press, pp. 114–62. Also see Chandler (1988d), 'Development, Diversification

and Decentralization', in Thomas K. McCraw (ed.), *The Essential Alfred Chandler: Essays Toward a Historical Theory of Big Business*, Boston: Harvard Business School, pp. 91–6; and Chandler (1977), *The Visible Hand: The Managerial Revolution in American Business*, Cambridge, MA: Belknap, pp. 456–63.

5. Robert Pollin (1993), 'Public Credit Allocation Through the Federal Reserve', in Gary A. Dymski, Gerald Epstein and Robert Pollin (eds), *Transforming the U.S. Financial System: Equity and Efficiency for the 21st Century*, Armonk: M.E. Sharpe, Inc., pp. 321–54; esp. pp. 335–9 and 346–7.

6. For similar arguments concerning problems with a competition in laxity and the need for heightened Federal Reserve control, see Jane D'Arista (1994), *The Evolution of U.S. Finance, Volume II: Restructuring Institutions and Markets*, Armonk: M.E. Sharpe, Inc., pp. 168, 323–5 and 453–4.

Bibliography

Andrews, P.W.S. (1949), *Manufacturing Business*, London: Macmillan & Co. Ltd.

Baumol, William J. (1959), *Business Behavior, Value and Growth*, New York: The Macmillan Company.

Bearle, Adolph A. and Gardiner C. Means (1932), *The Modern Corporation and Private Property*, New York: Harcourt, Brace & World.

Benston, George J. (1990), *The Separation of Commercial and Investment Banking: The Glass–Steagall Act Revisited and Reconsidered*, New York: Oxford University Press.

Benston, George J. and George G. Kaufman (1988a), 'Regulating Bank Safety and Performance', in William S. Haraf and Rose Marie Kushmeider (eds), *Restructuring Banking and Financial Services in America*, Washington, DC: American Enterprise Institute, pp. 63–99.

Benston, George J. and George G. Kaufman (1988b), *Risk and Solvency Regulation of Depository Institutions: Past Policies and Current Options*, New York University: Salomon Brothers Center for the Study of Financial Institutions; Monograph Series in Finance and Economics, No.1.

Benston, George J. and George G. Kaufman (1986), 'Risks and Failures in Banking: Overview, History, and Evaluation', in George G. Kaufman and Roger C. Kormendi (eds), *Deregulating Financial Services: Public Policy in Flux*, Cambridge, MA: Ballinger Publishing Company, pp. 49–77.

Benston, George J., Robert A. Eisenbeis, Paul M. Horvitz, Edward J. Kane and George G. Kaufman (1986), *Perspectives on Safe and Sound Banking: Past, Present, and Future*, Cambridge, MA: MIT Press.

Calamoris, Charles W. (1989a), 'Do "Vulnerable" Economies Need Deposit Insurance? Lessons from the U.S. Agricultural Boom and Bust of the 1920s', Federal Reserve Bank of Chicago, Working Paper Series; **WP–89** (18), October.

Calamoris, Charles W. (1989b), 'Deposit Insurance: Lessons from the Record', *Economic Perspectives*, The Federal Reserve Bank of Chicago, **XII** (3), May/June, 10–30.

Chandler, Alfred D., Jr. (1994), 'The Competitive Performance of U.S. Industrial Enterprise Since the Second World War', *Business History Review*, **69**, Spring, 1–72.

Chandler, Alfred D., Jr. (1990), *Scale and Scope: The Dynamics of Industrial Capitalism*, Cambridge, MA: Belknap.

Chandler, Alfred D., Jr. (1988a), 'Administrative Coordination, Allocation and Monitoring: Concepts and Comparisons', in Thomas K. McCraw (ed.), *The Essential Alfred Chandler: Essays Toward a Historical Theory of Big Business*, Boston: Harvard Business School, pp. 398–424.

Chandler, Alfred D., Jr. (1988b), 'The Beginnings of "Big Business" in American Industry', in Thomas K. McCraw (ed.), *The Essential Alfred Chandler: Essays Toward a Historical Theory of Big Business*, Boston: Harvard Business School, pp. 46–73.

Chandler, Alfred D., Jr. (1988c), 'Decision Making and Modern Institutional Change', in Thomas K. McCraw (ed.), *The Essential Alfred Chandler: Essays Toward a Historical Theory of Big Business*, Boston: Harvard Business School , pp. 343–54.

Chandler, Alfred D., Jr. (1988d), 'Development, Diversification, and Decentralization', in Thomas K. McCraw (ed.), *The Essential Alfred Chandler: Essays Toward a Historical Theory of Big Business*, Boston: Harvard Business School, pp. 74–116.

Chandler, Alfred D., Jr. (1988e), 'Recent Developments in American Business Administration and Their Conceptualization', in Thomas K. McCraw (ed.), *The Essential Alfred Chandler: Essays Toward a Historical Theory of Big Business*, Boston: Harvard Business School, pp. 117–55.

Chandler, Alfred D., Jr. (1988f), 'Scale, Scope, and Organizational Capabilities', in Thomas K. McCraw (ed.), *The Essential Alfred Chandler: Essays Toward a Historical Theory of Big Business*, Boston: Harvard Business School, pp. 472–504.

Chandler, Alfred D., Jr. (1988g), 'Introduction to the Visible Hand', in Thomas K. McCraw (ed.), *The Essential Alfred Chandler: Essays Toward a Historical Theory of Big Business*, Boston: Harvard Business School, pp. 382–97.

Chandler, Alfred D., Jr. (1977), *The Visible Hand: The Managerial Revolution in American Business*, Cambridge, MA: Belknap.

Chandler, Alfred D., Jr. (1962), *Strategy and Structure: Chapters in the History of Industrial Enterprise*, Cambridge, MA: MIT Press.

Chandler, Alfred D., Jr. and Stephen Salsbury (1971), *Pierre S. du Pont and the Making of the Modern Corporation*, New York: Harper & Row.

Corrigan, E. Gerald (1991), 'The Banking–Commerce Controversy Revisited', *Quarterly Review*, Federal Reserve Bank of New York, **16** (1), Spring, 1–13.

Corrigan, E. Gerald (1987), 'A Framework for Reform of the Financial System', *Quarterly Review*, Federal Reserve Bank of New York City, **12** (2), Summer, 1–8.

Corrigan, E. Gerald (1986), 'Financial Market Structure: A Longer View', *Federal Reserve Bank of New York, 72nd Annual Report*, 3–54.

Corrigan, E. Gerald (1985), 'Are Banks Special?', in Thomas M. Havrilesky, Robert Schweitzer and John T. Boorman (eds), *Dynamics of Banking*, Arlington Heights: Harlan Davidson, Inc., pp. 205–19.

Crotty, James (1994), 'Are Keynesian Uncertainty and Macrotheory Compatible? Conventional Decision Making, Institutional Structures, and Conditional Stability in Keynesian Macromodels', in Gary Dymski and Robert Pollin (eds), *New Perspectives in Monetary Macroeconomics: Explorations in the Tradition of Hyman P. Minsky*, Ann Arbor: University of Michigan Press, pp. 105–39.

Crotty, James R. and Don Goldstein (1993), 'Do U.S. Financial Markets Allocate Credit Efficiently? The Case of Corporate Restructuring in the 1980s', in Gary A. Dymski, Gerald Epstein and Robert Pollin (eds), *Transforming the U.S. Financial System: Equity and Efficiency for the 21st Century*, Armonk: M.E. Sharpe, Inc., pp. 253–86.

D'Arista, Jane W. (1994), *The Evolution of U.S. Finance, Volume II: Restructuring Institutions and Markets*, Armonk: M.E. Sharpe, Inc.

D'Arista, Jane W. (1993), 'No More Bank Bailouts: A Proposal for Deposit Insurance Reform', in Gary A. Dymski, Gerald Epstein and Robert Pollin (eds), *Transforming the U.S. Financial System: Equity and Efficiency for the 21st Century*, Armonk: M.E. Sharpe, Inc., pp. 201–20.

D'Arista, Jane W. and Tom Schlesinger (1993), 'The Parallel Banking System', in Gary A. Dymski, Gerald Epstein and Robert Pollin (eds), *Transforming the U.S. Financial System: Equity and Efficiency for the 21st Century*, Armonk: M.E. Sharpe, Inc., pp. 57–199.

Donaldson, Gordon and Jay W. Lorsch (1983), *Decision Making at the Top: The Shaping of Strategic Direction*, New York: Basic Books, Inc.

Dymski, Gary (1994), 'Asymmetric Information, Uncertainty, and Financial Structure: "New" versus "Post" Keynesian Microfoundations', in Gary Dymski and Robert Pollin (eds), *New Perspectives in Monetary Macroeconomics: Explorations in the Tradition of Hyman P. Minsky*, Ann Arbor: University of Michigan Press, pp. 77–103.

Dymski, Gary (1993), 'How to Rebuild the U.S. Financial Structure: Level the Playing Field and Renew the Social Contract', in Gary A. Dymski, Gerald Epstein and Robert Pollin (eds), *Transforming the U.S. Financial System: Equity and Efficiency for the 21st Century*, Armonk: M.E. Sharpe, Inc., pp. 101–32.

Dymski, Gary A., Gerald Epstein and Robert Pollin (1993a), 'Introduction', in Gary A. Dymski, Gerald Epstein and Robert Pollin (eds), *Transforming the U.S. Financial System: Equity and Efficiency for the 21st Century*, Armonk: M.E. Sharpe, Inc., pp. 3–20.

Dymski, Gary A., Gerald Epstein and Robert Pollin (eds) (1993b), *Transforming the U.S. Financial System: Equity and Efficiency in the 21st Century*, Armonk: M.E. Sharpe, Inc.

Dymski, Gary and Robert Pollin (eds) (1994), *New Perspectives in Monetary Macroeconomics: Explorations in the Tradition of Hyman P. Minsky*, Ann Arbor: University of Michigan Press.

Dymski, Gary and Robert Pollin (1992), 'Hyman Minsky as Hedgehog: The Power of the Wall Street Paradigm', in Steven Fazzari and Dimitri B. Papadimitriou (eds), *Financial Conditions and Economic Performance: Essays in Honor of Hyman P. Minsky*, Armonk: M.E. Sharpe, Inc., pp. 27–61.

Edwards, Franklin R. (1988), 'The Future Financial Structure: Fears and Policies', in William S. Haraf and Rose Marie Kushmeider (eds), *Restructuring Banking and Financial Services in America*, Washington, DC: American Enterprise Institute, pp. 113–55.

Edwards, Franklin R. (1987), 'Can Regulatory Reform Prevent the Impending Disaster in Financial Markets?', in *Restructuring the Financial System: A Symposium Sponsored By The Federal Reserve Bank of Kansas City*, August, pp. 1–17.

Eisenbeis, Robert A. (1990), 'Restructuring Banking: The Shadow Financial Regulatory Committee's Program for Banking Reform', in George G. Kaufman (ed.), *Restructuring the American Financial System*, Boston: Kluwer Academic Publishers, pp. 23–34.

Eisenbeis, Robert A. (1987), 'Eroding Market Imperfections: Implications for Financial Intermediaries, the Payments System, and Regulatory Reform', in *Restructuring the Financial System: A*

Symposium Sponsored By The Federal Reserve Bank of Kansas City, August, pp. 19–54.

Eisenbeis, Robert A. (1983), 'Bank Holding Companies and Public Policy', in George J. Benston (ed.), *Financial Services: The Changing Institutions and Government Policy*, Englewood Cliffs, NJ: Prentice-Hall, pp. 127–55.

Ely, Bert (1988), 'The Big Bust: The 1930–33 Banking Collapse – Its Causes, Its Lessons', in Catherine England and Thomas Huertas (eds), *The Financial Services Revolution: Policy Directions for the Future*, Boston: Kluwer Academic Publishers, pp. 41–67.

England, Catherine (1988), 'Agency Costs and Unregulated Banks: Could Depositors Protect Themselves?', in Catherine England and Thomas Huertas (eds), *The Financial Services Revolution: Policy Directions for the Future*, Boston: Kluwer Academic Publishers, pp. 317–43.

England, Catherine and Thomas Huertas (eds) (1988), *The Financial Services Revolution: Policy Directions for the Future*, Boston: Kluwer Academic Publishers.

Fazzari, Steven (1992), 'Introduction: Conversations with Hyman Minsky', in Steven Fazzari and Dimitri B. Papadimitriou (eds), *Financial Conditions and Macroeconomic Performance: Essays in Honor of Hyman P. Minsky*, Armonk: M.E. Sharpe, Inc., pp. 3–12.

Fazzari, Steven and Dimitri B. Papadimitriou (eds) (1992), *Financial Conditions and Macroeconomic Performance: Essays in Honor of Hyman P. Minsky*, Armonk: M.E. Sharpe, Inc.

Federal Home Loan Bank of San Francisco (1988), *The Future of the Thrift Industry*, Proceedings of the Fourteenth Annual Conference, 8–9 December.

Federal Reserve Bank of Kansas City (1987), *Restructuring the Financial System: A Symposium Sponsored By The Federal Reserve Bank of Kansas City*, 20–22 August.

Fickle, James E. (1980), *The New South and the 'New Competition'*, Chicago: University of Illinois Press.

Friedman, Milton (1962), *Capitalism and Freedom*, Chicago: University of Chicago Press.

Friedman, Milton and Rose Friedman (1979), *Free to Choose*, New York: Harcourt Brace Jovanovich.

Galambos, Louis (1966), *Competition and Cooperation: The Emergence of a National Trade Association*, Baltimore: Johns Hopkins Press.

Garrison, Roger W., Eugenie D. Short and Gerald P. O'Driscoll, Jr. (1988), 'Financial Stability and FDIC Insurance', in Catherine England and Thomas Huertas (eds), *The Financial Services*

Revolution: Policy Directions for the Future, Boston: Kluwer Academic Publishers, pp. 187–207.

Gerschenkron, Alexander (1962), *Economic Backwardness in Historical Perspective*, Cambridge, MA: Harvard University Press.

Goldenweiser, E.A. (193X), *Bank Suspensions in the United States, 1892–1931*, Material prepared by the Federal Reserve Committee on Branch, Group and Chain Banking, 5.

Goldstein, Donald (1995), 'Financial Structure and Corporate Behavior in Japan and the U.S.: Insulation vs. Integration with Speculative Pressures', Manuscript, Department of Economics: Allegheny College, July.

Goldstein, Donald (1991), 'Takeover and the Debt Assessments of Firms and the Stock Market', Dissertation, Department of Economics, University of Massachusetts.

Greenbaum, Stuart I. and Byron Higgins (1983), 'Financial Innovation', in George J. Benston (ed.), *Financial Services: The Changing Institutions and Government Policy*, Englewood Cliffs, NJ: Prentice-Hall, pp. 213–34.

Haraf, William S. and Rose Marie Kushmeider (1988a), 'Redefining Financial Markets', in William S. Haraf and Rose Marie Kushmeider (eds), *Restructuring Banking and Financial Services in America*, Washington, DC: American Enterprise Institute, pp. 1–33.

Haraf, William S. and Rose Marie Kushmeider (eds) (1988b), *Restructuring Banking and Financial Services in America*, Washington, DC: American Enterprise Institute.

Havrilesky, Thomas M. (1985), 'Theory-of-the-Firm Models of Bank Behavior', in Thomas M. Havrilesky, Robert Schweitzer and John T. Boorman (eds), *The Dynamics of Banking*, Arlington Heights: Harlan Davidson, Inc.

Havrilesky, Thomas M., Robert Schweitzer and John T. Boorman (eds) (1985), *The Dynamics of Banking*, Arlington Heights: Harlan Davidson, Inc.

Hawtrey, R.G. (1923), *Currency and Credit*, London: Longmans, Green & Co.

Hay, Donald A. and Derek J. Morris (1979), *Industrial Economics: Theory and Evidence*, Oxford: Oxford University Press.

Horvitz, Paul M. (1988), 'Commentary', in William S. Haraf and Rose Marie Kushmeider (eds), *Restructuring Banking and Financial Services in America*, Washington, DC: American Enterprise Institute, pp. 100–104.

Huertas, Thomas F. (1988), 'Can Banking and Commerce Mix?', in Catherine England and Thomas Huertas (eds), *The Financial Services*

Revolution: Policy Directions for the Future, Boston: Kluwer Academic Publishers, pp. 289–307.

Huertas, Thomas F. (1987), 'Redesigning Regulation: The Future of Finance in the United States', in *Restructuring the Financial System: A Symposium Sponsored By The Federal Reserve Bank of Kansas City*, August, pp. 139–66.

Jacobs, Michael T. (1991), *Short-term America: The Causes and Cures of Our Business Myopia*, Boston: Harvard Business School.

Kane, Edward J. (1990), 'Defective Regulatory Incentives and the Bush Initiative', in George G. Kaufman (ed.), *Restructuring the American Financial System*, Boston: Kluwer Academic Publishers, pp. 117–27.

Kane, Edward J. (1989), *The S & L Insurance Mess: How Did it Happen?*, Washington: The Urban Institute.

Kane, Edward J. (1988), 'The Looting of FSLIC: What Went Wrong?', in Federal Home Loan Bank of San Francisco, *The Future of the Thrift Industry*, Proceedings of the Fourteenth Annual Conference, 8–9 December, pp. 49–59.

Kane, Edward J. (1985), *The Gathering Crisis in Federal Deposit Insurance*, Cambridge, MA: MIT Press.

Kaufman, George G. (ed.) (1990), *Restructuring the American Financial System*, Boston: Kluwer Academic Publishers.

Kaufman, George G. (1988), 'The Truth About Bank Runs', in Catherine England and Thomas Huertas (eds), *The Financial Services Revolution: Policy Direction for the Future*, Boston: Kluwer Academic Publishers, pp. 9–40.

Kaufman, George G. (1986), 'Banking Risk in Historical Perspective', *Staff Memoranda*, Federal Reserve Bank of Chicago, SM–86–3.

Kaufman, George G. and Roger C. Kormendi (eds) (1986), *Deregulating Financial Services: Public Policy in Flux*, Cambridge, MA: Ballinger.

Kaufman, George G., Larry R. Mote and Harvey Rosenblum (1983), 'The Future of Commercial Banks in the Financial Services Industry', in George J. Benston (ed.), *Financial Services: The Changing Institutions and Government Policy*, Englewood Cliffs, NJ: Prentice-Hall, pp. 94–126.

Keynes, J.M. (1937), 'The General Theory of Employment', *Quarterly Journal of Economics*, **51**, 209-33.

Kindleberger, Charles P. (1989), *Manias, Panics, and Crashes: A History of Financial Crises,* Revised Edition, New York: Basic Books, Inc.

Lazonick, William (1992), 'Controlling the Market for Corporate Control: The Historical Significance of Managerial Capitalism', *Industrial and Corporate Change*, **1** (3), 445–88.

Lazonick, William (1990), 'Organizational Capabilities in American Industry: The Rise and Decline of Managerial Capitalism', *Business and Economic History*, **19** (Second Series), 35–54.

Litan, Robert E. (1988), 'Reuniting Investment and Commercial Banking', in Catherine England and Thomas Huertas (eds), *The Financial Services Revolution: Policy Directions For the Future*, Boston: Kluwer Academic Publishers, pp. 269–87.

Marris, Robin (1964), *The Economic Theory of 'Managerial' Capitalism*, New York: Free Press of Glencoe.

Mayer, Martin (1990), *The Greatest-Ever Bank Robbery: The Collapse of the Savings and Loan Industry*, New York: Charles Scribner's Sons.

Mayer, Martin (1984), *The Money Bazaars: Understanding the Banking Revolution Around Us*, New York: E.P. Dutton, Inc.

McCraw, Thomas K. (ed.) (1988), *The Essential Alfred Chandler: Essays Toward a Historical Theory of Big Business*, Boston: Harvard Business School.

Means, Gardiner C. (1962), *The Corporate Revolution in America: Economic Reality vs. Economic Theory*, New York: Crowell–Collier Publishing Company.

Means, Gardiner C. (1959), *Administrative Inflation and Public Policy*, Washington: Anderson Kramer Associates.

Mengle, David L. (1990), 'The Case for Interstate Branch Banking', *Economic Review*, Federal Reserve Bank of Richmond, **76** (6), November/December, 3–17.

Minsky, Hyman P. (1988), 'Back from the Brink', *Challenge*, **31** (1), January/February, 22–8.

Minsky, Hyman P. (1986), *Stabilizing an Unstable Economy*, New Haven and London: Yale University Press.

Minsky, Hyman P. (1982), *Can 'It' Happen Again?: Essays on Instability and Finance*, Armonk: M.E. Sharpe, Inc.

Minsky, Hyman P. (1977), 'A Theory of Systemic Fragility', in Edward I. Altman and Arnold W. Sametz (eds), *Financial Crises: Institutions and Markets in a Fragile Environment*, New York: John Wiley & Sons, pp. 138–52.

Minsky, Hyman P. (1975), *John Maynard Keynes*, New York: Columbia University Press.

Morris, Charles S. and Gordon H. Sellon Jr. (1991), 'Market Value Accounting for Banks: Pros and Cons', *Economic Review*, Federal Reserve Bank of Kansas City, March/April, 5–19.

Moss, Scott J. (1981), *The Economic Theory of Business Strategy: An Essay in Dynamics Without Equilibrium*, New York: John Wiley & Sons.

Penrose, Edith T. (1968), 'The Growth of the Firm – A Case Study: The Hercules Powder Company', in Alfred D. Chandler, Jr., Stuart Bruchey and Louis Galambos (eds), *The Changing Economic Order: Readings in American Business and Economic History*, New York: Harcourt, Brace & World, Inc., pp. 411–26.

Penrose, Edith T. (1959/1980), *The Theory of the Growth of the Firm*, White Plains: M.E. Sharpe, Inc.

Pizzo, Stephen, Mary Fricker and Paul Muolo (1989), *Inside Job: The Looting of America's Savings and Loans*, New York: McGraw-Hill.

Pollin, Robert (1996), 'Financial Structures and Egalitarian Economic Policy,' *International Papers in Political Economy*. Also in (1995) *New Left Review*.

Pollin, Robert (1993), 'Public Credit Allocation through the Federal Reserve: Why It Is Needed; How It Should Be Done', in Gary A. Dymski, Gerald Epstein and Robert Pollin (eds), *Transforming the U.S. Financial System: Equity and Efficiency for the 21st Century*, Armonk: M.E. Sharpe, Inc., pp. 321–54.

Pollin, Robert and Gary Dymski (1994), 'The Costs and Benefits of Financial Stability: Big Government Capitalism and the Minsky Paradox', in Gary Dymski and Robert Pollin (eds), *New Perspectives in Monetary Economics: Explorations in the Tradition of Hyman P. Minsky*, Ann Arbor: University of Michigan Press, pp. 369–401.

Porter, Michael E. (1992a), *Capital Choices: Changing the Way America Invests in Industry*, Washington, DC: Council on Competitiveness.

Porter, Michael E. (1992b), 'Capital Disadvantage: America's Failing Capital Investment System', *Harvard Business Review*, September–October, 63–82.

Poterba, James M. and Lawrence H. Summers (1992), 'Time Horizons of American Firms: New Evidence from a Survey of CEOs', Manuscript, Department of Economics: Massachusetts Institute of Technology.

Richardson, G.B. (1960), *Information and Investment: A Study in the Working of the Competitive Economy*, London: Oxford University Press.

Richardson, G.B. (1959), 'Equilibrium, Expectations and Information', *Economic Journal*, **69** (274), June, 223–37.

Rolnick, Arthur I. and Warren E. Weber (1984), 'The Causes of Free Bank Failures', *Journal of Monetary Economics*, October, 267–91.

Rolnick, Arthur I. and Warren E. Weber (1983), 'The Free Banking Era: New Evidence on Laissez-Faire Banking', *American Economic Review*, December, 1080–91.

Saunders, Anthony (1988), 'Bank Holding Companies: Structure, Performance, and Reform', in William S. Haraf and Rose Marie Kushmeider (eds), *Restructuring Banking and Financial Services in America*, Washington, DC: American Enterprise Institute, pp. 156–202.

Schwartz, Anna J. (1988), 'Financial Stability and the Federal Safety Net', in William S. Haraf and Rose Marie Kushmeider (eds), *Restructuring Banking and Financial Services in America*, Washington, DC: American Enterprise Institute, pp. 34–62.

Scott, Kenneth E. (1990), 'Never Again: The S&L Bailout', in George G. Kaufman (ed.), *Restructuring the American Financial System*, Boston: Kluwer Academic Publishers, pp. 71–94.

Shadow Financial Regulatory Committee (1992), Statement nos 1–69, *Journal of Financial Services Research* (Special Edition).

Shadow Financial Regulatory Committee (1990), Statement nos 36, 39, 41 and 43, in George G. Kaufman (ed.), *Restructuring the American Financial System*, Boston: Kluwer Academic Publishers, pp. 157–73.

Simison, Robert L. and Oscar Suris (1995), 'Alex Trotman's Goal: To Make Ford No. 1 In Auto Sales', *The Wall Street Journal*, Western Edition, A1 and A5, 18 July.

Smith, Adam (1937/1965), *The Wealth of Nations*, New York: Modern Library Edition.

Spellman, Lewis J. (1982), *The Depository Firm and Industry: Theory, History, and Regulation*, New York: Academic Press.

Tobin, James (1987), 'The Case for Preserving Regulatory Distinctions', in *Restructuring the Financial System: A Symposium Sponsored By The Federal Reserve Bank of Kansas City*, August, pp. 167–183.

Warburton, Clark (1963), *Depression, Inflation, and Monetary Policy: Selected Papers, 1945–1953*, Baltimore: Johns Hopkins University Press.

Wojnilower, Albert M. (1991), 'Some Principles of Financial Regulation: Lessons from the United States', Booklet, First Boston Asset Management: A slightly edited version of a paper delivered at the Reserve Bank of Australia Conference on Financial Deregulation, Sydney, Australia, 21 June.

Wojnilower, Albert M. (1990), 'Financial Institutions Cannot Compete', Booklet, First Boston Asset Management: Paper delivered at the Fourth Special Financial Conference sponsored by the American Committee on Asian Economic Studies, in cooperation with the Federal Reserve Bank of San Francisco, and the Institute of Business & Economics Research and the Center for German and European Studies, University of California at Berkeley, 30 November.

Wojnilower, Albert M. (1988), 'A Shock But No Surprise', Booklet, First Boston Corporation: Paper presented to The Money Marketers of New York University, 20 January.

Wojnilower, Albert M. (1987), 'Spaceships Not Satellites', Booklet, First Boston Corporation: Paper prepared for the Seventh International Symposium on Forecasting, Boston, Massachusetts, 28 May.

Wojnilower, Albert M. (1985a), 'Financial Change in the United States', Booklet, First Boston Corporation: Paper presented at the Conference on the Origins and Diffusion of Financial Innovation at the European University Institute, Florence, Italy, 7–9 October.

Wojnilower, Albert M. (1985b), 'Private Credit Demand, Supply, and Crunches – How Different are the 1980s?', *American Economic Review*, **75** (2), May, 351–6.

Wojnilower, Albert M. (1980), 'The Central Role of Credit Crunches in Recent Financial History', *Brookings Papers on Economic Activity*, **2**, 277–339.

Wolfson, Martin H. (1994), *Financial Crises: Understanding the Postwar U.S. Experience*, Second Edition, Armonk: M.E. Sharpe, Inc.

Wolfson, Martin H. (1993), 'The Evolution of the Financial System and the Possibilities for Reform', in Gary A. Dymski, Gerald Epstein and Robert Pollin (eds), *Transforming the U.S. Financial System: Equity and Efficiency in the 21st Century*, Armonk: M.E. Sharpe, Inc., pp. 133–55.

Wolfson, Martin H. (1986), *Financial Crises: Understanding the Postwar U.S. Experience*, Armonk: M.E. Sharpe, Inc., Second Edition 1994.

Wray, L. Randall (1992), 'Minsky's Financial Instability Hypothesis and the Endogeneity of Money', in Steven Fazzari and Dimitri B. Papadimitriou (eds), *Financial Conditions and Economic Performance: Essays in Honor of Hyman P. Minsky*, Armonk: M.E. Sharpe, Inc., pp. 161–80.

Zweig, Phillip L. (1985), *Belly Up: The Collapse of the Penn Square Bank*, New York: Crown Publishers, Inc.

Index

NEW DIRECTIONS IN MODERN ECONOMICS

Post-Keynesian Monetary Economics
New Approaches to Financial Modelling
Edited by Philip Arestis

Keynes's Principle of Effective Demand
Edward J. Amadeo

New Directions in Post-Keynesian Economics
Edited by John Pheby

Theory and Policy in Political Economy
Essays in Pricing, Distribution and Growth
Edited by Philip Arestis and Yiannis Kitromilides

Keynes's Third Alternative?
The Neo-Ricardian Keynesians and the Post Keynesians
Amitava Krishna Dutt and Edward J. Amadeo

Wages and Profits in the Capitalist Economy
The Impact of Monopolistic Power on Macroeconomic Performance in
the USA and UK
Andrew Henley

Prices, Profits and Financial Structures
A Post-Keynesian Approach to Competition
Gokhan Capoglu

International Perspectives on Profitability and Accumulation
Edited by Fred Moseley and Edward N. Wolff

Mr Keynes and the Post Keynesians
Principles of Macroeconomics for a Monetary Production Economy
Fernando J. Cardim de Carvalho

The Economic Surplus in Advanced Economies
Edited by John B. Davis

Foundations of Post-Keynesian Economic Analysis
Marc Lavoie

The Post-Keynesian Approach to Economics
An Alternative Analysis of Economic Theory and Policy
Philip Arestis

Income Distribution in a Corporate Economy
Russell Rimmer

The Economics of the Profit Rate
Competition, Crises and Historical Tendencies in Capitalism
Gérard Duménil and Dominique Lévy

Corporatism and Economic Performance
A Comparative Analysis of Market Economies
Andrew Henley and Euclid Tsakalotos

Competition, Technology and Money
Classical and Post-Keynesian Perspectives
Edited by Mark A. Glick

Investment Cycles in Capitalist Economies
A Kaleckian Behavioural Contribution
Jerry Courvisanos

Does Financial Deregulation Work?
A Critique of Free Market Approaches
Bruce Coggins